Deepak Thapa is a writer and book editor based in Kathmandu. He has written extensively on the Maoist movement in various Nepali and international publications. He is also the editor of *Understanding the Maoist Movement of Nepal* (Martin Chautari, Kathmandu, 2003).

Bandita Sijapati has a Master's degree in development economics from Columbia University and is currently a PhD student at the Maxwell School of Citizenship and Public Affairs, Syracuse University, New York.

A KINGDOM
UNDER SIEGE

Nepal's Maoist Insurgency, 1996 to 2003

Deepak Thapa
with
Bandita Sijapati

the printhouse
Kathmandu

Zed Books
London & New York

All interpretations of events and views expressed in this book are the authors' and do not necessarily reflect the interpretations or views of any person or organisation the authors have been associated with or of any person or organisation who has assisted in the publication of this book.

Front cover: Sakar and Chingar (both noms de guerre) sport a 7.62 calibre SLR and a 12-bore rifle as they pose for the camera at a Maoist camp in Surkhet district, July 2003. Back cover: Faded Maoist flags fly high above the Bheri river in Surkhet near the Jajarkot border, July 2003. Background: Remains of a police post destroyed by the Maoists in Rolpa district, February 2001. Frontispiece: Maoists training in Sindhupalchowk district, October 2002.
All cover pictures by Dhurba Basnet.
Frontispiece by Sagar Shrestha.
Design by Chandra Khatiwada.

© *Deepak Thapa and Bandita Sijapati*

First published by the printhouse in July 2003
Updated edition, September 2004

Published in Nepal by the printhouse, GPO Box 637, Kathmandu, Nepal
Phone: +977-1-4476871, email: printhouse@wlink.com.np

Published in the rest of the world by Zed Books Ltd, 7 Cynthia Street, London N1 9JF, UK and Room 400, 175 Fifth Avenue, New York, NY10010, USA in 2004

www.zedbooks.co.uk

Distributed in the USA exclusively by Palgrave Macmillan, a division of St. Martin's Press, LLC, 175 Fifth Avenue, New York, NY 10010

A catalogue record for this book is available from the British Library

Library of Congress cataloging-in-publication data available

ISBN: 1 84277 570 7 (hb)/1 84277 571 5 (pb)

Preface to the Updated Edition

MUCH HAS changed since this book was first published in mid-2003. An uneasy peace was holding out due to a ceasefire between the government and the Maoists. Although a recent change in government had introduced a measure of political uncertainty, there were hopes that meaningful talks would begin soon and bring an end to the eight years of fighting that had engulfed the country. There was reason for optimism since a high-powered team of Maoists were above ground and attending rallies like regular politicians. Two rounds of meetings had been held and although there was nothing much to show for it, both sides continued to profess their commitment to dialogue, and the occasional misunderstanding that cropped up did not actually sour the atmosphere.

Everything unravelled within a month. First came rumours in July that the Maoists were rethinking their strategy and that their leaders were slowly slipping back underground. An alarmed government managed to convince the Maoists to meet once again and hurriedly put together a proposal of reforms for consideration at the talks. But the rebels rejected it outright and pulled out of the ceasefire.

The fighting renewed with greater ferocity and in about a year a further 3000 people have been killed. Numerous others have disappeared as silent victims of a conflict in which human rights abuses have become routine. Another government has come to power in Kathmandu, but chances of a negotiated peace seem as slim as ever. That, in effect, sums up the tragedy that has overtaken Nepal yet again.

This updated edition bring the reader up-to-date on events surrounding the Maoist insurgency until the middle of 2004. The update forms a separate chapter at the end of the book. And apart from the one change in the number of deaths mentioned on pg. 10, necessitated by the resumption of hostilites, and the addition of a couple of annexes, the core of the book retains its previous form. Even the tenor of the writing in Chapter 7 has not been tampered with although it is clearly influenced by the promise of peace, a promise that did not seem improbable at the time it was written.

Deepak Thapa

Preface

BETWEEN ITS founding as a modern state in 1768-69 and the year 1996, only one event had posed a serious threat to Nepal's integrity: the 1814-16 war with the English East India Company. Since then the country had been more or less at peace with the world outside and with itself. This peace was broken when the Communist Party of Nepal (Maoist) launched its *janayuddha*, a 'people's war', in 1996, to start a conflict that has led to the gravest internal crisis Nepal has faced since the standoff against the British nearly two centuries ago.

This portrayal of Nepal's Maoist movement attempts to provide a greater understanding of the nature of the 'revolutionary war' that has engulfed the country. Focusing on the major political developments since the creation of modern Nepal, it provides an up-to-date historical overview and attempts to explain the rise of the Maoists (Maobaadi, in Nepali) by going back to the successive events that radicalised sections of the Nepali Left culminating in the Communist Party of Nepal (Maoist) taking up arms in 1996.

The evolution of the Maoist movement was until recently a little known feature of Nepal's political history. As one of the several ultra-left groups, the CPN (Maoist) and its earlier incarnations did not attract much attention in the immediate post-1990 world of multiparty politics, dominated as it was by the Nepali Congress and the Communist Party of Nepal (Unified Marxist-Leninist). It did have a parliamentary presence in the form of a political wing, the United People's Front Nepal, but its voice was lost in the babel that characterised the first few years of a nascent democracy. Within the party, however, there was a dynamic at play, a dynamic that called for an armed uprising against the state. And when this occurred, like the rest of society, the government was caught totally unawares.

This present work provides a concise account of how the Maoist movement transformed from an idea into a full-fledged rebellion; what the motive force was that propelled it; and how it has been able to sustain itself for so long. It looks at defining moments on its career path, and at the actions taken by the government to contain it. It provides an analysis of events along the way that helped fuel the movement, and looks at where the state may have erred in judgement. It also deals with the effect the fighting has had on the country's social and economic structure, and the havoc it has wreaked on the politics of the country.

Most of the material used is based on published sources, both scholarly and journalistic (and unless specified all translations from Nepali-language texts are by myself). Books, documents, papers, and reports have been referred to. Where necessary, interviews have been conducted. This has been supplemented by field visits to the districts of Rolpa and Pyuthan. I have also drawn quite freely from my two essays that appeared in *Himal South Asia*, 'Day of the Maoist' (May 2001) and 'Erosion of the Nepali World' (April 2002), as well as from the paper 'Radicalism in the Left and the Emergence of the Maoists' I presented at the conference 'The Maoist Movement in Nepal: Context, Causes and Implications' organised by the School of Oriental and African Studies, London, in November 2001.

Because of the ongoing conflict during the time of primary writing, it was not possible to meet with the top leaders of the movement. I have attempted to fill that gap by studying the periodic statements issued by the leadership from their underground existence as well as voluminous literature they produced (most of which is available at www.insof.org and www.cpnm.org). Although there is the dilemma of falling prey to propaganda while using information put out by the Maoists (or for that matter, by the government), I believe that it does not detract from the narrative and that its inclusion is important to help readers form an opinion about the insurgency.

There were some issues that needed extra attention during the preparation of this book. Among them was the question of how to refer to the insurgency. Does one call it People's War or people's war; is it placed within quotes or not? I decided to go with 'people's war' since, apart from the Maoists and their sympathisers, I argue that the notion that it is an uprising by *all* the people in the manner that perhaps the 1990 People's Movement was, is still contested, and neither do I foresee such an eventuality.

I have also refrained from terming the Maoists 'terrorists' and this has nothing to do with the Nepali government's prevaricating position on the issue. Rather, I hold that even though the Maoists have definitely used terror in their campaign, it is quite difficult to justify categorising the CPN (Maoist) as a terrorist organisation despite the historical precedence of calling communist insurgents 'terrorists' — most notably by the British colonial government during the Malay Emergency — and notwithstanding the recent broadening of the definition of 'terrorism' by the American 'new right' and their followers worldwide.

There was also the question of tense. Events are still unfolding as this book goes to press. Since work on the book began, there have been three prime ministerial changes; a ceasefire has been declared; and the political situation has changed beyond recognition. As this book should hopefully serve as a useful reference in the future, I decided to mostly use the past tense to describe things that are actually current at the time of writing, in the optimistic assumption that peace will prevail.

Finally, I would like to thank the Enabling State Programme for funding the research and publication of this book. Thanks are also due to my editor, Stephen J. Keeling, for his meticulous handling of the text and providing the most useful suggestions at the time of writing; Sudheer Sharma for being ever-ready with his time to answer my queries; and Kanak Mani Dixit for providing the initial impetus for the book. I would, however, like to emphasise that my co-author and I are solely responsible for all the views expressed here as well as for any shortcomings or errors — inevitable in any undertaking such as this.

Deepak Thapa
Kathmandu, June 2003

Contents

Tables, figures and boxes

Tables

Figures

Boxes

Acknowledgements

Amnesty International for the quoted text on p. 6 and Box 6; *The Christian Science Monitor* for Box 12; Dhurba Basnet for Box 14; Harka Gurung for map on facing page; Himalmedia for quoted text on pp. 8-10, Box 7 and Box 8; John Whelpton for Figure 1; Kantipur Publications for Box 4 and Box 10; Rita Manchanda for quoted text on pp. 4-5 and Box 5; Shobha Gautam for Box 13; and *The Worker* for Box 3.

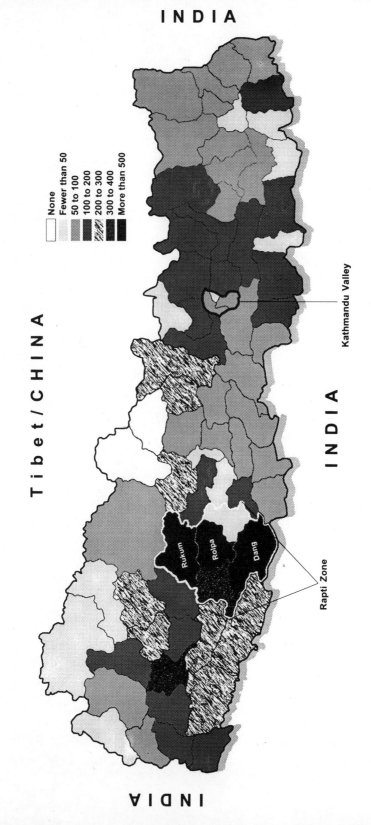

Number of people killed (classification by district)*

Legend:
- None
- Fewer than 50
- 50 to 100
- 100 to 200
- 200 to 300
- 300 to 400
- More than 500

T i b e t / C H I N A

I N D I A

I N D I A

I N D I A

Rukum

Rolpa

Dang

Rapti Zone

Kathmandu Valley

*Until mid-August 2004. Includes Maoist guerillas, policemen and soldiers killed in the field.
Scoure: www.insec.org.np*

Government classification of Maoist-affected districts, 2001*

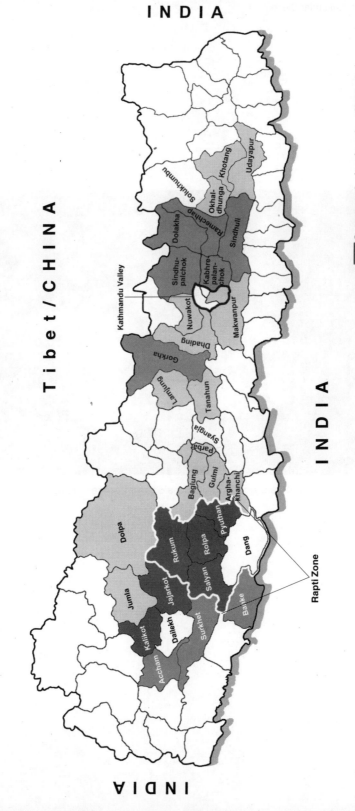

Category A (seriously affected)
Category B (moderately affected)
Category C (affected)

* This classification became redundant
after the breakdown of the ceasefire in November 2001.

DEEPAK THAPA

'To rebel is a people's right': Trailside slogan in eastern Rolpa.

When a ruling class resists fundamental reforms (which means reduction, if not liquidation, of its power and privileges), its confrontation with the new political forces becomes increasingly violent. A regime unwilling to satisfy popular aspirations begins to lose legitimacy. Coercion increasingly becomes its primary instrument of assuring obedience; 'law and order' becomes the favourite phrase of its governing groups. The revolutionary forces deliberately activate this process. By forcing the issues which augment the contradictions within the system and the divisions within the ruling class, they weaken the latter's efficacy and cohesion. By promoting activities which bring into sharp relief the parochial interests of the regime, they widen the perceptible gap between those in authority and expectations of the collective. By setting examples of defying and challenging established authority, they break the inhibitions of habitual or reflexive obedience and help transform private doubts into public actions; examples of overt resistance establish new standards of defiance and produce new alternatives and skills.

— Eqbal Ahmad in 'Revolutionary warfare and counterinsurgency'. Gerard Chaliand (ed), *Guerrilla Strategies: An Historical Anthology from the Long March to Afghanistan*, 1982.

The widow of constable Lokendra Giri of Rolpa breaks down over her husband's dead body. Giri was killed in the Maoist attack in Naumule, Dailekh district. April 2001.

Life and Death in the Time of War

HE WAS young, very young, and it was with childlike wonder he hung around as we went about our business collecting information for our reports. It was quite surprising to see him in that village in the northern reaches of Rolpa district, where we had arrived in June 2002. Young boys and girls were rarely seen in that area; they would either have left for safer places away from the fighting zone or they would have joined the 'People's Liberation Army' of the Communist Party of Nepal (Maoist).

We had met a detachment of the Maoist 'army' the day before as they lolled about in the grass and prepared a late afternoon meal. After some persuasion, they staged a short PT demonstration for our benefit. Later, in the fading light, they walked off in single file, crossed a small stream, and began their uphill climb to their night halt. We watched the hundred-odd young men and women, armed to the teeth and burdened with bulging backpacks, trudge up the mountainside before they disappeared from view. Soon after, it started raining, and we were thankful we were not out there with them.

It was the morning after that we met the young man. There were others on the periphery too, and from the civilian clothes they wore and the .303 Royal Enfield rifles they carried we could make out they were part of the Maoist village-based militia. Even though he was not armed, I asked the curiosity-struck boy if he too was village militia. Not me, he said, and, pointing to the others, said, *they* were the militia. He was a *ladakoo*, a fighter, he declared proudly. But hadn't all of them marched out yesterday evening? He had, too, but had come back in the night.

Finally, we were getting a chance to chat with one of the guerillas. We had been told to lay off them the previous evening, but here he was talking of his own volition. We asked him where he'd fought. Dang, Satbariya, Mangalsen, Lisne, Gam, Khara; he rattled off the names of the big battles. This young fellow was a real veteran. His group had just come back from the last-mentioned where the Maoists had suffered a setback, and as we learnt later, at that time they still did not know the extent of their losses. They would have to wait for official word on the battle from the party high command.

Asked why he had joined the Maoists, pat came the reply, 'For the country and the people.'

'Aren't you afraid you'll die?'

'No. Because our names will be inscribed in history,' he said promptly.

I never got to know the young fighter's name or where he came from; by now, he could even be dead. But his steely resolution gave us a glimpse of the kind of motive force that has driven the 'people's war'.

*   *   *

The political commissar attached to the armed company we had met told us that he 'injected' ideology into his young recruits' heads; and if the boy's commitment described above is any indication, it seems to have been very effective. That, however, is only part of the story. The sense of hurt is deep. There are instances aplenty where the state has made the mistake of using violence against villagers who had only been Maoist sympathisers to begin with, but who were then forced by circumstance to join the rebels. Take the following description of a village in Rolpa that was investigated by a group of journalists in 1998:[1]

> Mirul, a village in Rolpa district is a village without men. It is a Kham Magar village of 265 houses without men. In the first year of the insurgency, Mirul held the record for the largest number of killings in Rolpa district. This village is a case study in the 'making of Maoists'. Mirul's remoteness and inaccessibility reflects its abject neglect and backwardness. It is an arduous eight-hour walk from the district headquarters in Libang. The presence of the Nepali state is visible in the police post set up during Operation Romeo in 1995. The police stay on the other side of the river, watchful but do not cross over. When our all-women journalists' team went to Mirul, there seemed to be an apparent lull both in Maoist and police activity. But the women do not dare light a lamp, as dusk falls. The police have proscribed it. Outsiders are regarded with suspicion. 'This one or that one might be the man who puts on a mask and comes to kill at night or the informer who brings in the police,' a student said.
>
> Sympathisers of the UPF [United People's Front, the then political wing of the CPN (Maoist)], teachers, farmers and in the end, all the able-bodied men, had fled in the wake of arbitrary arrests and killings. It started with the killing of Mulman Budha, the 'smart' farmer of the village who was organising the community's drinking water project. Mane Karne, the son of the local village Mukhiya

(chief), now allied to the Nepali Congress, used the police to settle political and personal scores, targeting Mulman Budha. Just two days before, he [Mulman] had begun adult literacy classes. Maoists retaliated and killed the 'informer' Man Bahadur Roka. The police hit back charging 42 people with his murder, including in the charge-sheet the names of all those associated with the UPF and others whom Mane Karne wanted to get even with — women and men. Police justice was dramatically demonstrated when four men were picked up one night. Kumari Budha (23), the daughter of one of the men went with food and clothes for her father. She too was detained at the police post. Kumari Budha was raped and killed. The five half-burnt bodies were found smouldering the next day. It is a memory which even the children obsessively recall.

Those implicated in the omnibus charge-sheet did not wait around. They became *farari* (absconders). Raji Maya, who had been with her children in the fields staying in a *goth*, a cowshed, when Roka was killed, was also charged. She was arrested and imprisoned till she produced her land title deed as security for bail. Young men routinely harvesting potatoes in the upper slopes were picked up by the police and arbitrarily executed on the say so of village informers. Hundreds were arrested. For two years, Buji Maya (16), a Kham Magar girl, has been behind bars in Libang jail. She still does not know why she was arrested. She is charged with dacoity and murder. She was picked up on suspicion of feeding and sheltering the Maoists. It is not an unfounded suspicion, for who are the Maoists, but brothers, fathers, uncles and aunts in a tightly knit tribal village community. 'When they come for food, who can say no. Then, the police come,' said Asapura Gurung, a village ward member.

The men slipped away into the surrounding jungles, some to join the Maoists, others to melt into the crowds of the cities.

*　　*　　*

When it comes to atrocities, the Maoists have proved to be as ruthless as the state they oppose. One of the incidents that shocked the country was their brutal slaying of Mukti Nath Adhikari in January 2002, not long after the country had been placed under an emergency. A very popular teacher, Muktinath had rejected the advice of well-wishers not to remain in his home village of Duradanda in Lamjung district but to relocate to the relative safety of the district headquarters. But Muktinath was that rather rare breed—a committed teacher. Rather than opt for government service in Kathmandu, as was the norm, he had come back to his village after graduating from college and had taken up teaching. That fateful day, he was with his students in a classroom when he was asked to step out.

> A group of Maoists tied his hands behind his back, and took him about 200 metres from the school. There he was tied to a tree and shot in the head. He died on the spot. Muktinath Adhikari was convenor of Amnesty International's local group in Lamjung district and was acting headmaster of the school. It is suspected that he was killed because of his membership of the Nepal Teachers Association, considered close to the Nepali Congress. According to a communication, purportedly from the Maoists to Amnesty International, Muktinath Adhikari was killed because he was 'a person with a long record of anti-people activities and had proven charges against him of being an informer leading to the killing of a number of innocent people by the royal army in Lamjung'. According to other sources, however, he was killed because he had earlier refused to give 'donations' demanded by the Maoists and had received several threats as a result.[2]

* * *

Teaching is a risky job in areas where the Maoists are strong. Teachers are at the receiving end from both sides. As people living in Maoist areas, they are viewed with suspicion by the authorities, whilst their regular contacts with the district administration causes them to be viewed with equal distrust by the Maoists. A disproportionate number of teachers have been killed in the conflict. Certainly, examples abound of teachers working for one or the other side; but in the main they are only sons (very few daughters) of peasants trying to survive on the relative security of a government job. But that does not seem to impress the Maoists. Every month, they are forced to fork out a certain percentage of their meagre pay cheques for 'the cause'.

It has, of course, been far more dangerous to be a politician. Those allied to the Maoists have stayed underground throughout the conflict. They have after all been fighting the 'people's war', and are well aware of the risks involved. It has been the politicians belonging to other parties, especially the Nepali Congress, who have had it really tough in the face of Maoist atrocities. Many have left their villages to live in the district headquarters or moved on to Kathmandu. Govinda Shahi is one of them.[3] He was elected vice-chairman of Khagankot VDC in Jajarkot district on a Nepali Congress ticket in the local elections of November 1997. But since the Maoists had called for a boycott of those elections, fearing for his life, he mostly stayed away from his village and only went there with police protection. But he stopped going back altogether after December 2000, when the village police posts were shifted to the district headquarters. It was only after the July 2001 ceasefire that he was able to return home.

Back in his village Shahi was in for a shock. The Maoists had held elections to their own form of village government and the person elected chairman was someone with a grudge against him. Soon afterwards, the Maoists sent for him and accused him of corruption and told him he would not be set free until he paid a ransom of Rs 100,000. Shahi argued that that he could not have been guilty since he had hardly had the chance to work as VDC vice-chairman. The Maoists then said he was guilty of corruption when he had been the chairman of the village consumers' group, and reduced the fine to Rs 50,000. He heard the word *chalan* (literally, despatch) many times during their conversation, and aware that it was a euphemism for execution, he feared he would be killed. His family was informed about the ransom demand and they brought the Rs 50,000.

Shahi is lucky to have escaped with his life, and he was able to take advantage of the temporary ceasefire of 2001 to bring out his family with him. But many of the poorer or uninfluential supporters of non-Maoist parties were not able to do likewise. Stuck in their villages, they learnt to compromise and do as the Maoists told them, such as by taking up positions in the Maoist 'people's governments' even though they knew very well that this put them directly in the line of fire from the government side.

Ordinary villagers suffered the worst predicament caught in the crossfire between the two sides, particularly between the end of the first ceasefire in November 2001 and the second ceasefire in January 2003. Whole villages were subjected to terror as the 'people's war' became a no-holds-barred fight with random violence perpetrated by both sides. For the Maoists it was a fight for survival, while the army hungered for revenge, having been surprised by the sudden Maoist attacks and having suffered the ignominy of being worsted in the early battles.

One well-documented case happened in Akalgharuwa village, Banke district where armed Maoists arrived on the evening of 9 July 2002 and dragged all the males above 15 years of age out from their homes. They took around 25 of them to the nearby well and beat them severely, accusing them of handing over two of their comrades to the police. After the beating, Sohanlal Yadav and Moti Tamauli were hacked with an axe and a khukuri and shot dead. Not content with killing Yadav and Tamauli, both very poor, the Maoists also bombed and destroyed their houses and mercilessly beat and shot six others, injuring them seriously. Almost all the males in the village, including a few old men, were beaten up.[4]

As for the Royal Nepalese Army, it told Amnesty International that its mission was to 'disarm and defeat' the Maoists. Amnesty reported: 'The definition of what constitutes a "Maoist", according to army commanders interviewed by Amnesty International, includes civilians who give shelter, food, or money to the armed Maoists. The fact that much of this "assistance" is given under threat from the Maoists was not fully recognised… In this context, killings of "Maoists" in "encounters" with the security forces are reported on a daily basis compared to the very few reports of Maoists injured or arrested, suggesting that at least some units within the security forces have operated a policy of deliberately killing Maoist suspects instead of arresting them.'[5]

Writer Manjushree Thapa provides a very poignant account of one such case.[6]

Bhandariya is a cluster of three settlements in the open expanses of Bageshwari VDC (village development committee), Banke district, a mixed settlement that came into being in the 1970s, as official policies encouraging migration from the hills made neighbours of hill and tarai castes, majority and minority religions and many small ethnic groups. Most residents farm their own small plots and sharecrop the lands of those better off.

On the front porch of Mansaraa Budha's house, the teenage daughter of the house is urging bullocks to mill around in circles, threshing grains from the hay underfoot. She is a dishevelled girl with hard, watchful eyes. She has good reason to be mistrustful. It was the visit of four Maoists six months ago that left her bereft of a father, and of the will to better her life.

On the evening of 2 June 2002, four unarmed Maoists had asked for shelter at Mansaraa's house. 'Maoists would pass by here often', says a villager. 'They would come and go as they please'. They had never stayed before at this particular house, but like other villagers before them, Mansaraa and her husband Prem Bahadur could not turn away these unwelcome guests: who, after all, would protect them if the Maoists turned on them?

The family's clay house consists of two rooms, an alcove, and an attached cowshed. Mansaraa's youngest son, studying in class eight, slept on the porch with the visitors. Prem Bahadur, Mansaraa, their two daughters and their daughter-in-law, six months pregnant with her first child, slept indoors.

Villagers say that a large convoy of security forces drove into Bhandariya in the dead of the night and surrounded the nearby houses. In the dark, they dragged those sleeping on Mansaraa's porch to the front courtyard, making them all face down. They also stormed neighbouring houses, asking everyone to identify themselves and the men on Mansaraa's courtyard.

Villagers say that the uniforms worn by the security forces belonged to the army. Some of the army men were visibly drunk, they say. When one of the Maoists tried to run away, he was shot dead. Mansaraa's daughter — the one leading bullocks in the courtyard today — rushed out to see what was happening, only to be kicked and slapped around. 'Are you a Maoist girl?' asked two army men. Maoists had in the past held cultural programmes in the area to attract young cadres. The men asked, 'Do you know how to sing and dance?'

They let her go after her family identified her, but her face was marked and bruised. She was in such shock she did not notice that the army men were beating her brother along with the Maoists. According to villagers, they beat the three Maoists to death. They spared Mansaraa's younger son's life, but left him badly injured.

By this time Mansaraa had fainted. Her husband, convinced that he would be killed for housing Maoists, hid in a narrow space between the shingle roof and a tin sheet over the cowshed. There was just enough space there for one person to squeeze into. Army men hunted for him through the house, checking every grain vessel. When they found him, they killed him with two shots to the back.

They then hauled the bodies into an ambulance accompanying their convoy, and left. The family was in utter shock. 'What could we do?' Mansaraa says. 'We stayed, we cried. No, we could not even cry. We were afraid someone else might come, something else might happen'. She is bewildered: nobody from any of the other houses came to see how her family was doing. The next morning, some villagers said that they had not heard a thing.

They were too afraid to get involved.

The concept that citizens have rights — even if they are suspected Maoists — is clearly unfamiliar here. 'If the Maoists had not stayed at our house, none of this would have happened,' says Mansaraa, unable to blame the army for what, by all accounts, amounted to her husband's summary execution.

*　*　*

Mistaken identities have been all too common. One of the most tragic instances must be what occurred in Angapani village in Bajura district. Being about a day's walk from Martadi, the district headquarters, the villagers had been pretty much left to fend for themselves against the Maoists. But now and then the army and police would patrol their area, as happened on 28 October 2003. Having trekked the whole night and arrived in Angapani at the crack of dawn, they saw lights in a house and heard voices inside. They surrounded the house and ordered those inside to come outside. Instead the light was turned off and everything became silent. The order to open the door was given once again but there was no response. The troops then stormed into the house and killed everyone inside.

Seven people lost their lives; and all because of a misunderstanding. The seven were local villagers who had sat down for a night of gambling after harvesting their millet. 'Villagers think they may have suspected the people outside to be local Maoists, who have banned drinking and gambling. So they turned the lights off and kept quiet... Ironically, three of the dead were members of the "Kaal Sena", an anti-Maoist resistance group that the villagers had formed after they couldn't bear harassment by the Maoist militia any more.'[7]

Such then are the tragedies that have unfolded by the day since the 'people's war' began in 1996. One of the most widely accepted sources reports that 6,848 people had died until the end of August 2004.[8] The larger tragedy of the living is yet to be documented in full. That can happen only when permanent peace returns to the country.

Crowds fill up the avenue in front of Singha Durbar on the momentous day of 6 April, 1990.

Politics in Nepal
(1768–1996)

THE REASONS behind the Maoist 'people's war' are to be found in a complex of factors, not least of which is the historical legacy of Nepal's rulers ignoring the people's needs in pursuit of their personal gains. This trend continued even after the 1990 People's Movement had restored a working democracy. This chapter surveys the course taken by Nepali politics from 1768 to 1996 as the background to understanding the causes of the Maoist insurgency. It covers the autocratic Rana rule; the short-lived exercise of a form of democracy in the 1950s; the 1960 to 1990 authoritarian Panchayat regime; the growth and splintering of the Nepali communist parties; the 1990 People's Movement; and the (mis)rule of the post-1990 democratic governments. (A chronology from the founding of the Communist Party Nepal in 1949 through to the 4 June 2003 change of government is provided in Annex I).

The formation of the Nepali state

The history of the nation-state of Nepal is generally considered to have begun in 1768-69. This was when Prithvi Narayan Shah, the ruler of the small kingdom of Gorkha, completed the conquest of the Kathmandu Valley, culminating a military campaign he had begun nearly a quarter century before. Prior to Prithvi Narayan Shah's conquests, which ultimately resulted in the unification of the central Himalaya into one kingdom, the area covered by Nepal today was divided into dozens of principalities and kingdoms. By the time of his death at the age of 53 in 1775, the kingdom of Gorkha covered nearly the entire eastern half of present-day Nepal.

Prithvi Narayan Shah's descendants continued with the Gorkha conquest. Within 40 years of his death, the Gorkhalis had managed to bring under their control an area that extended from the Teesta River in the east up to the Sutlej River in the west, an area nearly twice the size of today's Nepal.

The rise of the Gorkhas coincided with the growing influence of the mercantile power, the English East India Company, in India. It was natural that the two expanding powers — the English East India Company and the Gorkha empire — should find cause for conflict. This happened in 1814 and the Gorkhalis were worsted in the war that followed. As per the terms of the 1816 peace treaty that ended the war, the geographical extent of Nepal was largely confined to its current boundaries.

On the political front in Kathmandu, the war with the British served to intensify the court rivalries and intrigues that had begun immediately after the demise of Prithvi Narayan Shah. This led ultimately, in 1846, to Jang Bahadur Rana usurping absolute power, and reducing the monarchy to a figurehead. By royal decree wrangled from the king, Jang Bahadur was able to ensure that the position of prime minister would be retained within his family, to be passed from brother to brother in terms of seniority.

The change of 1951

The following 104 years of Rana rule is a dark blot on the history of Nepal. All state power was vested in the prime minister, and the Ranas ruled Nepal as their personal fiefdom. The prime minister had the run of the country's treasury to use for whatever purpose he deemed fit, which usually meant the aggrandisement of himself and his family.

Apart from the rampant looting of the country's resources and the accompanying impoverishment of the countryside that led to large-scale migrations to India, the Ranas also imposed virtual isolation on the country since they were afraid of outside influences entering Nepal, possibly leading to a challenge to their hold on the state. And, in a sense, their policy of seclusion succeeded as the popular movements that buffeted the rest of South Asia during the first half of the twentieth century largely bypassed Nepal.

However, this isolationist policy was only one-sided, since although outsiders were not allowed in, Nepalis did go out of the country. For one, there was a continuous stream of people migrating to India in order to escape penury from their hill homesteads. These people either joined the Indian army or found some other form of employment, and settled in large numbers in India. And it was from among these groups that the first stirrings against the Ranas began.

Within Nepal, it was only in 1936 that a movement against Rana rule began with the formation of the Nepal Praja Parishad. The Praja Parishad advocated reforms and fomented anti-establishment sentiments among the people. But the Rana rulers quickly crushed the movement. However, the seeds had been sown, and the time for popular activity against the Ranas ripened with the end of British rule in India in 1947, since the government of the newly independent India was not particularly enamoured of the anachronistic Rana regime.

Earlier, in 1946, the Nepali National Congress had been set up in Banaras, India by a group of Nepali exiles. In 1950, the Nepali National Congress and the Nepal Democratic Congress, which had been founded in Calcutta in 1948, merged to form the Nepali Congress and decided to launch an armed movement against the Ranas. The Nepal Congress found an ally in King Tribhuvan, who also wanted the Rana yoke off his neck.

On 6 November 1950, as part of a coordinated effort, King Tribhuvan took refuge in the Indian embassy in Kathmandu along with Crown Prince Mahendra, grandson Birendra, and other members of his family. Four days later they were flown to Delhi by the Indian government.

Within days, the Nepali Congress began its armed insurrection by capturing the border town of Birganj. Armed groups made similar forays in various parts of Nepal. Over the next three months a see-saw battle raged between government troops and rebel forces. It was clear that the central authority of the Ranas had weakened. Battered on the battlefront by the rebels and unable to stave off Indian diplomatic pressure, Prime Minister Mohan Shamsher Jang Bahadur Rana capitulated. Delhi brokered a peace and on 7 February 1951 worked out a compromise between King Tribhuvan, the Ranas and the Nepali Congress. This has since become known as the Delhi Compromise. Under this arrangement, the king was to return with his powers restored and the Ranas and the Nepali Congress would jointly form an interim government that would hold elections to a constituent assembly to draw up a democratic constitution by 1952. (This demand to set up a constituent assembly remains unrealised to this day and, at the time of writing, continues to be one of the Maoists' central demands.)

Decade of instability: 1951-1960

King Tribhuvan returned home on 15 February and three days later made the historic proclamation that 'our wish and decision is that the government of our people will henceforth be carried out according to a democratic constitution prepared by a constituent assembly elected by them...'.[1]

The fall of the Rana regime meant a semblance of democratic governance was introduced in the country. The Interim Constitution promulgated in April 1951 provided various democratic safeguards such as establishing an independent judiciary, and limiting the king's role to a constitutional one. However, the Rana-Congress coalition government that took office on 18 February 1951 with Mohan Shamsher heading it, was doomed to failure from the very beginning. Stumbling from one crisis to another, B.P. Koirala, the home minister and the Nepali Congress' leader in the cabinet, finally resigned, and the other Congress cabinet ministers followed suit. This led to the downfall of the government itself in November 1951, an event that was to pave the way for a period of chronic instability.

As the largest political party and the one that had spearheaded the revolution, the Nepali Congress was the natural choice to lead the next government. But, surprisingly, instead of appointing the charismatic Congress leader, B.P. Koirala, as had been expected, the king nominated Matrika Prasad Koirala, B.P.'s elder brother, as the first commoner prime minister in 105 years. Unlike B.P., the senior Koirala did not have a support base within the party. King Tribhuvan seems to have calculated that appointing a prime minister without a personal following would mean that the new PM would have to rely more on the king's authority than party backing in order to rule.

Differences soon cropped up between the two Koiralas and less than a year later, Matrika Prasad resigned. This was to herald the beginning of a more active role for the monarchy in affairs of the state. With all the political parties in disarray, it provided just the right opportunity for the king to move out of the shadows of his constitutional role and begin participating actively in government decision-making.

King Tribhuvan died in March 1955, and his successor Mahendra, was to prove to be more than a match for the politicians. Despite street protests launched from various quarters, King Mahendra was able to hold the political parties at bay as he further consolidated the position of the monarchy. Beginning with the resignation of Matrika Prasad Koirala, the various governments appointed served in office at the king's pleasure and the politicians in their short-sightedness were only too willing to be pawns in the monarch's quest for a larger political role. Finally, when Mahendra reluctantly agreed to elections, it was not to be for a constituent assembly as promised by his late father, but to a parliament under a constitution that was to be 'granted' by him as the repository of the country's sovereignty. It is believed that given the intense internal conflicts within the political parties, King Mahendra calculated on no single party winning a majority, leaving a divided parliament that would be fair game for further manipulation by him.

The Constitution of the Kingdom of Nepal 1959, which was promulgated just a week before the elections, made it clear that the king was the source of all power.[2] Furthermore, its various clauses severely diluted the powers of the cabinet and provided the king with extraordinary powers that directly contradicted the principles of cabinet government. In effect, it created two power centres in the king and the prime minister.

The Nepali Congress and other political parties, including the Communist Party of Nepal (CPN), had no choice but to participate in the elections under such a constitution since the alternative would have been a renewed round of agitation, and after eight years of fruitless tussling with the throne,[3] the politicians seemed to have run out of steam.

The Nepali Congress government

In the first general elections held in February 1959, the Nepali Congress won a two-third majority in the 109-seat parliament. Although it secured just over 37 per cent of the vote, the first-past-the-post system enabled it to garner a clear majority of 74 seats.

Nepal's first democratically elected government took office in May 1959 with B.P. Koirala as prime minister. The Nepali Congress had adopted democratic socialism at its national conference in 1956, and the new government began to tread carefully along this path. Steps were taken towards providing free education and a health care system. A cautious attempt at land reform was initiated, mainly aimed at doing away with the tax-free *birta* landholding system, a legacy of Nepal's feudal past.

This government has been credited with having a 'record of accomplishment unparalleled by that of any previous government in Nepal'.[4] But its reformist policies did not go down well with all sections of society. The powerful landed class viewed the limited land reforms with alarm.

There was also the question of the personal dynamics between B.P. Koirala and King Mahendra. Relations between the two were never very smooth. While the king did not overtly interfere in the working of the government, his presence was never so far away. He continued to cultivate a base for himself through gestures such as receiving petitions and distributing state funds in a manner that was not quite becoming of the monarch in a parliamentary system.

Koirala's government lasted less than two years. On 15 December, 1960, King Mahendra dissolved parliament and arrested B.P. Koirala and some of his cabinet colleagues under the emergency powers vested in him by the constitution. This brought to an end Nepal's first experiment with democracy and King Mahendra took over total control of the country.

The Panchayat years

The takeover by King Mahendra laid the foundation for three decades of direct rule by the monarchy. Political parties were banned and many leaders were jailed or went into exile in India. The ban affected the Nepali Congress more than any other party, possibly because the king perceived it and its popular support to be the greatest threat to his authority.[5] In a bid to weaken it, defections from the Nepali Congress were encouraged and the ploy worked in that two of the prime ministers of the immediate post-1960 period belonged originally to the Nepali Congress.

Although some of the main leaders were imprisoned, others had escaped to India where they regrouped and planned an armed struggle against the king's regime. In late 1961, attacks by the Nepali Congress began with the covert support of Indian Prime Minister, Jawaharlal Nehru.[6] Although the Congress rebels were not able to repeat their successes of 1950, they did serve as irritants that a king still consolidating his position could have done without. The rebel activity, however, ceased abruptly when China invaded India in October 1962, and India could no longer afford to antagonise a buffer state like Nepal.

On 16 December 1962, King Mahendra proclaimed the 1962 Constitution of Nepal and established the Panchayat system. This was his own form of 'guided democracy' that was in vogue in many Third World countries at that time. The justification for the Panchayat system, touted as a partyless democracy, was made on the grounds that the country was not ready for multiparty politics and that the new system was suited to the 'climate and soil' of the country. In effect, it provided for a semblance of a national legislature – elected indirectly by the people through three tiers of village, district, and zonal assemblies – but which did not have any real legislative powers. The constitution did provide for a prime minister but he was beholden to the king for his office, and the ultimate source of his authority was the king. Because of the immense power the king wielded, the separation of powers between the legislature, the judiciary, and the executive became thoroughly blurred.

But the Panchayat system also spawned various groups that acted as an opposition from within. Factionalism resulted either from inter-personal feuds or from ideological considerations. In either case, the main goal was to reach positions of power. It, however, served to illustrate the hollowness of claims by Panchayat apologists that it would be free of the bickering that characterised parliamentary systems.

In 1980, King Birendra, who had ascended the throne eight years earlier, ordered a national referendum that offered people a choice between a 'reformed' Panchayat system and a multiparty system after student demonstrations snowballed into a situation of countrywide unrest against the government. This referendum provided an opportunity for the banned parties to reach out to the public for the first time in two decades. Many of the leaders who had been jailed for non-criminal offences were released and a measure of press freedom allowed. The Panchayat system won the vote in an election that was widely believed to have been rigged.

The promised 'reforms' were incorporated in the third amendment to the Panchayat constitution. The changes allowed for direct elections to the national legislature on the basis of universal franchise; the appointment of the prime minister on the recommendation of the legislature; and the cabinet becoming answerable to the legislature.[7] Although in practice, the king still wielded ultimate power, these provisions widened the political space for the political parties. Some became more involved in politics and began supporting candidates in the ostensibly partyless elections. Thus, for the first time in twenty years the country saw legislators with declared sympathies for the outlawed parties.

Another consequence of the referendum was that the Nepali Congress and certain factions of the communist movement began to work together against the Panchayat system. This cooperation was to pay dividends in 1985 when the Nepali Congress launched a *satyagraha*,[8] and the communists complemented this with a 'fill-the-jails' campaign. But a series of bomb blasts in the capital that resulted in a number of deaths led to the movement being called off. Although the India-based Popular Front led by Ram Raja Prasad Singh claimed responsibility for the attacks,[9] popular speculation was that the palace itself had been responsible for the explosions, which were used as a ruse to scuttle the opposition movement.

Direct opposition politics calmed down until the 1990 Movement for the Restoration of Democracy (also known as the People's Movement) faced up to a considerably weakened system. But the 1986 general election resulted in the presence of nine known leftist legislators in the Rastriya Panchayat along with an almost equal number with democratic sympathies, who were able to undermine the Panchayat system with their criticisms from within.[10] The staunch Panchayat supporters were also divided into various groupings, and their disunity and conflicting actions were to lead to the undoing of the Panchayat system in 1990.

Communist Party of Nepal

Although the Nepali Congress dominated the pre-1950 anti-Rana political space, a nascent communist movement had also become active around that time. It first emerged during the 1947 strike by workers at the Biratnagar jute and cloth mills in eastern Nepal. Leading the workers was Man Mohan Adhikari (Nepal's first and so far only communist prime minister, 1994-95). Adhikari was then a member of the Communist Party of India. There was no Nepali communist party and it wasn't until a couple of years later that one was formed.

When the Nepali National Congress was founded in 1946 as the first anti-Rana organisation, it drew in everyone committed to ending Rana rule. Among them was Pushpa Lal Shrestha, who served as the party's office secretary. But disillusioned by the policy of non-violent struggle and the leadership squabbles, Pushpa Lal quit the party and immersed himself in setting up a communist party. In April 1949, Pushpa Lal translated and published the *Communist Manifesto* in Nepali, making it the first Marxist work in the Nepali language. The Manifesto was made public on 15 September 1949, the date that is considered the founding day of the Communist Party of Nepal (CPN).[11]

At the time of the 1950 uprising, the CPN was just a fledgling entity. Apart from viewing the Nepali Congress as a party representing the moneyed classes, mainly because of its association with the disgruntled Ranas, the communists were not very clear about their role during the movement. Even though armed groups of communists had been active as part of the Mukti Sena ('Liberation Troops'), the Nepali Congress' forces against the Ranas, the CPN denounced the Delhi Compromise between the Nepali Congress, King Tribhuvan, and the Ranas, calling it a 'betrayal' of the revolution.[12] Later, during its First Congress of September 1951, the CPN maintained that the 1951 revolution had no political significance because it had not been a total revolution.

Pre-1960 CPN

During the immediate post-Rana period, the communists adopted a strongly anti-Congress position. They considered the Nepali Congress to be 'a 'stooge' of the Indian Government and called upon all 'progressive forces' to form a broad 'People's Front to fight it'.[13] Accordingly, the CPN entered into an alliance with the other virulently anti-Congress party, the Tanka Prasad Acharya-led Praja Parishad,[14] and formed the National People's United Front in July 1951. The Front's manifesto declared that the Nepali Congress was the 'Nehru government's toy'.[15] It further emphasised that a large proportion of Nepal's commercial and industrial enterprises were in Indian hands, and that India was trying to prevent Nepal from becoming friendly towards China. In other words, it tried to prove its credentials by adopting an anti-Indian stance, as opposed to the perceived pro-India bias of the Nepali Congress.

However, an incident during the tenure of the first Matrika Prasad Koirala government led to the gradual withering away of the Front. On 20-21 January 1952, the Raksha Dal, the paramilitary force that had been created largely out of the Mukti Sena, staged a revolt. The leadership of the mutiny fell on K.I. Singh, a Mukti Sena commander who had been imprisoned in Kathmandu since 1951 for not accepting the Delhi Compromise and continuing to lead his troops on a spree of 'revolutionary' violence. As the revolt continued, on 21 January Singh put forth his demands, which included the formation of an all-party government. The government troops were soon able to regain control of the situation and the revolt ended when Singh fled from the scene. The CPN, however, tried to claim responsibility for the revolt even though there was no indication of its direct involvement. This resulted in the party being outlawed, and from then on all its activities were carried out underground until the ban was lifted in April 1956 by the government led by Tanka Prasad Acharya.

The CPN did not let up in its activities during the ban period, but internally it was not faring so well. A leadership struggle had begun soon after the Rana regime ended. In 1951, the politbureau replaced Pushpa Lal with Man Mohan Adhikari as general secretary, a move that was 'the beginning of the never-ending leadership struggle within the party', and a bane that was to affect all factions that branched out of the main party.[16] The First Congress of the CPN was held in secret in January 1954. It confirmed Man Mohan Adhikari as general secretary, and again reiterated the CPN's opposition to the Delhi Compromise. It also 'adopted the resolution upholding "continuous struggle" against [the] "feudalist" regime and advocating replacement of the monarchy by a republic formed by an elected Constituent Assembly'.[17]

Another crisis erupted in 1955, when the CPN's leadership changed its stance on the monarchy and accepted the king as the country's constitutional head. This came in the form of a statement from the general secretary, Man Mohan Adhikari, and is believed to have been a compromise formula worked out with the then Tanka Prasad Acharya government in return for it lifting the ban on the CPN. Whatever may have been the rationale, the statement only served to exacerbate tensions within the party and accusations began to be heard that 'rightists' were beginning to use the party for their own ends.

Adhikari left Nepal for China for medical treatment soon after the ban on the party was lifted, and Keshar Jung Rayamajhi took over as acting general secretary. The radicals led by Pushpa Lal had opposed the pro-king statement 'as an inexcusable compromise with the basic tenets of the party ideology'[18] and Rayamajhi's assumption of the leadership during the party's Second Congress in 1957 led to further polarisation of the positions between the faction which favoured cooperation with other democratic forces and the one that was for 'an adventurist and fighting policy'.[19]

When King Mahendra announced parliamentary elections, the CPN central committee decided to take part in it, but, for the record it registered a protest that the elections were not being held for a constituent assembly. The decision to contest the elections was passed because the moderates were in a majority in the CPN central committee and their decision was motivated by pragmatism; Pushpa Lal, with his uncompromising stance against the elections, failed to persuade them otherwise.[20] The CPN's dismal performance at the 1959 polls, however, served to weaken the authority of General Secretary Rayamajhi, and led to a growing radicalisation of a section of the CPN.

The communist movement in the Panchayat era

The 1960 takeover by King Mahendra affected the CPN more than any other party. While it is true than many Congress stalwarts joined the Panchayat establishment, the party as such remained intact under the unchallenged leadership of B.P. Koirala, and, after his death in 1982, under the troika consisting of Ganesh Man Singh, Krishna Prasad Bhattarai, and Girija Prasad Koirala. In the case of the CPN, however, it saw the beginning of a process of splits and mergers that continue to this day—a process that led to the emergence of the Communist Party of Nepal (Maoist) more than three decades later.

CPN general secretary, Keshar Jung Rayamajhi was in Moscow at the time of the 'palace coup' and he welcomed the king's dissolution of parliament as a 'progressive' step. But in Kathmandu, Pushpa Lal issued a circular in the name of the politbureau demanding an end to the 'military terror' and calling for a conference of all parliamentary parties.[21] The communists had clearly divided into two factions: (1) the one led by Rayamajhi—the pro-Moscow faction; and (2) the group consisting of Pushpa Lal Shrestha, Man Mohan Adhikari, Tulsi Lal Amatya, among others—the pro-Peking faction. (This division also reflected the split in the Communist Party of India along similar lines.[22])

The Darbhanga plenum: In March 1961, the CPN held an expanded meeting of the central committee (known as a plenum) in Darbhanga, India, and after a month of heated debate, voting took place on which one of the three major 'political lines' it should adopt. The first was Rayamajhi's proposal that called for supporting constitutional monarchy and guided democracy; the second, proposed by Pushpa Lal, sought to restore the erstwhile parliament and favoured joint action with the Nepali Congress against the monarchy; whilst the third demanded an election to a constituent assembly, and opposed both support for a constitutional monarchy and working with the Nepali Congress. The third proposal came from Mohan Bikram Singh, who had been elected to the central committee during the Second Congress in 1957, and who was to make a name for himself as a radical in the left movement in the years to come.

Singh's proposal received the overwhelming majority of votes but the party's central committee chose to ignore that decision and chose to adopt Rayamajhi's proposal instead. Within a couple of months, Rayamajhi declared that he was in favour of a civil disobedience movement for the restoration of fundamental rights, but that any such movement should not have the overthrow of the monarchy as its objective.[23] This provoked the anti-Rayamajhi group to hold the party's Third Congress in Banaras in April 1962 and expel Rayamajhi and four others from the party on the charge of supporting King Mahendra's 'undemocratic' action. But this was only a formality because, in effect, the party had already split.

The Third Congress chose Tulsi Lal Amatya as the new general secretary. It also elected a National Council which passed a resolution that the Panchayat system was sustaining a 'military dictatorship', and that the 'highly exploitative' feudal system was destined to collapse. But because Pushpa Lal adopted a more extreme position, the CPN was to see yet another feud dominate its leadership, this time between Pushpa Lal and Tulsi Lal. In May 1968, Pushpa Lal and his associates held a meeting at Gorakhpur and announced the formation of a separate party with Pushpa Lal as general secretary.

(The fortunes of Pushpa Lal's new party turned out to be no different from that of the original CPN. Factionalism was rife and many splits had occurred by the time of his death in 1978. However, almost all left factions, including the Maoists, recognise his contribution to Nepal's communist movement, and his memory as the founder of the CPN is widely revered.)

The central nucleus: By the late 1960s the various divisions in the CPN's leadership were also affecting the party at the cadre level. With many of the leaders either in prison or in India, local units had begun operating independently. In theory, they were all affiliated to the CPN, but their activities were uncoordinated as there was no central command structure.[24] The existence of the party itself was at stake when some of the jailed leaders decided they had to find a way to get out of jail in order to revive it.[25] Accordingly, Man Mohan Adhikari and Sambhu Ram Shrestha signed a statement in which they agreed to assist and support the king without reservation. They were released in 1968.[26] And in December 1971, by when both Nirmal Lama and Mohan Bikram Singh had also been released, a 'central nucleus' was formed as a step towards creating a unified party apparatus. The aim was to bring the various strands of the communist movement under one party umbrella.[27]

The central nucleus also tried to include Pushpa Lal and his party. But it failed because the former wanted Pushpa Lal to dissolve his party, while Pushpa Lal proposed that everyone else should be subsumed within his party and remained staunch in his insistence on working with the Nepali Congress against the Panchayat system.[28]

The Fourth Congress: Differences soon arose within the central nucleus as well. But the Mohan Bikram group, which included Nirmal Lama, went ahead and held the 'Fourth Congress' of their faction of the CPN in September 1974 in Banaras, India.[29] Their faction called itself the CPN (Fourth Congress [Fourth Convention], or Chautho Mahadiveshan) with Mohan Bikram Singh as its general secretary. The Fourth Congress, which was to become the strongest communist grouping over the following decade, was very clear on the question of armed revolution. At the party's Nationwide District Secretaries' Conference held in 1979, Nirmal Lama, who had replaced Mohan Bikram as general secretary, proposed 'training guerillas, proletarianising party cadre, creating separate base areas, taking action against local cheats, and initiating an agrarian uprising'. His proposal was duly adopted.[30] (This was the very course that the CPN [Maoist] was to take from the mid-1990s.) But this campaign ended with the announcement of the national referendum in May 1979.

Although initially hesitant about an appropriate response to the referendum call, the Fourth Congress appealed to all left parties to collectively demand a free and fair referendum. It also worked with other communist forces to lead an agitation insisting that five pre-conditions be fulfilled before they took part in the referendum.[31] Nirmal Lama was thus able to bring about a working understanding among the Left; but, as general secretary, he faced criticism within his own party for accepting a referendum proposed by the king, and was forced to quit his post.[32]

After the referendum and the disputed victory for the Panchayat system, Nirmal Lama was in favour of taking the opportunity to penetrate the Panchayat bodies,[33] while Mohan Bikram preferred boycotting elections.[34] Finally, in 1983, the two leaders decided to go their own ways and the Fourth Congress broke up into the Nirmal Lama and the Mohan Bikram factions.

The Jhapa uprising and the CPN (ML): A real communist uprising took place in Jhapa around the time Mohan Bikram, Nirmal Lama and others were busy with the central nucleus. The Jhapa uprising (Box 1) may have just been naïve romanticism fuelled by the youth of its leaders but its significance lay in the fact that it was the first armed communist rebellion in Nepal. Its long-term impact, however, was much greater since out of this movement grew the largest communist party the country has ever seen—the CPN (Unified Marxist-Leninist).

The first steps towards establishing the CPN (ML) began at the June 1975 conference held by the Jhapa District Committee with representatives from others districts, leading to the formation of

---

Box 1. The Jhapa uprising

In 1967, a radical grouping within the Communist Party of India (Marxist) began a peasants' movement in the Naxalbari area of West Bengal, India. Although the rebellion, which has since spawned several similar uprisings all over India, was soon put down, one of its repercussions was the formation of the CPI (Marxist-Leninist) in 1969 by disgruntled elements in the CPI (Marxist). The CPI (ML) recognised Mao Tse-tung as 'our chairman' and believed revolution was the only way to fell the old state. This was around the time of the Cultural Revolution in China, and Beijing encouraged the would-be revolutionaries by reporting extensively on their activities in its press.

Jhapa lies just across the border river of Mechi from Naxalbari. The goings-on in both India and China were noticed by some young communist organisers who were active in the Jhapa District Committee of the East Kosi Coordination Committee (nominally under Man Mohan Adhikari). The CPI (ML) did not only provide ideological inspiration; they also 'loaned' two activists to the Nepalis.[35] The Coordination Committee began its campaign to eliminate 'class enemies' in May 1971, and managed to wipe out eight of them.[36] But the 'revolution' was soon crushed by the government which executed seven of the leaders and imprisoned many others. The Jhapa uprising was not able to achieve much in terms of fostering a communist revolution, but its leaders did succeed in building the largest communist organisation in the country, the Communist Party of Nepal (Unified Marxist-Leninist).

the All Nepal Communist Coordination Committee. Over the next few years, other localised movements joined the Coordination Committee and in December 1978 the CPN (Marxist-Leninist, or ML, pronounced Ma-Le) was established at a national conference. The process of incorporating smaller groups within the CPN (ML) continued and by the time of the 1990 People's Movement, it had become the largest communist organisation in the country with a claimed network in 50 districts.[37]

Fourth Congress, Masal, and Mashal: After breaking off with Nirmal Lama, Mohan Bikram Singh set up his own party in November 1983 called the CPN (Masal).[38] In 1984, Masal became one of the founding members of the Revolutionary Internationalist Movement (RIM), the worldwide grouping of Maoist parties. Box 2 gives a brief description of RIM and jumps ahead to outline its supposed contribution to the growth of the Maoist movement in Nepal.

In 1985, after its Fifth Congress, Masal broke up once more, this time into CPN (Masal) and CPN (Mashal), with the latter led by Mohan Baidya.[39] Under Baidya's leadership, the CPN (Mashal) adopted the doctrine of a violent movement in the hope of instigating a mass uprising. The so-called 'Sector Incident' of 1989, in which King Tribhuvan's statue at Tripureshwor was blackened and some police posts attacked, was part of that strategy. But, because the accompanying publicity resulted in the party becoming publicly known, the central committee deemed it a mistake, and Mohan Baidya was removed to make way for Pushpa Kamal Dahal (better known by his nom de guerre Prachanda) as general secretary.[40]

The second coming of democracy

With the death in 1982 of B.P. Koirala, the Nepali Congress was being led by the triumvirate of Ganesh Man Singh, Krishna Prasad Bhattarai (as acting president), and Girija Prasad Koirala (as general secretary). But apart from the aborted satyagraha in 1985, the oldest political party in the country seriously lacked direction. A number of its leaders had entered the Panchayat system after the 1980 referendum and by the late 1980s there was speculation that more were ready to follow. On the other side, preparations were on to amend the constitution further to allow political parties to participate in Panchayat politics.[41]

Box 2. Revolutionary Internationalist Movement (RIM)

The Revolutionary Internationalist Movement is a worldwide grouping of revolutionary parties committed to the 'scientific principles of Marxism-Leninism-Mao Tsetung Thought'. Its origins can be found in the first international conference of Maoist parties held at an unspecified location in the autumn of 1980. It was during the second conference in London in March 1984 that RIM was formed. The task it laid before itself was to 'hasten the development of the world revolution—the overthrow of imperialism and reaction by the proletariat and the revolutionary masses; the establishment of the dictatorship of the proletariat in accordance with the necessary stages and alliances in different countries; and the struggle to eliminate all the material and ideological vestiges of exploiting society and thus achieve classless society, communism, throughout the world'. It identified the following 'preliminary steps' to achieve its objectives:[42]

1. An international journal must be developed as a vital tool in reconstructing the international communist movement. It must be at once both an organ of analysis and political commentary as well as a forum for debating the questions of the international movement. It must be translated into as many languages as possible, vigorously distributed in the ranks of the Marxist-Leninist parties and among other revolutionary forces. The Marxist-Leninist parties must correspond regularly with the journal and contribute articles and criticism.

2. Helping the formation of new Marxist-Leninist parties and the strengthening of existing ones is the common task of the international communist movement. The ways and means must be found for the international movement as a whole to assist Marxist-Leninists in different countries in carrying out this crucial task.

3. Joint and coordinated campaigns should be conducted by the Marxist-Leninist parties and organisations The First of May activities should be carried out under unified slogans.

4. The different Marxist-Leninist parties and organisations should carry out the political line and decisions adopted by the International Conferences and agreed to by these parties, even while continuing to carry out principled struggle over differences.

5. All Marxist-Leninist parties and organisations should, within the measure of their capacity, contribute financially and practically to the tasks involved in furthering the unity of the communists.

6. An interim committee—an embryonic political centre—must be set up to lead the overall process of furthering the ideological, political and organisational unity of communists, including the preparation of a draft proposal for a general line for the communist movement.

The CPN (Masal) was among the signatories establishing RIM. Andrew Nickson wrote that Baburam Bhattarai was RIM's main contact in Nepal until at least 1992.[43] That was long after Masal had split and the breakaway Mashal itself had become part of the Unity Centre, a grouping Bhattarai had himself joined. Thus, for a time, Nepal was represented in RIM by both Masal and the Unity Centre. In 1996, Masal was expelled from RIM because of differences, among other things, over the RIM committee's support to the CPN (Maoist), which remains the only Nepali communist party within RIM at present.[44]

The only tangible contribution of RIM's to the growth of the Maoist movement in Nepal seems to have been publicising it in its journal, *A World to Win*, which is also published in Nepali. However, Prachanda refers appreciatively to RIM in his paper 'The Great Leap Forward: An Inevitable Need of History', that was adopted by the CPN (Maoist)'s Second National Conference in February 2001:

> Now, Marxism-Leninism-Maoism is there as an ideological foundation for the creation of a new communist international. All the communist revolutionaries need to march forward seriously to give it an organised form through class and ideological struggle. Today RIM has already emerged as an embryo of it. Everybody has to attempt to refine and develop it. Special attention must be paid to conducting discussions and interactions with revolutionaries outside RIM and uniting them in the movement.

> Further down, Prachanda also acknowledged the role of the 'high level of theoretical interaction with the RIM committee', in the development of 'Prachanda Path'.[45]

But the winds of change that had blown across eastern Europe in 1989 also reached Nepal towards the end of the year and political parties began hectic parleys to prepare for a new stage of struggle against the king's autocracy. There was no doubt that the politicians calculated on their agenda of change becoming more amenable to the people for, apart from the general disenchantment with the Panchayat system, the population was also undergoing considerable hardship due to a situation that had arisen through no cause of the establishment. This was the expiry of a trade and transit treaty between Nepal and India in March 1989, which India refused to renew. It resulted in what has been called an economic blockade, with only two transit points kept open by India along its entire border with Nepal. For a country so overwhelmingly dependent on its southern neighbour, both for trade and transit, these restrictions entailed considerable hardship to the people who had to experience the rationing of essential supplies. This blockade, which nearly brought about the collapse of Nepal's economy, led to further bitterness against the government.

The People's Movement

The 1980 referendum and the aborted satyagraha had proved that the Congress and the communists working together were a potent political force. But it had also become clear that neither side could hope to lead a movement on its own. Although there was still the outstanding issue of the Left's division into a dozen or so parties and factions, the differences were overcome in the spirit of the longing for change when seven of them, including the CPN (ML) and the CPN (Marxist), came together to form the United Left Front. Sahana Pradhan, Pushpa Lal's widow and leader of the CPN (Marxist), was made chairperson.[46] The formation of the Front was announced on 15 January 1990, and three days later a national convention was held by the (still-outlawed) Nepali Congress in Kathmandu, during which Ganesh Man Singh announced that beginning on the 18th of February a national movement would be launched against the Panchayat system to restore multiparty democracy.

The 18th of February had been chosen for its historic significance since it was on the same date precisely 39 years previously that King Tribhuvan had declared the end of the Rana regime and heralded the dawn democracy in Nepal. Four decades later, the same day was to initiate a new struggle to usher in democracy once again.

Political activities for the movement began well in advance. A Joint Coordination Committee was set up to liaise between the two main constituents of the Movement for the Restoration of Democracy, the Nepali Congress and the United Left Front.

The Movement kicked off as planned on 18 February, but its progress was hardly up to expectations. Although anti-Panchayat demonstrations did take place in many parts of the country, the alacrity with which the Panchayat establishment reacted, which included police firings, seemed to be working. Because the government had rounded up leaders from both the Congress and the Left prior to the initiation of the movement, most known opposition leaders were in jail and the activities outside were being carried out in an uncoordinated way. The movement was not able to carry the masses along with it and towards the end of March, there seemed to be no evidence of a People's Movement.[47]

The tide turned when the local population of Kathmandu Valley came out in support of change. It began with the daily ' blackouts' in the evening when on cue people would switch off their lights for ten minutes and the valley was plunged into darkness. People would then take advantage of the cover of dark and come out on the streets to shout slogans against the Panchayat system.[48]

The People's Movement received new momentum after this. Demonstrations became a regular feature in Patan, and slogans were raised against the monarchy. Public meetings and processions were held every day, and barricades set up to prevent the police from entering the city. The demonstrations then spread to Kathmandu.

Meanwhile, cracks had begun to appear in the Panchayat edifice. The foreign minister resigned, calling for negotiations with the opposition. The cabinet was reshuffled, but four new ministerial appointees refused to take office. Prime Minister Marich Man Singh Shrestha came under criticism for letting things get out of control. He was sacked and replaced by Lokendra Bahadur Chand.

If King Birendra had hoped to assuage a public that seemed to be reacting to government high-handedness in dealing with the movement, he was thoroughly mistaken. Although implicit was recognition of what the government had taken to calling the 'so-called people's movement', there was nothing in his early morning public address announcing Chand's appointment that indicated he was ready to introduce multiparty democracy. The extent to which he was ready to make concessions was made clear when he said: '[W]e will…be constituting a constitutional reforms commission to make recommendations for political reforms which the Nepali people desire.'[49]

The change of prime minister only served to inflame the people further. They had hoped that after more than a month of vicious crackdowns by the government, and given that popular support was clearly on the side of the anti-Panchayat forces, the king would be ready for some sort of dialogue with the political opposition. The people poured out on the streets from all directions, and headed towards central Kathmandu.

It just so happened that the United National People's Movement (UNPM), a grouping of radical communist parties that had not joined the United Left Front and which was carrying out its own programme of protest, had called for a general strike on that day, 6 April. The people were out on their own volition to show disapproval of the king's action. One of the common slogans of the day was: *'Bire chor, desh chhod'* (Thief Bire[ndra], leave the country.) By late afternoon, the streets around Tundikhel in central Kathmandu were full in what was perhaps the largest-ever gathering in Nepal's history.[50]

No one was leading the crowd; it followed its own momentum. Things came to a head when a section began surging towards the royal palace. Army soldiers had taken up position between the palace and the police who were trying to control the protestors. Police began firing when the statue of King Mahendra in Durbar Marg was vandalised.

Accounts vary as to how many people were killed, but more important than the tally was the fact that the events proved to be the turning point for the movement. A curfew was clamped on Kathmandu and Patan. But behind the scenes events began to move quickly. Negotiations between the Panchayat side led by Lokendra Bahadur Chand, and the opposition resulted in a breakthrough agreement which was presented to the king for approval on 8 April. Under the agreement, the ban on political parties was to be lifted and the term 'partyless' dropped from the Panchayat constitution.

The 9th of April dawned on a new Nepal. The movement had been called off and political parties were free to operate once again after a gap of 30 years.

The interim government and the new constitution

The transition from Panchayat to multiparty democracy proved a rocky one. The opposition had to wrangle concessions from the king one by one. The palace seemed inclined to believe that changes in the 1962 constitution alone would suffice to placate the opposition. This was despite the fact that the latter had called for the dissolution of the national legislature and other Panchayat institutions; the removal of provisions from the constitution that went against the spirit of a multiparty system; and the formation of an interim government. And rather than direct negotiations with the king, the parties had to be content with talking to the middleman, Prime Minister Chand.

Sensing the public mood, however, Chand resigned after 10 days in office and the king invited Ganesh Man Singh to form an interim government. Singh declined and suggested Krishna Prasad Bhattarai's name instead. Accordingly, on 18 April 1990 an interim government was formed with Bhattarai as prime minister. The rest of the cabinet consisted of three representatives each from the Congress and the Left Front, two independents and two royal nominees.

A week later, the Nepali Congress and the United Left Front made clear their joint stand on the shape on the new constitution when it issued a directive to the interim government:

> The new constitution must be fully democratic; the king must become a constitutional monarch; the king must act only on the advice of the council of ministers. All institutions and laws not conducive to democraticisation must be repealed. Democratic rights must be ensured for all citizens. Institutions and processes must be developed for the protection of democracy. A free election must be held as soon as possible, and an independent election commission must be formed for this purpose. There should be press and academic freedom, and equal rights for women.[51]

The task before the interim government was not an easy one. Perhaps the June 1990 agreement with India on trade and transit that allowed for the smooth flow of goods into Nepal was the most easily accomplished task since people like Chandra Shekhar, who were on intimate terms with Nepali Congress leaders, had come to power in India. But, domestically, it was an uphill battle, and that had mainly to do with the general intransigence shown by the monarchy to let go of its hold on power.

The palace continued to throw up surprises such as forming a Constitution Reforms Recommendation Committee without consulting the cabinet. The political parties were furious and demanded that the Committee be disbanded immediately. Luckily for all sides, there was no need for a showdown since the chairman of the commission, Chief Justice of the Supreme Court, Biswanath Upadhyaya, resigned and three of the members did not even join it at all.[52] The commission was dissolved and a Constitution Recommendations Commission, again with Upadhyaya as chairperson and members chosen by Bhattarai, was set up.

Since the political parties had specified the form of the constitution it desired in their mandate to the interim government, the Commission knew what was expected of it. Initially, the Left was not too happy about a constitution drawn up by committee and had insisted on an election to a constituent assembly, with the radicals from the UNPM raising up a chorus in support. But since the Nepali Congress was not ready to take up the matter and because of the uncertain political situation, the Left Front agreed to drop it.[53]

There were many challenges before the Constitution Recommendations Commission (CRC), but the two most important were the issue of the country's demographic diversity and that of binding the monarchy constitutionally. One of the first moves of the Constitution Recommendations Commission seemed propitious enough when it asked the public to provide it with suggestions on the shape of the future constitution. That gave hope to those who felt discriminated against by a state led by Bahuns and Chhetris (Brahmins and Kshatriyas from the midhills) because of their ethnicity, caste, language, region of origin, or religion. They hoped the new constitution would incorporate their aspirations to define a document that recognised the plurality of Nepali society. That hope was to remain unfulfilled and the various suggestions made by these groups were ignored in totality. Krishna Bhattachan writes that 'The CRC was concerned about the nature of sovereignty, constitutional monarchy, fundamental structure of the Constitution, various organs of the Constitution including the Executive, Legislature and Judiciary, and their checks and balances. The public, on the other hand, were concerned about the role of the king, the possibility of [a] federal structure, reservation of seats, and inheritance rights.'[54]

The only gestures made towards the country's diversity in the new constitution was the definition of the nation as 'multiethnic' and 'multilingual', and recognition of the various languages spoken in the country as the 'national languages of Nepal' (while the status of Nepali was defined as the official 'language of the nation').[55] On the question of religion, the demands that Nepal be declared a secular state were opposed vigorously by orthodox Hindu organisations (with a fair bit of prodding and assistance from their fundamentalist brethren in India).

The question of the role of the monarchy was a trickier one for the Commission to handle. The palace was still not giving in easily to the proposed changes, and it even showed its hand in a circular it sent out to units of the army. This asked them to propose to the Commission that the country's sovereignty should rest with the king who should retain overall command of the army and appoint the commander-in-chief, and also that Nepal should continue to be a Hindu state.[56]

Following one controversy after another, a compromise document was finally agreed on in which the basic features of a multiparty democracy were evident, and in which the executive authority was to be wielded by the prime minister. The issue of control over the army was resolved by providing the king with the authority to mobilise the army, but on the recommendation of a Security Council, comprising the prime minister, the defence minister, and the army chief (which, theoretically, gave the civilian government the upper hand). Certain powers and privileges were, however, accorded to the monarch, including the prerogative to nominate 10 members to the 60-member upper house of parliament and the incongruous one to appoint ambassadors. Louise Brown writes that these '...retained, to a limited degree, the palace's ability to dispense patronage'.[57]

Although none too happy, the moderate left kept quiet. On the other hand, the radical communists and the country's various minority groups condemned the constitution outright since their respective demands for a constituent assembly and the recognition of a multiethnic Nepal went unfulfilled.

The far left

At the time the 1990 People's Movement was launched, there were only three avowedly Maoist parties that could each boast of a significant enough following: the CPN (Fourth Congress), the CPN (Masal), and the CPN (Mashal). The latter two viewed any compromise with the palace or cooperation with the Nepali Congress as out of the question. Thus while the Fourth Congress joined the moderate left parties to form the United Left Front and cooperate with the Nepali Congress against the Panchayat system, Masal (led by Mohan Bikram Singh) and Mashal (led by the newly elected general secretary, Prachanda) formed the UNPM with other smaller radical factions in pursuit of the same goal. Baburam Bhattarai of the CPN (Masal) was chosen to lead this grouping.[58]

During the People's Movement, the UNPM went its own way. The climax on 6 April 1990, when the crowds pushed towards the palace, is said to have been goaded by UNPM activists.[59] After the movement was called off by the Nepali Congress and the Left Front, the UNPM described the accord with the palace as a betrayal of the movement, and asked the people to continue with the movement.[60] Although they were not able to elicit much response, the parties in the UNPM were forever ready to denounce any perceived attempt by the monarchy to strengthen its bargaining position during the drafting of the constitution. Their two main demands were that the country's sovereignty should be vested in the people and not, as it had been until then, in the king, and that the election should first be held for a constituent assembly, which would then draw up a 'people's constitution'.

The demand to recognise the sovereignty of the people was incorporated in the new constitution promulgated on 9 November 1990 since the Nepali Congress and the Left Front were in favour of it as well. But, the UNPM's demand for a constituent assembly went unheeded.

The 1991 election

The drafting of a new constitution was the first of the Krishna Prasad Bhattarai government's twin objectives. The other was holding elections to a parliament under the new constitution. In the months leading up to the election, political parties were formed by the dozen in the euphoria of a newfound freedom. By early 1991, the number of parties had reached 74, although only 47 sought recognition from the Election Commission; whilst of these, three were denied registration.[61]

The Nepali Congress was obviously the main contender for power, with the ULF providing the main challenge. The Left Front proposed going into the first elections together with the Nepali Congress, but received a rebuff from the latter. Explains Andrew Nickson: 'Although the interim Prime Minister Bhattarai was disposed to continue collaboration with the ULF, an electoral alliance was bitterly opposed by Girija Prasad Koirala. The United States government was also averse to the prospect of a "united front government" at a time when its global ideological onslaught against communism was reaping enormous dividends. When Ganesh Man Singh met President George Bush and the right-wing pressure group, National Endowment for Democracy, in Washington in December 1990, he was left in no doubt that US support for his party would be conditional on a break with the ULF.'[62]

The ULF splintered soon after because of the perception of the smaller parties that they were being ignored. The two major players in the Left Front, the CPN (Marxist) and the CPN (ML), however, united to form the CPN (Unified Marxist-Leninist). This was a formidable combination since it injected the new party with the cadre strength of the CPN (ML), which itself was led by those completely unknown to the public at large, while the CPN (Marxist) provided leaders with a larger profile such as Sahana Pradhan and Man Mohan Adhikari. The latter became the president of the CPN (UML), while the general secretary of the CPN (ML), Madan Bhandari, continued as general secretary in the new party as well. The new party was later joined by the CPN (Amatya), adding yet another known name to its ranks in the person of Tulsi Lal Amatya.

Those formerly with the Panchayat polity, the erstwhile *panchas*, also formed a party of their own, but no sooner had they decided on the name, Rastriya Prajatantra Party (RPP), than they divided into two factions. Thus, there was the RPP (Chand), led by former prime minister, Lokendra Bahadur Chand, and the RPP (Thapa), led by yet another former prime minister, Surya Bahadur Thapa.

The other party of national significance was the Nepal Sadbhavana Party, dedicated to championing the cause of the people of the tarai, who, like the ethnic peoples of the hills and the mountains, had a history of grievances against the state, although, in their case, it was in their perceived domination by the hill people.

On the radical left, three of the Maoist parties, including the Fourth Congress and Mashal, united in November 1990, and announced the formation of a new party, the CPN (Unity Centre) or (Ekata Kendra), with Prachanda as general secretary. (In a very significant development, the new party was later joined by a breakaway faction from Masal led by Baburam Bhattarai, who parted ways with Mohan Bikram Singh on the issue of taking part in elections.)[63] Even though the constituents of the Unity Centre were opposed to the constitution and multiparty elections, it decided to take part in them 'in order to gain a platform to "expose" the inadequacy of the parliamentary system' even as it retained its ultimate goal of 'new people's democracy'.[64] Accordingly, it was decided that the United People's Front Nepal (UPFN—Samyukta Jan Morcha Nepal) would be its political wing and Baburam Bhattarai its convenor.[65] Thus, the country saw the creation of a political front of a self-proclaimed, semi-underground revolutionary party (not unlike the relationship between Sinn Fein and the Irish Republican Army).

The results of the May 1991 elections gave the Nepali Congress an outright majority (Table 1). Although that was more or less expected, what was not was the almost total decimation of the RPP as well as the exceptionally strong showing by the CPN (UML). The biggest surprise was the nine seats won by the UPFN. The communists together mustered an impressive 36 per cent of the vote, a five-fold increase over what the undivided Communist Party of Nepal had received in the 1959 elections.

Table 1. Results of the 1991 general elections (Total seats: 205)			
Party	Seats contested	Seats won	Percentage of votes
Nepali Congress	204	110	38
Communist Party of Nepal (UML)	177	69	28
United People's Front Nepal	69	9	4
Nepal Sadbhavana Party	75	6	4
Rastriya Prajatantra Party (Chand)	154	3	7
Rastriya Prajatantra Party (Thapa)	162	1	5
Communist Party of Nepal (Democratic)	75	2	2
Nepal Workers' and Peasants' Party	30	2	1
Independents	291	3	4

Source: Hoftun, Martin et al, People, Politics and Ideology, 1999.

Elected governments, 1991-1996

One of the biggest upsets of the 1991 elections was the defeat of Krishna Prasad Bhattarai, president of the Nepali Congress, who went down to Madan Bhandari, general secretary of the CPN (UML). Apart from the ignominy of an electoral loss at the hands of a practically unknown adversary, Bhattarai's defeat was to have far-reaching consequences for the Nepali Congress and with that, for the country as well.

With prime ministerial-aspirant Bhattarai out of the way, it fell on the general secretary, Girija Prasad Koirala, to take the reins of the Nepali Congress government—the first of three tenures he was to serve in the next 10 years. But soon, factionalism, which had always been present in the party but which had not been allowed to overshadow the larger goal of overthrowing the Panchayat system, now reared its head.[66] Dissension had been simmering during the nomination of electoral candidates. After the elections, it came out into the open. Koirala was accused of cronyism in making government appointments from within his own party. Although, initially, Bhattarai made the charge, Ganesh Man Singh too joined the fray, accusing the prime minister of practising *bahunbad* (favouring people from the Bahun community, to which Koirala belonged) in his appointments,[67] and even threatened to quit his honorary position as 'Supreme Leader' of the Nepali Congress.

In parliament and on the streets, Koirala was continuously criticised by the communist opposition. Within his own party, he was being forced to tread warily. There was also resentment at the entry of former *panchas* into the Nepali Congress and at their growing influence. Not long into Koirala's first prime ministership, a clear division emerged in the Congress parliamentary party between the pro-Koirala and pro-Bhattarai factions. The antagonism between the two sides was exacerberated after Madan Bhandari, the CPN (UML) general secretary died in a highway accident in May 1993. Bhattarai stood as the Nepali Congress candidate in the February 1994 by-election for the seat left vacant by Bhandari's death. He was beaten once again, this time by Madan Bhandari's widow, leading to accusations against Koirala that he had taken it upon himself to ensure Bhattarai's defeat, thereby scuttling the latter's chances of replacing him. In July 1994, after Bhattarai's group failed to turn up for the vote of thanks to the royal address, Koirala dissolved parliament amid protests from his own party.

The mid-term elections held in November 1994 resulted in a hung parliament, and although the Nepali Congress received a higher percentage of votes, the CPN (UML) emerged as the party with the largest number of seats (Table 2). Significantly, the share of the (now-united) Rastriya Prajatantra Party saw a big leap as it won 20 seats, while the United People's Front (which had by then split— see details below) failed to win a single seat.

As the largest party in parliament, the CPN (UML) was invited to form the government, and the party president, Man Mohan Adhikari, became prime minister heading a minority government. Although he earned the distinction of being the first-ever communist prime minister under a monarchy, the 'communist' tag was only really for public consumption since the party was hardly a communist party in the orthodox sense. Not long after the May 1991 general elections, in October, the party's central committee had opted for a new political programme known as 'multiparty people's democracy' *(bahudaliya janbad)* to replace the Maoist 'new people's

Table 2. Results of the 1994 general elections			
Party	Seats contested	Seats won	Percentage of votes
Communist Party of Nepal (UML)	196	88	31
Nepali Congress	205	83	33
Rastriya Prajatantra Party	202	20	18
Nepal Workers' and Peasants' Party	27	4	1
Nepal Sadbhavana Party	86	3	3
Independents	385	7	6

Source: Hoftun, Martin et al, People, Politics and Ideology, 1999.

democracy' as its official line. 'Multiparty people's democracy' was basically a form of democratic socialism; but, given the CPN (UML)'s identity as a communist party, it did not dare change its name as well.

The CPN (UML) government did not last long. In May 1995, the opposition called for a special session of parliament to vote on a no-confidence motion against the Adhikari government. Rather than face the House where he was certain to lose, Prime Minister Adhikari recommended dissolution of the parliament and the holding of fresh polls. But in August 1995, the Supreme Court ruled that his move was unconstitutional. By withholding in effect the prime minister's prerogative to seek a fresh mandate, this judgement signalled a period of instability that led to makeshift arrangements at the centre throughout the term of the second parliament.

In September 1995 the Nepali Congress formed a coalition government under the Congress parliamentary party leader, Sher Bahadur Deuba, with support from the Rastriya Prajatantra Party (the party of former panchas, and political pariahs until then), and the tarai-based Nepal Sadbhavana Party.

Left unrest

This chapter, which ends with the start of the 'people's war' in February 1996, needs to go back a few years to trace the development of the left parties in the years after 1990. The realignments within the left movement after the People's Movement had seen the polarisation of communist forces into blocs in which the CPN (UML) had emerged as the strongest, followed by the UPFN (or, in other words, the CPN-Unity Centre), which had performed rather creditably in the 1991 elections. There were other smaller groups that had done well enough as well, namely, the Nepal Workers' and Peasants' Party and Communist Party of Nepal (Democratic). The Left was thus represented in strength in the first parliament, and could together prove to be a threatening opposition on the streets as well.

While the stated position of a party like the UPFN was that they were only 'using' the parliament to reach out to the people, the CPN (UML) had more or less accepted multiparty democracy (underscored by its adopting 'multiparty people's democracy'). Therein lay the catch for the CPN (UML), for while their schooling for more than a decade had been based on a revolutionary agenda, their official position now was adherence to adversarial parliamentary politics. As Nickson noted at the time: 'Despite tortuous efforts by its secretary-general to reconcile multi-party democracy with communist orthodoxy, large sectors of the youth wing of the UML are known to be ambivalent about the value of parliamentary democracy'.[68]

In other words, the CPN (UML) wanted to be accepted as a responsible parliamentary opposition, even though it could not afford to alienate its supporters, and, more importantly its cadre, by completely shedding the radical image of its past. It was this contradiction that was to be reflected in the party's actions in the years that followed.

The first sign of trouble came with the civil servants' agitation in July 1991, barely three months after the Nepali Congress had come to power. Having begun a strike over the government's alleged discrimination against those with leftist sympathies, the agitation was supported by the CPN (Unity Centre) with its political wing, the UPFN, leading the attack on the government in the parliament. Other opposition parties, including the CPN (UML), supported it.[69] The protest died out soon enough without a satisfactory resolution (although a few employees were sacked), but this rekindled the traditional mutual antipathy between the Left and the Nepali Congress.

The relationship soured further due to the government's economic policies, which veered away from the Congress's professed ideology of democratic socialism. Explains Brown: 'The gulf between the party's theory and practice can also be attributed to Nepal's poverty, to the exigencies of the international political environment and to the strategy of economic liberalisation which the

World Bank, the IMF and other donor agencies deemed it correct for Nepal to pursue.'[70]

Political and fiscal exigencies may have led the Nepali Congress government along the path of a market-oriented fiscal policy, but it had the larger effect of unsettling an economy that had been firmly controlled by the government and cushioned by subsidies. Waiting on the sidelines to take advantage of any sign of public disenchantment with the government were the parties of the radical left. They made their move in February 1992 when the Unity Centre/UPFN joined hands with Masal and two other smaller parties to launch a series of protests against the Girija Prasad Koirala government under the banner of a Joint People's Agitation Committee.[71] In March, the committee handed the prime minister a memorandum consisting of 14 demands (which had been expanded from the earlier eight points — see Annex II).[72] Thereafter, a succession of protest programmes were organised, which included the observance of 6 April as a People's Movement Day to be marked with a *bandh* (general strike).[73] The protests on 6 April turned violent and more than a dozen people were killed in the police firing to disperse the demonstrators.

The killings served to further radicalise the leftists. The CPN (UML) had initially found itself in the awkward position of not being able to join its hardliner comrades nor come out in support of the government. It was roundly criticised for simply protesting against the police firing and asking for the resignation of the home minister, Sher Bahadur Deuba. But the CPN (UML) managed to force an agreement with the government on the issue of the police action as well as some of the issues that had incensed the radicals such as an increase in the electricity tariff. In this way, the CPN (UML) was able to undermine the movement launched by the Unity Centre, and at the same time earn credit for having forced the government to an understanding.[74] That nothing came of the agreement is a different matter.

A pattern had been established: the Left would take to the streets and the Congress government would use brute force to maintain law and order. The next sustained spell of disturbances came with the death of Madan Bhandari, general secretary of the CPN (UML), in the May 1993 highway accident. The CPN (UML) and other communist parties claimed foul play, and when a government probe concluded it had been an accident, the entire Left launched a countrywide, often-violent agitation. The movement might have taken a turn for the worse had it not been for the devastating floods of July 1993 in central Nepal, which caused tempers to cool down and the government and the CPN (UML) reached an agreement to form another inquiry commission.

There were further street protests by the communist parties after Koirala dissolved parliament in July 1994 and called for fresh elections, but that too petered out soon enough after what seemed 'more of a ritual performance than a full-hearted confrontation.'[75]

The CPN (Maoist)

While it may have been clear that the CPN (Unity Centre) was a radical party, what was not so well known was that the 'unity congress' of December 1991 had passed a resolution to initiate a 'people's war to bring about a new democratic revolution in Nepal'.[76] The CPN (Unity Centre) had been formed by the coming together of the CPN (Fourth Congress) and the CPN (Mashal). These parties, along with the CPN (Masal), had a common pedigree in the Fourth Congress of 1974, and had gone their own ways due mainly to personal animosities between the leaders that were masked under the veneer of ideological differences. Given this history of mutual distrust and hostility, it was natural that sparks would also fly within the newly formed Unity Centre.

The actual unity of the Unity Centre was suspect right from the time of the 1991 'unity congress'. This meeting had rammed through Prachanda's political line that called for 'a clear-cut political line of protracted people's war for carrying out the New Democratic revolution in the country with a Marxist-Leninist-Maoist ideological perspective'.[77] Since Nirmal Lama was not particularly in favour of an armed uprising immediately, even though the 1991 UPFN election manifesto did state that it was for establishing a communist republic, presumably through a revolution, the differences grew wider and, in May 1994, the party split into a Unity Centre led by Prachanda and another by Nirmal Lama.[78] (Figure 1 shows the development of the branches of the Nepal communist movement that led to the formation of the CPN [Maoist]).

The UPFN also divided, reflecting the developments in the mother party, with Baburam Bhattarai heading the one allied to Prachanda's Unity Centre (although for some time it was called the UPFN–Bhusal, after Pampha Bhusal, now a senior figure within the

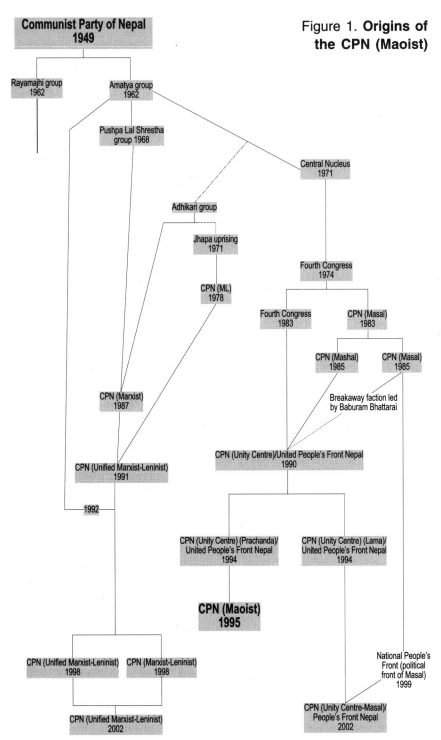

Figure 1. **Origins of the CPN (Maoist)**

Communist Party of Nepal 1949

Rayamajhi group 1962

Amatya group 1962

Pushpa Lal Shrestha group 1968

Central Nucleus 1971

Adhikari group

Jhapa uprising 1971

Fourth Congress 1974

CPN (ML) 1978

Fourth Congress 1983

CPN (Masal) 1983

CPN (Mashal) 1985

CPN (Masal) 1985

Breakaway faction led by Baburam Bhattarai

CPN (Marxist) 1987

CPN (Unity Centre)/United People's Front Nepal 1990

CPN (Unified Marxist-Leninist) 1991

1992

CPN (Unity Centre) (Prachanda)/ United People's Front Nepal 1994

CPN (Unity Centre) (Lama)/ United People's Front Nepal 1994

CPN (Maoist) 1995

National People's Front (political front of Masal) 1999

CPN (Unified Marxist-Leninist) 1998

CPN (Marxist-Leninist) 1998

CPN (Unified Marxist-Leninist) 2002

CPN (Unity Centre-Masal)/ People's Front Nepal 2002

Adapted from Hoftun, Martin et al, People Politics and Ideology, *1999.*

CPN [Maoist]), and Niranjan Govinda Vaidya (incidentally, one of the founders of the original CPN in 1949) leading the one allied to Lama's Unity Centre.[79] Both factions of the UPFN approached the Election Commission for recognition. The commission recognised the one supported by Nirmal Lama in August 1994.[80] Baburam Bhattarai responded by calling for a boycott of the mid-term elections scheduled for November.[81] Although his reaction was seen as a face-saving measure at the time, the Election Commission slamming the door on the Bhattarai-led UPFN paved the way for its giving up electoral politics in favour of armed revolt.[82]

After the 1994 split, the Unity Centre led by Prachanda went completely underground as it began preparations for its next phase of struggle. It held its Third Plenum in March 1995. This was to be the turning point in their campaign for a number of reasons. This meeting decided to rename their party the Communist Party of Nepal (Maoist).[83] It also decided that for 'the true liberation of the people all efforts must be concentrated for the development of a people's war that would usher in the new people's democratic form of government', and decided to give up its policy of taking part in parliamentary elections. (This last presumably at the insistence of the Revolutionary Internationalist Movement.[84]) Further, it analysed the other left parties' positions in order to justify its extremist position. It considered the CPN (UML) to be a party that had degenerated into 'revisionist reactionarism' for having 'taken up the responsibility of protecting the cause of the monarchy, feudalism, imperialism, and expansionism' by forming the government after the mid-term elections. It termed Masal 'rightist neo-revisionist' for having entered parliamentary politics, for having supported 'reactionaries' like the CPN (UML), for promoting the formation of a permanent front with rightist opportunists (the rival Unity Centre), and for treating 'true communist revolutionaries' (their party), as enemies.[85]

Initial rumblings and the beginning of the 'people's war'

The March meeting 'was followed by six months of hectic preparations primarily to recast the old organisational structure into a fighting machine'.[86] And, in September 1995, the 'Plan for the Historic Initiation of the People's War' was adopted by the Central Committee of the Party, in which the 'Theoretical Premises for the Historic Initiation of the People's War' were laid out as follows:[87]

A. This plan of ours would be based on the lessons of Marxism-Leninism-Maoism regarding revolutionary violence. On the occasion of formulation of the plan for initiation of the process that will unfold as protracted people's war based on the strategy of encircling the city from the countryside according to the specificities of our country, the Party once again reiterates its eternal commitment to the theory of people's war developed by Mao as the universal and invincible Marxist theory of war.

B. This plan of initiation of the people's war would be based on the principle that everything is an illusion except state power. While remaining firm on the principal aim of the armed struggle as to capture political power for the people, the Party expresses its firm commitment to wage relentless struggle against all forms of deviationist thoughts and trends including economism, reformism and anarchism.

C. This plan would be based on the aim of completing the new democratic revolution after the destruction of feudalism and imperialism, then immediately moving towards socialism, and, by way of cultural revolutions based on the theory of continuous revolution under the dictatorship of the proletariat, marching to communism — the golden future of the whole of humanity. We are firm that it is a crime against the proletariat and the general masses of the people to start an armed struggle without the firm conviction of carrying it out to the end. We shall never allow this struggle to become a mere instrument for introducing partial reforms in the condition of the people, or terminating in a simple compromise by exerting pressure on the reactionary classes. Thus, our armed struggle will be totally free of all sorts of petty bourgeois, narrow nationalist, religion-communal and casteist illusions.

D. This plan of ours would be based on the great spirit of proletarian internationalism. The Nepalese revolution is an integral part of the world proletarian revolution and this will serve the world revolution. In this context our Party takes it as a serious responsibility to contribute towards the further development of Revolutionary Internationalist Movement (RIM) (of which our Party is a participating member), which is marching forward to advance world revolution under the guidance of Marxism-Leninism-Maoism and to create a New International.[88]

E. This plan would be based on the theoretical premises of building a revolutionary united front and a revolutionary army under the leadership of the Party of the proletariat in the phase of the new democratic revolution. The Party is firmly committed to establish the leadership of the Party in every sphere by maintaining its vitality by way of conducting inner-party struggle in a dialectical manner according to the principle of universality of contradictions, to serve the people wholeheartedly, to maintain close relations with the people, and to adhere to the principle of mass line.[89]

F. This plan would be formulated on the principle of the right to self-determination of the Party of the proletariat. Armed struggle will be carried out by uniting all strata and categories of anti-feudal and anti-imperialist masses of the people under the leadership of the Party. Our armed struggle will be conducted by taking agrarian revolution as the axis and by relying on the labouring masses, particularly the poor peasants, and the Party will never and under no circumstances succumb to the pressures, threats and enticements of the internal and external reactionary forces.

G. The war will develop according to its own laws not in a straight line but in a complex zigzag path. It is necessary to acknowledge the importance of Lenin's saying that the revolution always creates in its course of development an unusual and complex situation. The people's war will triumph after going through cycles of victory and defeat and gain and loss. We shall be able to lead the people's war only by correctly grasping the law of contradiction of transformation of wrong into right.

There then began a series of public meetings held all over the country under the aegis of the UPFN 'as part of the final politico-ideological preparation'.[90] Part of this preparation process was the Sija campaign in Rolpa and Rukum, so named after the two prominent mountains of Rukum and Rolpa, Sisne and Jaljala, respectively. This was a purely political campaign to mobilise party members to propagate the ideology of Marxism-Leninism-Maoism. Apart from party propaganda the cadre also carried out some social work.[91]

In October 1995, while the Sija campaign was underway, a fight broke out between supporters of the UPFN/CPN (Maoist) and the other parties, mainly the Nepali Congress and the Rastriya Prajatantra Party, at a village fair in the eastern part of Rolpa district. The newly appointed government of Sher Bahadur Deuba moved swiftly to arrest UPFN supporters, accusing them of creating public disorder. The police then launched 'Operation Romeo' in November, an action which was characterised by random arrests, torture, rape, and extra-judicial killings, leading to the complete alienation of a large part of the local population from the government. (A fuller description of Operation Romeo is given in Chapter 3).

This was a situation that suited the Maoists very well. As their mouthpiece put it, the 'vicious armed police operation, code-named "Romeo Operation", launched by the reactionary state against the rural class struggle going on for some time in Rolpa district in [the] Western Hills and a countrywide public outcry against this state repression, provided a perfect setting to initiate the people's war... In this light the Political Bureau of the Central Committee of the Party that met briefly in January 1996 made the final selection of the date of the historic initiation [of the "people's war"] for February 13'.[92]

The rest is history. On 4 February 1996, Baburam Bhattarai led a three-member delegation of the UPFN to present a memorandum to Prime Minister Sher Bahadur Deuba (Annex III). The memorandum warned that unless the government initiated appropriate measures towards fulfilling their 40 demands by 17 February, the UPFN would begin an armed struggle. The implied threat was taken lightly by everyone, and the government was no different (although the then parliamentary affairs minister, Narahari Acharya, claims that the prime minister had asked him to look into the matter and that before the government could formulate a response the Maoists had begun their attacks).[93]

On 11 February, Prime Minister Deuba left on a state visit to India, and was still there on 13 February 1996, when the office of the Small Farmer's Development Programme run by the Agricultural Development Bank was overrun in Gorkha district and the loan papers destroyed. This was followed in the evening by attacks on police posts in Rolpa, Rukum, and Sindhuli districts (Box 3). The 'People's War' to establish 'the dictatorship of the proletariat, marching to communism — the golden future of the whole humanity' had begun.

Box 3. 13 February 1996

On 13 February 1996, at about 3:45 pm a group of people, both men and women, (the mainstream media later reported it to number about 300, which was in reality an overestimation) took possession, almost without any resistance, of the office of the Small Farmer's Development Programme of the state owned Agricultural Development Bank in Chyangli VDC (village development committee) in Gorkha district, in central Nepal. At first the masses gathered outside the office, located in a small village bazaar, and, while one of the youths gave a brief speech exposing the mechanism of exploitation of poor peasants by the Bank and highlighting the need of capturing it by the peasants, another group overpowered the staffs inside the office and took possession of all the official papers. As they do not generally keep cash in such offices, the loan papers signed by the peasants and the land registration certificates (known as *lalpurja*) deposited by the peasants as collateral were seized. While the *lalpurjas* were kept safe to be returned later to the respective peasants in the surrounding villages, a bonfire was made out of the loan papers worth several million rupees and other documents. Then after [...] a brief parting speech by one of them, the mass of the people dispersed quickly and safely to their respective places. The whole thing was over within about half an hour and the nearest police outpost about a kilometre away was caught totally unawares.

The same day in the evening (between 8 pm and 11 pm) three police outposts, one each in Rolpa and Rukum districts in western Nepal and one in Sindhuli district in eastern Nepal, were seized by armed youths shouting Marxist-Leninist-Maoist slogans. In Rolpa district, which has been in the forefront of militant resistance struggle for several years, the police outpost at Holeri was stormed by a militant team armed with local weapons and explosives. As the policemen were ready to surrender everything except their rifles, there ensued an exchange of fire from both sides for almost two hours. Ultimately, bound by the policy of not killing any policemen at this initial stage, the militants ransacked the office, seized the store and took hold of a substantial amount of high explosives and other utilities and escaped to safety. Before departure, they made their revolutionary political motives clear to the policemen and a crowd of curious villagers which had gathered outside the police station. In a similar move at the Athbiskot-Rari police outpost in the neighbouring Rukum district, also known as a stronghold of Maoist communists, the outpost was easily captured without any resistance from the policemen. The armed raiding team took possession of a large amount of explosives and other utilities and valuables and escaped safely after making their revolutionary intentions clear to the captured policemen. In the third case of Sindhuli district, with a glorious revolutionary tradition, the police outpost at the historic Sindhuligarhi (or the fort where the powerful British interventionist army was defeated by the then Gorkhali soldiers in an epic battle using guerilla tactics in 1766) was captured without any resistance whatsoever. After making a long discourse on New Democratic

Revolution to the captured policemen and their families, the militants escaped with substantial amount of high explosives and other utilities. The anecdote goes that before their departure the militants tied down the policemen and covered them with warm quilts to safeguard them from the biting winter cold, which the policemen later publicly acknowledged in the national media.

On February 13 itself, planned assaults were made against three more targets. In the capital city of Kathmandu a soft-drink bottling factory owned by a multinational company [Pepsi] was attacked and a portion of the building torched. Surprisingly the company chose not to publicise the incident for unknown reasons. In Gorkha district a liquor factory owned by a comprador bourgeois was blasted. As the police personnel in the hectic running around after the bank action earlier in the day in nearby Chyangli VDC incidentally happened to be enjoying the liquor session there at the time, this action was also hushed up maybe to hide their own embarrassment. In another highly successful action, the house of a notorious feudal-usurer in Kavre district in eastern Nepal was raided at night by a large group of men and women and properties and cash worth Rs 1.3 million seized and loan documents worth several million rupees destroyed. Nobody was physically harmed in all these actions.

The same night, thousands of leaflets and posters containing the appeal of the Party to the general masses to march along the path of people's war to smash the reactionary state and establish a New Democratic state, were distributed in major cities and headquarters of more than 60 districts (out of a total of 75 districts).

Excerpted from 'The Historic Initiation and After', The Worker, no 2, June 1996.

MIN BAJRACHARYA

Maoist leaders Pampha Bhusal (extreme left), Krishna Bahadur Mahara (fifth from left) and Baburam Bhattarai (fourth from right) at one of their periodic *mashal julus* (torch rallies) just before they went underground in February 1996.

Understanding the Causes of the 'People's War'

ALMOST EVERY attempt to explain the Maoist insurgency customarily refers to the 40-point charter of demands (see Annex III) presented by UPFN chairman Baburam Bhattarai to Prime Minister Sher Bahadur Deuba on 4 February 1996. And practically everyone agrees that, barring one or two points, it would be quite difficult to take issue with that wish list; most of the demands are reasonable and not dissimilar in spirit to the election manifestoes of mainstream parties. In hindsight, therefore, it seemed a major faux pas on the part of the government of the day not to have engaged the Maoists, and, in a sense, to have provided an excuse for the Maoist uprising. It was quite unlikely, however, that the Maoists would have come for talks even if the government had invited them. The January 1996 central committee meeting of the CPN (Maoist) had already decided that the uprising would begin on the 13th of February 1996[1] and, as is well known, the first attacks on government installations began even before the 17 February deadline expired.

For the next few years, the Left, especially the CPN (UML), found it convenient to blame the Nepali Congress over the Maoist issue for the simple reason that the latter was in power when the 'people's war' broke out.[2] The CPN (UML) conveniently glossed over the fact that the UPFN had presented a similar list of 38 demands to the CPN (UML) government in December 1994, which it chose to ignore in the same way as the following Congress government did.[3] The demands, thus, seem to have been only a feint. The reasons for the CPN (Maoist) taking to the gun, and its rapid success within a few years, have to be sought elsewhere.

Early warnings
In the early 1990s, two western scholars wrote very prophetic articles arguing that Nepal provided a perfect setting for a Shining Path-like Maoist insurgency to take root. These two articles are remarkable in that they both make comparisons with the Peruvian movement to support their conclusions, which they had most likely arrived at independent of each other.

In 1992, Andrew Nickson had warned in his essay mentioned earlier:

> The future prospects of Maoism in Nepal will...depend largely on the extent to which the newly elected Nepali Congress government addresses the historic neglect and discrimination of the small

rural communities which still make up the overwhelming bulk of the population of the country. As in the case of Peru, this would require a radical reallocation of government expenditure towards rural areas in the form of agricultural extension services and primary health care provision. Successful implementation of such a programme would mean a radical shake-up of the public administration system in order to make it both more representative of the ethnic diversity of the country and more responsive to the needs of peasant communities.

However, such a scenario is extremely unlikely…[4]

A year later, Stephen Mikesell noted:

The London staff of the International Emergency Committee to Defend the Life of Abimael Guzman, the imprisoned leader of the Shining Path guerrillas of Peru, has been astounded by the volume of mail received from Nepal in support of him. From nowhere in the world has such a large number of letters been sent by so many members of a national legislature, to say nothing of common citizens.

Perhaps this support from a world away springs from ignorance of the less than complementary picture portrayed by the international press and western analysts of the Sendero Luminoso (the party's name in Spanish). Or does it derive from a naïve romance of Nepal's intellectuals with the revolutionary tradition? Or could the affinity for Comrade Gonzalo's ideology have deeper underpinning, based on similarity of certain underlying characteristics of Himalaya society with those of the Andean hinterland of Peru? If this were the case, could we then expect tendencies similarly violent to emerge in Nepal?[5]

That neither of these two articles received what in retrospect should have been the required attention was probably due to two factors. The first was that both were written in English, whereas in Nepal the language of the intelligentsia is Nepali. The second factor, and this was probably the more likely reason, was that for a country just coming out of a long spell of authoritarian rule, and given the various dislocations and expectations the changeover had caused, it seemed only natural that all kinds of voices would find their way into the politics of the day, including espousals of armed struggle. Therefore, cautionary words like the ones above could be treated with disdain. But as Nickson warned elsewhere in his article, it was precisely in a situation of euphoric stupor that the Maoists were likely to begin operating. The developments since then proved that he was on target.

At the time of writing this book — almost a dozen years and an equal number of governments later — there has been no substantial change in the conditions that the two writers observed. As the parliamentary exercise proceeded, there was no improvement in the socio-economic conditions of the people. Governance remained in shambles as political parties expended their energy in power plays. Corruption soared unchecked. The gap between the poor and the rich grew wider while conspicuous consumption became the norm in the capital and other urban centres. It was as if the 1990 movement, which people expected so much of, had not even happened. The only difference now is that the country is in the eighth year of a violent conflict that has eaten into the vitals of the nation-state of Nepal.

Economic factors

The Maoists claimed in 1996 that the introduction of a 'new democratic system' through a protracted 'people's war' was inescapable because all the attempts to carry out reforms within the old 'semi-feudal' and 'semi-colonial' system had failed. That such an assertion could be made at all was a definite indication that the Maoist movement was no longer a temporary phenomenon without social bases but had (and has) roots deep in the country's social and economic order, and is a by-product of Nepal's unsuccessful development endeavours. That the Maoist insurgency was able to survive and grow in the following seven years has been a clear indication of this.

The possibility of the politicisation of the country's sorry economic conditions had been considerable for some time in Nepal. In the late 1960s and early 1970s the problems of absolute poverty had become unbearable for many Nepalis as sustaining the Panchayat regime took precedence over all other values and objectives, corruption became institutionalised, and the duality in Nepali society became sharper since only a small coalition of privileged classes and groups derived benefits from the system. As a result, places like the tarai witnessed sporadic outbursts of popular protest, as less privileged social groups and classes such as the lower-echelon bureaucrats, small-scale businessmen, industrial labourers, teachers, students, and unemployed graduates became increasingly frustrated with the Nepali elite that continued to retain much of the restrictive characteristics of old-style feudal politics. The protests reflected the less-privileged groups' political impotence to do anything about it.[6] Towards the end of the 1970s it became apparent that, even with relatively optimistic projections, economic growth was likely to be inadequate to meet popular expectations. It was argued that 'it seems likely that before long, if economic and social conditions do not improve rapidly, such unrest will become more pervasive and better organised.'[7]

The predictions were quite on the mark since in 1985 the Nepali Congress launched a campaign of civil disobedience while the communists started a 'fill the jails' campaign.[8] Thereafter, the introduction of the IMF and World Bank-sponsored structural adjustment programmes, together with a government basic needs programme in 1986-87, led to a significant increase in GDP growth. However, the benefits of these interventions were offset by a steady rise in inflation as between 1980 and 1987 there was an average annual increase of over 10 per cent in consumer prices.[9] This had a considerable effect on the household budgets of the urban poor and the lower income middle classes who rely heavily on purchased food grains. In the years 1988 and 1989, the government lost much credibility in the face of deepening economic problems, compounded by the trade and transit embargo put in place by India. The government's critics argued that the economic crisis could be resolved only if the political system was reformed and multiparty politics reinstated.[10]

The interim government formed after the capitulation of the Panchayat system found an economically ravaged country. The 1989 World Development Report ranked Nepal as one of the world's poorest countries. Ranked 115th out of 120 countries in terms of per capita GNP, it had a particularly low rate of growth, and the heaviest reliance on agriculture of any country in the world (57 per cent of GDP and 93 per cent of the labour force). At the same time, inflation, already running at over 10 per cent in the 1980s, shot up. The first post-People's Movement prime minister, Krishna Prasad Bhattarai, promised that prices would come down by 35 per cent; instead they rose by nearly 30 per cent during his tenure.

Besides the criticism of being unrepresentative, the Panchayat system was also reviled for its susceptibility to corruption. Ironically, scandals faced by several ministers in the interim government, in particular those relating to corruption and other illegal activities, emerged as core political grievances against the interim government as well. This increasingly undermined the legitimacy of the administration as evidence of inefficiency and malpractice mounted. Divisions within the coalition cabinet, which had always remained considerable, became more pronounced. The overall concern among many who had been active in the democracy movement was that their 'demands for radical reform were being ignored in favour of a compromise with the palace and other conservative forces.'[11]

The Nepali Congress government, elected in 1991, made a public commitment to institute 'a new order' in Nepal, in which democracy and development were to move forward in concert. In October 1991, the National Planning Commission presented the Eighth Five-Year Plan (1992-1997), which provided guidelines for the next five years. The Plan maintained that 'development is not just a mechanistic function of capital and technology. It is a social and political process of mobilising and organising people to the desired goals. This will be possible only when people themselves are associated in the decision-making process ... and, more importantly, in benefit sharing [with regard to development activities].'[12] Crucially, it was recognised that the pace of development in Nepal could only be accelerated, and some measure of sustainability assured, by actively involving people in the development process through grassroots activities.

The fiscal year 1993/94 saw some promising results. There was an unprecedented growth in agriculture of 7.6 per cent; GDP registered a 7.9 per cent increase; the tourism sector was able to contribute 4 per cent to the GDP; and in the manufacturing sector, the carpet industry emerged as a major foreign-exchange earner with the value of its exports tripling within three years. Furthermore, per capita GDP rose from around US$ 170 in the mid-1980s to US$ 202 by 1994. But the momentum did not last long. These economic advances did not have enough of a foundation, and the growth rates decelerated rapidly in 1995 due to political instability, bad governance, and rampant corruption among party politicians. These politicians translated the increased freedom and openness of the polity into an open house of nepotism, bribery, and corruption.[13] As a result, many people bemoaned that their standard of living was lower under the democratically elected governments of the 1990s than during the Panchayat era.

Poverty outpaces growth

According to official statistice, 42 and a half per cent of Nepal's population still live below the poverty line. This is despite the many attractive slogans that have promised development over the last 50 years and the implementation of nine five-year plans. Annual per capita income is only US$ 220, and Nepal is 142nd on the UNDP's Human Development Index. Only Laos, Bangladesh, and Afghanistan are worse off in Asia.[14] Similarly, throughout much of the country's development experience, growth rates in both the agricultural and non-agricultural sectors have remained low and highly erratic and without a base for sustained growth of output at a satisfactory rate.[15] A close look at the pattern of growth (Figure 2) reveals that the overall growth rate of 5 per cent over the last 15 years has been due largely to the growth of the non-agricultural sector. While this has significantly changed the structure of the economy, mainly to the benefit of urban areas, economic opportunities in the country have been very unevenly distributed as rural and semi-rural areas have benefited little and employment has failed to keep pace with the transformation. About 80 per cent of Nepal's people still work in agriculture, an arena where growth has been erratic and fallen below expectations.[16]

At the same time, the number of educated unemployed people has continued to increase. The close to 100,000 rural youths who fail the high school board examinations every year are unable to find either a job or keep themselves busy with further studies. The average economic growth of approximately 4 per cent annually since 1998, has been insufficient to absorb the estimated 500,000 young people who join the labour force each year.[17] This has widened the gross income inequalities that lie within the growth rates. The more remote districts of the mid-west and far-west, have average annual incomes well below the US$ 220 national figure. Per capita income is less than US$ 100 in the Maoist stronghold of Rolpa. In some parts of Nepal the average life expectancy is only half of that in Kathmandu. According to the UN Human Development Report 2001, 38 per cent of Nepal's population is extremely poor and cannot meet its basic needs. Other indicators are equally stark. Life expectancy is 59 years, and the adult literacy rate is roughly 51 per cent. Yet here, too, there is sharp divergence between the 'two Nepals'. For example in the mountains of the far west, life expectancy is only 42 years and adult literacy, 37 per cent.[18]

Figure 2. GDP growth rates (average annual)

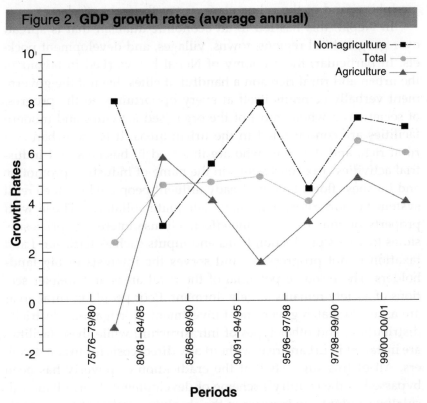

Source: Ministry of Finance, Economic Survey, *several years.*

This pervasive poverty can to some extent be attributed to the neo-classical development philosophy Nepal adopted, which, instead of emphasising distributive justice or equity, has led to the uneven distribution of income and wealth. Property or inherited property rights are protected by law, keeping society sharply divided between the rich and the poor. Land reform efforts aimed at limiting the amount of land an individual can own have been half-heartedly enforced. As a result, the practice of large landowners thriving on the servitude of dependent farmers and bonded labourers, although now illegal, continues. Furthermore, the rich have a say in policy-making and programme formulation, and hence usually enjoy most of the opportunities and facilities of skill development and participation. Consequently, in the absence of an effective national strategy for economic planning, the role of the state has historically been one of surplus appropriation through taxation and other means to reinforce the control of the 'centre' over the 'periphery' and of the ruling classes over the 'subject' classes.

In Nepal, this has led to an economic dualism that is spread over geographical regions, towns, villages, and development pockets. In particular, the economy of Nepal has worked in favour of the urban and rural rich and a handful of elites. Even if the government verbally commits itself at every opportunity to the progress of society as a whole, most of the organised activities and modern facilities are concentrated in the urban areas. It is the urban and rural rich, and the elites who are involved in business and industrial activities. Tax concessions in the name of industrial promotion and business flows favour already affluent people whilst the credit system favours those who have adequate collateral. Those with property or sources of income effectively use interest or price subsidies to access production loans and inputs such as fertiliser. Land taxation is not progressive, and serves the interests of big landholders. The resource potential of the rural areas and weaker sections of society remains largely dormant. Poor people in rural areas are asked to match government investment in irrigation, electricity distribution, and other types of infrastructure while these facilities are installed in urban areas without any direct costs for urban dwellers. All of this suggests that the eradication of poverty has been bypassed in the country's scheme of development. World Bank calculations point to an increase in the absolute number of poor people in Nepal between the late 1970s and late 1990s.

Centre–periphery demarcations

The neo-Marxist analysis and the concept of centre and periphery and its inherent structure of inequality that allows the centre to appropriate surplus from the periphery mostly for its own benefit and to maintain domination and dependency, describes very well the uneven development that has happened in Nepal both internally and in terms of its relations with India.

Nepal's economy is irrevocably tied to India's. Nepal's geographical position and its scarcity of the natural resources needed to produce industrial goods has meant that its economy has always been subject to fluctuations from changes in its relationship with India, and particularly with New Delhi's ability to use economic pressures to manipulate foreign policy and water concessions. This was evident in the 1989 trade and transit dispute that led to economic growth declining from the 1980s average of 4 per cent to only 1.5 per cent that year owing largely to the disruption of supplies of imported raw materials for export industries. Furthermore, Nepal relies heavily on remittances from India sent home by military and non-military workers. Hundreds of thousands of Nepalis live and work in India.

Even more significant is Nepal's landlocked position that makes it depend on India as both the source and transit point for almost all of its imports and exports. The existence of a national frontier does provide a modicum of protection to Nepal's nascent productive enterprises. But class interests on both sides continue to maintain the 'leaky' nature of the frontier, making it easy for the centre (India) to appropriate labour and primary products from its periphery (Nepal). India also benefits from largely unrestricted access to Nepali markets. [19]

One of the main manifestations of the internal centre-periphery relations is that Kathmandu — the nation's capital which contains all forms of economic and political power — is the place where decisions regarding the appropriation, distribution and realisation of surpluses generated by production in peripheral areas, mainly the tarai and the hills outside the valley, are made. The negative consequences of this lopsided polity are that first, because the major decisions are taken in the centre, the perspectives, aspirations, and needs of people from the periphery do not get represented. They are often ignored, or the decision-makers are unaware of the needs of the rural regions. As Pashupati S.J.B. Rana and K.P. Malla have pointed out:

> In terms of development expenditure, a large part of the total investment in the last two decades has gone to Kathmandu and its surrounding areas...this has gone so far that the gulf between Kathmandu Valley and the subsistence economies of the hills areas of Nepal is growing similar to the gulf between the developed countries and the under-developed 'third world'...To the problems of cultural heterogeneity...the process of development is adding the problem of economic heterogeneity to such a degree that truly

disturbing dualities may emerge in the nation. These differences between areas are echoed by differences between social strata. The two decades of development have seen the emergence of a privileged stratum which skims the cream of development opportunities and benefits.[20]

Second, this centralisation has resulted in the concentration of power in a few state agencies and others that ensure that decisions are in line with the needs of the most prominent private vested interests. And, despite the expectations engendered by the 1990 movement, not one of the 13 governments[21] that have held power since then has done anything to liberate the rural peasantry, who constitute a majority of the population, from the exploitative land relationships existing in the villages.

Take the instance of budgetary allocations. In 2000, 82 per cent of the budget was for central level programmes. Within the budget line for district development, about a third went to employee benefits and other expenses, and only two-thirds on specific targeted programmes. Consequently, in some districts, especially in the mid-western and far western regions, virtually everyone is poor and has been so for generations.[22] Indeed, large segments of these populations are what development experts call the 'hardcore' poor: people who barely manage to survive.

Supporting the idea that Nepal's development is urban-biased, the year 2000 HDI for urban areas (0.616) was far above that for rural areas (0.446), where more than 80 per cent of the population live. Among the development regions, the central region had the highest HDI (0.493), followed closely by the eastern (0.484) and western regions (0.479) (see Figure 3). This stems largely from the fact that most of Nepal's trading centres and productive economic activities are concentrated in the east and centre. The mid-western (0.402) and far western (0.385) regions, which lie far from the centre of power, have traditionally been neglected by both the government and development agencies.

These high levels of poverty, especially in the hill areas which are characterised by physical and economic as well as social backwardness, provide a starting point to understand why the CPN (Maoist) could count on popular support for a 'people's war'. Even with the coming of multiparty democracy the prospects for socio-economic transformation in Nepal remained dim because of the lack

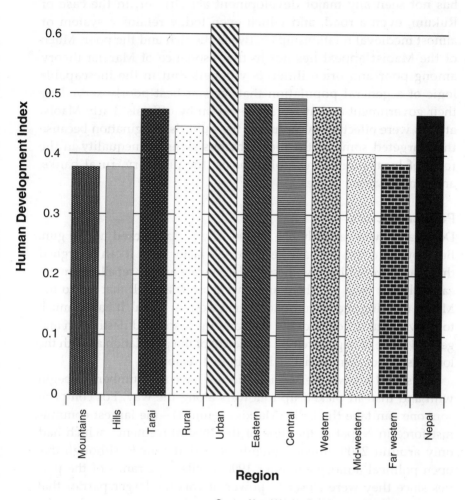

Figure 3. Regional Human Development Index, 2000

Source: Nepal Human Development Report, 2001, *2002.*

of adequate focus by government and development agencies on rural areas and the unchanged character of Nepal as a society in which pre-capitalist relations of production dominate.

Due to the structural inequalities inherent in the system, the Maoists found fertile grounds for their ideas to grow, and found ready support for their promises of an alternative to an economically, socially, culturally, and politically flawed system that they sought to replace. It is no coincidence that the epicentre of the Maoist movement has been the poverty-stricken contiguous districts of northern Rolpa and Rukum in the western mid-hills—an area that has not seen any major development activity, or, in the case of Rukum, even a road; and which even today retains a system of almost medieval relationships between the rich and the poor. Much of the Maoist appeal lies not in the resonance of Marxist theory among poor and often illiterate villagers, but in the inescapable logic of a general population that feels at best poorly served by their government and at worst preyed on by officials. Early Maoist attacks were effective in capturing the public's imagination because they targeted some of the most obvious signs of inequality in the form of local politicians, police posts, the judiciary, rural banks, and land revenue offices.

Political factors

Deprivation was certainly one reason why people picked up the gun. But, poverty could not have been the sole factor since it can be argued that Nepal would have witnesssed large-scale armed rebellions much earlier had it been so. There are other reasons as well that led to the Maoist uprising and its consolidation in western Nepal. It had as much to do with the structure of the state and the associated destitution and general sense of neglect felt by a majority of the population as with the long history of communist activity in that region.

It is well known the Maoists did not have the numbers to begin with and instead picked up followers along the way. For comparison, one can take the CPN (Marxist-Leninist)—the largest communist force in Nepal at the time of the 1990 movement—which had only around 2000 enlisted members at that time.[23] Although the open political atmosphere after 1990 swelled the ranks of the parties since they were closer to power, it was the larger parties that benefited the most. The Maoists were rather hard-pressed in the beginning to muster the numerical strength required to carry out their programme of armed rebellion. But as events have since shown, they ultimately prevailed. The following two sections look at some of the factors that helped the Maoists during the crucial initial phase of the 'people's war'.

Mohan Bikram Singh's legacy

After the first round of peace talks between the CPN (Maoist) and the government in August 2001, the rebels had suggested the second phase be held in Libang, the district headquarters of Rolpa. Commentators at the time had likened their invitation to the Maoists' inviting the government to come to their 'capital'. That the Maoists should consider the western Nepal districts of Rolpa, Rukum, Salyan, Jajarkot and Pyuthan as their base, and that it should be equally recognised as such by the outside world, provided a considerable psychological boost to the rebels. It can be quite forcefully argued that without the support of the local people of those districts, the 'people's war' would have been a non-starter and without such a 'base' totally in their grip, notwithstanding their activities in other districts, the Maoist mystique would perhaps not have spread so widely and so quickly.

This mass support in those districts did not result from Maoist mobilisation alone. It owed, and owes, a lot to the decades of work by veteran communist leaders like Khagu Lal Gurung and Barman Budha (who was elected MP on a UPFN ticket to the 1991 parliament), and later by people such as Krishna Bahadur Mahara (another UPFN MP in 1991). If, however, there is any single person who can be credited with the growth of radical communism in the mid-west (and even in Nepal), it has to be Mohan Bikram Singh.

Mohan Bikram has long been identified with the extremist left in Nepal, not least because he was one of the founders of the CPN (Fourth Congress), the ideological school for leaders of the CPN (Maoist). Like Nirmal Lama, his long-time associate in the Fourth Congress, Mohan Bikram Singh began his political career as a Nepali Congress worker and was active in his home district of Pyuthan in the immediate aftermath of the 1951 revolution. Soon after, he joined the CPN, and became the party's district secretary in Pyuthan. His rise within the CPN was quite meteoric, being elected to the central committee at the 1957 Second Congress.

During the CPN's 1961 Darbhanga plenum, held after the 1960 takeover by King Mahendra, it was Mohan Bikram who had advocated the constituent assembly option and opposed support for a constitutional monarchy or working with the Nepali Congress. Similarly, at the formation of the CPN (Fourth Congress), general secretary Mohan Bikram presented the political programme for the party and at the top of his priority list was again elections to an assembly which would be entrusted with drawing up a new constitution. (It is also instructive that the other focus areas he outlined at that time were not very dissimilar from either the UPFN's 1991 election manifesto or Baburam Bhattarai's 40-point list of demands.[24] Despite personal differences with Mohan Bikram, it seems the leaders of the offshoot parties continued to follow a programme that had been charted out under his tutelage two decades earlier, although the Maoists would be quite loathe to admit it.)

Mohan Bikram's single-minded pursuit of a constitution drawn up by a constituent assembly was to drive his politics for more than three decades. It was this hard-line posture that led his party, the CPN (Masal), to reject the 1990 constitution as well as the first parliamentary elections under it (which resulted in Baburam Bhattarai and a few others quitting the party and joining the Unity Centre). But, most importantly, his brand of extreme communism was to have a deep impact in Pyuthan and other neighbouring districts, which today constitute the backbone of the Maoist movement.

This is especially true for the eastern part of Rolpa, which was earlier part of Pyuthan district, and which today is known as the Maoists' birthplace. As early as 1957, the large northern village of Thawang had already become communist.[25] During the 1959 parliamentary elections, the CPN candidate received 700 of the 703 valid votes cast in Thawang—that at a time when the Nepali Congress landslide had swept across the country. Mohan Bikram's call for a boycott of the 1980 referendum meant that not a single vote was cast in Thawang, and after the plebiscite the portraits of the king and queen, which were mandatory in government offices such as the village panchayat office, were replaced with those of Marx and Lenin, an action that invited severe police repression.[26]

During the campaign for the 1991 elections, the call by the CPN (Masal) for a boycott translated into a voter turnout lower than the national average of 65 per cent in four adjoining districts in western Nepal. Pyuthan recorded the lowest with just 36.7 per cent, followed by Baglung (49.5 per cent), Myagdi (52.2 per cent), and Rolpa (58.5 per cent). Nickson points out the anomaly of a low voter turnout in these districts that 'were characterised by higher than average levels of literacy and political consciousness. The low turnout was attributed to Masal's national election boycott campaign in this area of the country where its political work was concentrated.'[27] (When Masal decided to opt for parliamentary politics in the 1994 parliamentary elections by supporting 'independents', it won one seat each in Baglung and Pyuthan, while in the 1999 elections, both the Pyuthan seats were won by the National People's Front [Rastriya Jana Morcha], the political wing of the CPN [Masal]. The Front won two of the three seats in Baglung and one of two in Arghakhanchi, another district adjoining Pyuthan.)

Mohan Bikram Singh had painstakingly cultivated a strong organisational structure for the radical left in and around Pyuthan since the 1950s. It was this solid bloc of left supporters that the Maoists were able to exploit to their advantage when the time came to begin an armed struggle. Also, it is likely that by opting to participate in the 1994 elections, Mohan Bikram made it easier for the Maoists to sway a population his party had already indoctrinated against parliamentary politics.

The Nepali Congress in government

If certain parts of the country had been primed for a revolutionary movement over the years, the coming to power after the 1990 movement, first of a Nepali Congress majority government and then, with a nine-month communist interregnum, of a Nepali Congress-led coalition provided the spark that led to the ensuing conflagration. Amik Sherchan, a UPFN MP in the 1991 parliament who survived a brutal police attack in 1993, has said: 'If it hadn't been for Girija Prasad Koirala and Khum Bahadur Khadka, there would perhaps have been no Maoist war.'[28] His reference is to Koirala as prime minister in the first government and Khadka as the home minister in the second, but his statement needs some elucidation.

There has been a long-standing and deep-seated antagonism between the Nepali Congress and the communists. It goes back to the 1951 movement, the settlement of which, with the Nepali Congress as a party to it, was vociferously denounced by the communists. The latter had always viewed the Nepali Congress as its main opponent and even suggesting cooperation with the Nepali Congress in the fight against the monarchy by the founder of the CPN, Pushpa Lal, had been enough for him to be branded a 'traitor' in the eyes of the more radical elements in the Left. It was a sentiment that was reciprocated in full measure by the Nepali Congress. B.P. Koirala was cool towards Pushpa Lal's proposal for joint action. The fact that the royal palace cultivated some sections of the communists during the Panchayat years to serve as a counterweight to the popularity of the Nepali Congress was not hidden from the Congress either.[29] It was only during the 1990 People's Movement that the two sides were able to work together for the first time. Even then, the hardliners among the communists opted for an independent course of action. During the 1991 election campaign, even the future prime minister, Girija Prasad Koirala, had to taste first-hand the extent of left hostility during the course of his election campaign when he had to flee from an election meeting in Pyuthan that was attacked by Masal supporters.[30] It was this history of antipathy and distrust that Girija Prasad Koirala brought with him when he became prime minister in 1991, and soon enough communist activists in outlying districts began facing harassment from the local administration, working in league with local Congress politicians.[31]

But, here, another factor came into play as well.

To begin with, the Nepali Congress did not have much of an organisational base in many districts.[32] Compared to the numbers the communists could muster, the Congress presence at the grassroots was pitiful, and in order to bolster its strength it began inducting into the party people who had been active in the Panchayat system, especially in the lower tiers of the party organisation. One survey of the background of Nepali Congress leaders found that around 40 per cent of the Nepali Congress leaders at village and town levels had switched their allegiance from the Panchayat system to the Congress party after 1990 (as opposed to only 10 per cent in the case of CPN–UML).[33] 'Ex-panchas flocked into the ranks of the Nepali Congress from the very first day after the revolution,' wrote Hoftun et al.[34] Some people even claimed that within six months the ex-panchas outnumbered the original Congress members.

An exodus of this kind into the Nepali Congress seems natural in hindsight, primarily because it would have been the local influentials who were in politics in the first place, and the party of choice would have been the Nepali Congress, which seemed to be the brightest star in the political firmament. But the entry of rural politicians into the Congress had another effect. In areas where communist organisers had been active, people who had lived through the Panchayat-era rule by their local leaders automatically began supporting the left parties. In districts like Rolpa and Rukum, this meant backing the UPFN.

There was another reason for popular support for the UPFN. After the 1990 People's Movement, the situation in the districts was rather fluid and the government had not been able to exert its full authority. In districts where they were in strength, activists of the UPFN began taking account of Panchayat-time development projects. At impromptu hearings, many of the village officials of the previous regime were found guilty of taking advantage of their office and were punished through 'people's action'. Anyone considered to be 'exploiters', 'usurers', or just generally 'cheats', which in many cases would often be the same ones accused of pilfering state resources, also found themselves targets of similar 'people's action'. For a population which had not experienced any form of governance except what came in the form of the local politician, the realisation that the UPFN spoke in their favour led to mass sympathy for the party.

In the 1991 parliamentary elections, the UPFN won both seats from Rolpa and one in Rukum (the second Rukum seat went to the Nepali Congress). But the election also provided an absolute majority to the Nepali Congress at the centre, and the same people who had been cowed down by the activities of the UPFN and who had by then joined the ruling party, struck back. And this time, with the help of the state machinery, which was being 'congressised', the distinction between the state and the Nepali Congress became more or less blurred. This was especially pronounced in remote areas.

Girija Prasad Koirala, with his well-known aversion to communists, did little to control such acts of harassment, and even terror. The police arrested UPFN supporters on trumped-up charges and often tortured them. The *Human Rights Yearbook 1992*, brought out by Kathmandu-based human rights organisation Informal Sector Service Centre (INSEC), reported that in Rolpa, '...political workers, employees and teachers have been the victims of arrest and torture because of political revenge... [S]peeches, processions and mass meeting had been prohibited in that area [Libang, the district headquarters]. There are many incidents that political parties with support from the ruling power had taken political revenge in this district... Local elections were held in a one-sided manner in this district... and candidates of other political parties [non-Nepali Congress] were not allowed to file their nominations...'[35]

Although the situation appeared slightly better in Rukum, there was still evidence of the administration's high-handedness. '[U]pon arrival of the Prime Minister Girija Prasad Koirala in the district

69

headquarters Muskot, a rally led by local member of parliament [belonging to the UPFN] had shown protest and black flag against the PM [sic]. The local administration and the ruling party arrested 27 people and political workers.'[36]

It is a similar story over the successive years. According to the *Human Rights Yearbook 1993*: 'There have been a number of incidents of human rights violations by the state machinery using force. In Libang of Rolpa district, regarded as a stronghold of United People's Front, an armed force of 80 men including six inspectors and District Police Officers ... launched a suppression campaign ... Women were misbehaved [with], chickens and goats were slaughtered and eaten, and citizens were widely charged with false allegations.'[37]

The Yearbook's coverage of Rukum for that year shows the manner in which state violence was carried out in these far-off regions. A village dispute that had broken out between two sides led to a cow, frightened by the commotion, jumping to its death over a cliff. The owner of the cow charged 21 UPFN activists (his opponents in the quarrel) with killing the cow and the police obliged him by arresting five of them.

People in Rolpa tell stories galore of such incidents where disputes between opposing political sides led to the large-scale arrest of UPFN supporters. Baburam Bhattarai had visited Rolpa to take stock of the situation but was not allowed to visit the jail. He condemned the police behaviour and demanded that all false cases be withdrawn and an investigation conducted by a neutral committee.[38]

(The year 1993 was also when the countrywide agitation against the Koirala government took place over the death of Madan Bhandari, the CPN [UML] general secretary, who died in a highway accident. The UPFN was active in the movement as well. It was in the course of a transportation strike that the party's MP from Chitwan, Amik Sherchan, was severely beaten by the police and escaped death only by sheer chance.[39])

This is not to imply that the UPFN was entirely blameless. The human rights yearbooks for this period are full of incidents of UPFN supporters attacking Nepali Congress activists. But the state's responses against the former were always out of proportion to their so-called crimes such as in the indiscriminate manner in which it arrested scores of people, tortured them, and even executed some of them.

Operation Romeo: In September 1995, the same month that the coalition government under Sher Bahadur Deuba of the Nepali Congress came to power, the UPFN (and the CPN-Maoist) began the Sija Campaign in Rolpa and Rukum as part of their 'politico-ideological preparation'. By this time, the UPFN was clashing not only with Nepali Congress workers, but also with those from the Rastriya Prajatantra Party and even the CPN (UML).[40] The home minister in the new cabinet was Khum Bahadur Khadka, whose home district is Dang, just south of Rolpa. Known to be a ruthless politician, he had been accused in a shooting incident during the 1994 election campaign in which two people were killed and 29 others wounded.[41] Given Khadka's violent politics, it was no surprise that his response to the UPFN's activities was a violent police action under the codename Operation Romeo.

A hint of what was actually taking place in Rolpa at that time can be found in the explanation Khadka gave parliament on the 'special security programme'. One newspaper report quoted him as saying that 'some criminal-minded persons carried out such activities as murdering and assaulting local residents, stopping the victims from informing the police about the incidents, and the patients from going to hospital, and violently attacking security personnel, thereby creating tension and terror in the district.' According to Khadka, police teams had been despatched to eight village development committees, 70 persons had been arrested before the security operation and 117 since then, and a number of guns and khukuris had been recovered from houses.[42]

In a television interview, Khadka further said that action had been taken against people who were indulging in anti-monarchy and anti-democracy activities.[43] The next day, Baburam Bhattarai slammed Khadka, arguing that protesting against the monarchy and democracy *was* allowed under the constitution, and that it was no secret that his party had always been in favour of a republic.[44] Bhattarai also said that the weapons mentioned in the minister's statement were only muzzle-loaders and khukuris and that his party activists were accused of being terrorists for possessing such traditional arms. He claimed that all village development committee chairmen in Rolpa elected on the UPFN ticket had been arrested.[45]

Talking to a newspaper almost a month later, Baburam Bhattarai gave his version of what had gone on during the Operation Romeo:

[A]round 1500 policemen including a specially trained commando force sent from Kathmandu have been deployed to let loose a reign of terror against the poor peasants of that rugged mountain district in western Nepal. So far about one thousand people have been arrested, of whom about three hundred are kept in police custody or sent to jails under fictitious charges while the rest have been released on bail or after severe torture. The people arrested range from 12 to 70 years of age and most of them have been subjected to inhuman torture while in police custody... More than ten thousand rural youths, out of a population of two hundred thousand for the whole district, have been forced to flee their homes and take shelter in remote jungles. The armed police operation is still continuing and the virtual reign of white terror seems endless at the moment.[46]

The *Human Rights Yearbook 1995* reported how after a clash at a village fair, 'The government initiated ... suppressive operations to a degree of state terror. Especially, the workers of United People's Front were brutally suppressed.' Under the direct leadership of local ruling party workers, the police searched UPF cadre's homes in 11 villages of Rolpa district, and tortured and arrested many of them. Nearly 6000 locals left the villages due to this police operation. One hundred and thirty-two people were arrested without being served with warrants. Among the arrested were some who were over 75 years of age. 'All the detained were subjected to torture.'[47]

If Khum Bahadur Khadka, and by default, the government, had thought it could curb the UPFN's activities by sending in the police, it was to prove a huge miscalculation. The affected people had begun to view the government as the enemy. In the words of a Maoist party worker, 'They picked up a rock to drop it on their own feet.'[48]

The 'official' explanation
It was only to be expected that the various political parties of the country would have differing views on the origins of the Maoist movement. In its study of the Maoist movement, the Nepali Congress did not find it necessary to look into the underlying causes that had fed the insurgency over the years. It chose to deal more with the politics of the Unity Centre in the period before the conflict began in order to explain the rise of the Maoists, and preferred to attribute it to a (perhaps inadvertent) meeting of minds of ex-

treme forces of both the right and the left, as well as of 'unseen powers'.

> [T]he seeds of the CPN (Maoist)'s ideology can be found in the extremist powers that have not accepted the Constitution of the Kingdom of Nepal (1990) that was established as one of the gains of the 1990 People's Movement. That is why Maoist activities have found sustenance in the various activities of extreme leftists and extreme rightists that do not want a democratic system for Nepal and of forces that do not want political stability in Nepal. [49]

It is also instructive that the High-Level Committee to Provide Suggestions to Solve the Maoist Problem that was formed in 1999 by Prime Minister Krishna Prasad Bhattarai under Sher Bahadur Deuba concluded that the spread of Maoist activities was not due to any failure of the democratic system. It asserted that it was due to 'weaknesses in the management and administration of the state as well as to the frequent changes in government. Rather than a growth in the people's support of the Maoists it [was] the inability of the state machinery to assert itself forcefully.' Again, no attempt was made to identify the 'root causes'.

The official Congress position thus refused to admit that the Maoist movement could be a manifestation of forces other than petty political conspiracies. Interestingly the document on the Integrated Internal Security and Development Programme (IISDP), which was mooted as a holistic solution to the Maoist problem, saw it otherwise. Because it was prepared when the Nepali Congress itself was in power, it is worth recounting some of the points listed as the 'reasons that played a role in the complexity of this [Maoist] problem' as it dealt with matters other than the purely political.[50]

1. Local bigwigs had for long ruled over oppressed groups and deprived them of access to resources, even as they exploited them.
2. Because basic humanitarian needs such as education and health services were at a minimum, the people of these regions score very low on the human development index.
3. Hopelessness among the youth because of the lack of employment opportunities.
4. An absence of influential political leadership committed to the

welfare of the people as well as an absence of influential government institutions together with a system of justice that is not easily available or easy to avail of.

5. The people from this region have been bypassed by development due to a lack of development and welfare programmes.

6. The participation of locals has not been sought by ongoing development programmes and neither have development programmes been able to include locals in their implementation.

Expectedly enough, the Left is not willing to let the Nepali Congress off so easily, if only because the Congress has ruled the country for almost the entire period since 1990. The CPN (UML) has capitalised on this fact to the extent that of its sum total of 77 'reasons for the origins of the Maoist problem' enumerated in its evaluation of the Maoist movement, practically all have either directly to do with the Nepali Congress governments or with governance in general.[51]

The other communist parties generally play on the same themes that are dealt with in this chapter, but a recurring one is the attitude of the Nepali Congress towards communists and the brutality of the police.

Social factors

There is also a pronounced ethnic and class dimension to the problem of poverty and hence the rise of the Maoists in Nepal. While Nepal is essentially a country of minorities comprising more than sixty ethnic and caste groups; three of them—Bahun, Chhetri, and Newar—are economically and politically dominant. This disparity is rooted in the history of giving land grants to military and civil officials who came to inhabit the fertile and commercially and politically important Kathmandu valley. Under the Ranas, as under the Shah kings of Gorkha before them, the ruling class, most of whom belonged to the three above-mentioned groups, always adopted a mode of government which permitted them to remain in Kathmandu. As a result, Kathmandu became the geographical centre where surpluses appropriated from other regions were realised.

On the other hand, many of Nepal's socio-cultural groups have never had access to the state apparatus. The presence of Dalit (so-called untouchables), Madhesi (people of tarai origin) and janjati (members of ethnic groups) in the state has been negligible.

Because of this polarisation, Nepali civil servants operate from Kathmandu, are oriented to the Kathmandu valley—seen to be the real hub of national life—and the welfare of ethnic villagers in remote places is completely ignored.[52] As a result, the incidence of poverty is higher among ethnic groups such as Tamangs, Magars, and Tharus, while the other hardest-hit have always been Dalits.

The Pakistani scholar, Eqbal Ahmad, wrote back in 1970 that the 'pressures for change in the political, economic, and social relationships of the past inevitably lead to a confrontation with those whose interest lie in the maintenance of the status quo.'[53] Ahmad's understanding of the causes that lead to revolution could have served as a warning to those who took it upon themselves to remake the political order in Nepal after 1990. But as things turned out observations such as his would have gone unnoticed.

The re-establishment of democracy engendered expectations among the hitherto quiescent population groups that the new political setup would be more amenable to their aspirations. Most vociferous among these were the ethnic groups who make up about 35 per cent of Nepal's population. These communities nurse a historic sense of marginalisation from the national power centre. Groups like the Magars and the Gurungs were themselves part of the Gorkha expansionary war, and constituted part of the ruling elite in the initial years of the Gorkha empire. But they soon found themselves sidelined by the ruling coalition of the Shah-Chhetris.[54] Other population groups, such as Rais, Limbus and Tamangs, and those of tarai origin, who were subjugated in the course of the unification campaign, have never been considered for state positions.

This situation remained unchanged during the century-long rule by the Ranas. In fact, the Rana era, which provided a period of relative political stability, saw a speeding up of the process of moulding Nepal into a Hindu state at the expense of other religious belief systems and ways of life. With state sanction provided only to the Hindu religion, which was clearly identified with the ruling group, and with an emphasis on the Nepali language, the languages, religions, and cultures of the various ethnic groups gradually lost importance. (It has often been argued that this may have happened in the natural course of events, but because it was imposed from above, the supremacy of Hinduism and the Nepali language is resented.) The codification of the social do's and don'ts in the *Muluki Ain* of 1854 led to the inferior placement of ethnic groups in the social hierarchy by law, and raised the status of the Hindu 'upper castes'.

When the Panchayat system was instituted in 1962, the constitution, for the first time, defined Nepal as a Hindu kingdom and Nepali as the country's national language. The attempt seems to have been to subsume ethnic identities within the national rubric of a Nepaliness.[55] Anything that strayed from the Panchayat ideal of 'one nation, one language' (one religion was implicit) was prohibited by the government. But that did not prevent the various groups from organising themselves, albeit in a roundabout manner, such as the Nepal Sadbhavana Parishad (which became the Nepal Sadbhavana Party after 1990) to serve the interests of the tarai people and the Nepal Langhali Association[56] (which became the Nepal Magar Association after 1990). For some reason, these organisations were countenanced by the state even though they threatened the Panchayat's characterisation of Nepal as a homogeneous state. These early attempts at ethnic and regional assertions, however, provided the perfect setting for the welter of expectations to burst out into the open after 1990.

Ethnic groups (also called janjatis or nationalities), together with other disadvantaged groups such as Dalits, non-Hindus, Madhesis, and women, saw in the re-establishment of democracy an opportunity to set right the inequities that had characterised two centuries of domination in all spheres of the state by 'upper-caste' Hindus. There was a rush to form political parties with distinct ethnic agendas. And when the Constitution Recommendations Commission asked for suggestions on the shape of the new constitution, the response was overwhelming.

There were demands asking for constitutional recognition of all languages of Nepal, not only Nepali, and for all religions, not only Hinduism. There were calls to ensure representation of all population groups in the legislature as well as for the division of the country into autonomous units reflecting the demographic dominance of particular groups. 'Rather than attempting to accommodate these grievances, the commission and the interim government simply perceived them as a threat to national unity, and virtually dismissed them out of hand.'[57] The 1990 constitution thus provided for the formal trappings of parliamentary democracy but true representation, besides the quite perfunctory recognition of the country's 'multiethnic, multilingual' character, was lacking. The paramountcy accorded to the Hindu religion and the Nepali language was carried over from the 'undemocratic' 1962 constitution. Demands to make the upper house of parliament into a 'house of nationalities' to ensure the representation of all ethnic groups in the legislature and to introduce affirmative action in government employment were also ignored. The stranglehold of the Bahun-Chhetri combine on the state not only remained intact, but grew firmer over the years.

The levels of representation in parliament and the civil service both illustrate the last point. In the two elected Panchayat legislatures (of the 1980s), the share of Bahuns and Chhetris was 50 per cent. This proportion increased to 55, 63, and 63 per cent respectively in the 1991, 1994, and 1999 parliaments.[58] (Most strikingly only one Dalit was elected MP in these three elections.) The imbalance has been even more striking in the bureaucracy. Between 1983 and 1985, 69 per cent of those who passed the civil service examination were Bahuns and Chhetris. This figure rose to 81 per cent in 1992/93; and by 2001 it stood at 98 per cent![59]

Bahuns and Chhetris together constitute only 29 per cent of the population, and yet have almost total command over the state's resources. As Pfaff-Czarnecka observes: 'Nepal lacks a clear majority in its population that would render the political dominance of one particular group more self-evident. Ethnic activists in Nepal increasingly point out that a minority is running a multiethnic nation.'[60]

Nickson foresaw little likelihood of change 'given the entrenched power of the landed aristocracy supported by the armed forces, the highly traditional and Brahmin-dominated public administration, and the shallow and ambivalent ideology of the Nepali Congress Party itself'.[61] He could have said the same of the CPN (UML) as well since for all its revolutionary rhetoric, there was nothing in its short spell in power to indicate it was any more progressive than the Nepali Congress. In fact, it was during the CPN (UML) rule that the government decided to broadcast news in the Sanskrit language despite the fact that Sanskrit is the mother tongue of no one in Nepal. This added insult to injury for the janjatis, who were still smarting under the imposition of Nepali as the national language in the 1990 constitution and the introduction of compulsory Sanskrit up to high school level.[62] (Anti-Sanskritism is one of the rallying cries of the Maoists, and one that finds favour even among ethnic activists who otherwise see Magars being 'used' by the Maoists.[63])

The state thus continued with a policy of exclusion even as there were demands for recognising the country's pluralist character. And it was quite natural that with some nurturing, the historical hurt festering deep inside would find expression in support for an insurgency that aimed to reverse these wrongs. By providing an outlet for the expression of ethnic and other discontent, where the state had all but shut it out, the Maoists seem to have succeeded remarkably in securing the backing of a large number of people.

The advocacy of minority rights has been a constant feature in the Left's stated programmes. It finds explicit mention in the founding document of the Fourth Congress, which emphasised the need for 'effective action' to 'develop the language, culture and society of oppressed and backward groups'.[64] The UPFN manifesto for the 1991 election was full of such sentiments, and it is worth noting that of the nine UPFN MPs in the 1991 parliament, six were janjatis. The Maoists went one step further and in the leaflet that was distributed with the beginning of the 'People's War' in 1996, declared:

> To maintain the hegemony of one religion (i.e. Hinduism), language (i.e. Nepali), and nationality (i.e. Khas), this state has for centuries exercised discrimination, exploitation and oppression against other religions, languages and nationalities and has conspired to fragment the forces of national unity that is vital for proper development and security of the country.[65]

Baburam Bhattarai has provided further elaboration:

> The oppressed regions within the country are primarily the regions inhabited by the indigenous people since time immemorable [sic]. These indigenous people dominated regions that were independent tribal states prior to the formation of the centralised state in the later half of the eighteenth century, have been reduced to the present most backward and oppressed condition due to the internal feudal exploitation and the external semi-colonial oppression. They have been left behind [in] the historical development process because of [the] blockade of their path of independent development and imposition of socio-cultural along with economic oppression upon them with the backing of the state by those forces

who had come from outside. Thus it is quite natural that the question of regional oppression of Mongol dominated eastern, central and the western Hilly regions or the Austro-Dravid dominated Inner Terai and Terai regions are manifested in the form of national oppression. There the regional and the national questions have intertwined with one another. Besides this, the problem of the Khas dominated far western Karnali region can occur as regional question instead of a nationality question and it will have to be tackled accordingly. Thus, according to the concrete situation it is necessary to solve the problem of oppressed regions and nationalities by granting regional and national autonomy.[66]

It is therefore no coincidence that the Maoists strongholds are in west Nepal, and particularly, Rolpa and Rukum, where the Magars are dominant. The mobilisation techniques of the UPFN/CPN (Maoist) alone, and these were certainly very effective,[67] would not have moved them to embrace the Maoist ideology so easily. A letter by a foreigner to a Kathmandu weekly while Operation Romeo was underway explains just how easy it was for the Kham Magar of Rolpa to be swayed by Maoist rhetoric. 'The problem lies in the situation many young Magars are in,' she writes. 'Education in the Magar areas is bad to non-existent, the health status in parts catastrophic, and no interest from the official side in improving anything or even lending an open ear to their problems and needs. Money and big projects are brought to the lower areas [where Bahuns and Chhetris are dominant] but never reach the Magars [who live in the high mountains in the north]. So they see their only hope in a radical solution which they think the [Maoists] can bring.'[68]

Social dislocation

Social and economic change – urbanisation, increases in literacy and education, industrialisation, mass media expansion – extend political consciousness, multiply political demands, broaden political participation. These changes undermine traditional sources of political authority and traditional political institutions; they enormously complicate the problems of creating new bases of political association and new political institutions combining legitimacy and effectiveness. The rates of social mobilisation and the expansion of political participation are high; the rates of political organisation and institutionalisation are low. The result is political instability and disorder.

This statement by Samuel P. Huntington[69] is eerily familiar to what happened in the Nepal of the early 1990s.

For all its drawbacks, the Panchayat system had brought 'development' in the form of highways and schools to the country-side. Roads allowed village youth to see life elsewhere, and literacy allowed them access to the tools to understand, compare, and contrast their lives with life in the outside world. The country has always had a vibrant media culture, and with the introduction of press freedom in 1990, all the deeds and misdeeds of politicians were widely debated in the papers. Political leaders thoroughly failed to provide any meaningful programme to their workers, busy as they were in playing power games at the centre and openly amassing personal fortunes. This led to disenchantment among their followers who 'were ready for picking up by the Maoists'.[70] In other words, young Nepalis 'politicised by literacy and the ability to read the newspapers and yet frustrated by poor and unresponsive education, the age-old route down the mountains to menial labour in the Indian plains was no longer a path that could be trod unthinkingly'.[71]

In the same vein, French scholar Anne de Sales has written of villages full of individuals 'who have had experience of realities other than those of the daily life of the village'.

Whether their personal journeys have been in search of a better education or, more commonly, in search of work, whether they have gone to the flatlands of the tarai, to the capital, or abroad, they have come into contact with a modernity which, even if it is not viewed as 100 per cent positive, marks a Rubicon. The perception of rural areas like theirs as dead ends and going nowhere, forgotten by the rest of the world, discourages the young people, who are more inclined than in previous times to join a militant project for a society where they would have a more respected place and a better life.[72]

Although Sales was referring to the Kham Magar youth of Rolpa (her area of fieldwork); her observation would be true for the young anywhere in Nepal. A politically conscious and aware youth population that saw no succour coming from the political establishment was easily swayed by Maoist rhetoric — rhetoric which claimed: 'This state that does not manufacture even a needle in the name of self-reliant and national economy, has handed over the whole economy of the country to a dozen families of foreign compradors and bureaucratic capitalists.'[73]

Maoist guerrillas and militia line up for a rally in Dolakha district. July 2001.

The Growth of the Maoist Movement

THE 'PEOPLE'S war' caught the Nepali public totally by surprise. People were generally quite unaware of even the existence of the CPN (Maoist) and had only vague knowledge of the UPFN's memorandum enumerating the 40-point list of demands to Prime Minister Sher Bahadur Deuba. In fact, even after the fighting had actually begun, the sketchy information filtering out of the remote districts did not lend any urgency to the situation. Reports of disturbances in the countryside were a regular feature in newspapers, and there seemed nothing novel in the news to warrant extra attention. Soon, however, it became clear that something out of the ordinary was taking place in the hills of Nepal.

Among the actions that signalled the initiation of the conflict on 13 February 1996, was an attack on a police station in the district of Rolpa (along with two others in Rukum and Sindhuli — see Box 3). Groups shouting 'Love Live Maoism' surrounded the police post at Holeri in southwestern Rolpa and demanded that the policemen inside surrender their weapons. When the latter refused, the attackers searched the office and made off with some explosives.[1]

Six years later, on 8 September 2002, the Maoists launched a devastating attack on a police station in eastern Nepal and a day later overran the district headquarters of Arghakhanchi in the western part of the country. In the fighting in the two places, more than 110 security personnel, including army soldiers, lost their lives, and the rebels captured more than two hundred pieces of small arms.[2]

These two events serve to illustrate the spectacular gains made by the Maoists between 1996 and 2002, and the reason they have been so successful has particularly to do with the manner in which the state has responded to the crisis.

The government's ad hoc response

When Baburam Bhattarai submitted his demands on 4 February with the warning that an armed uprising would begin if the grievances outlined were not looked into, Deuba virtually ignored it and went off on a visit to India. There is no evidence that the police were kept on alert during that period. The lackadaisical manner in which the authorities treated the possibility of an armed revolt has partly to do with the fact that after the 1990 political changeover few thought the radical left posed a credible threat. (This was notwithstanding Nickson's warning that 'Masal, which had also remained quiescent during the Panchayat regime, is following the strategy of Sendero Luminoso and that it has decided to launch its armed struggle to coincide with the establishment of parliamentary democracy in Nepal.'[3]).

The largest pre-1990 communist grouping, the CPN (ML) had given up Maoism and embraced multiparty democracy. Fringe Maoist parties like the Unity Centre and Masal were certainly vocal in their opposition to the constitution and their commitment to establishing a republic. But given the divisions within these parties and their lack of mass support, they were seen as little more than nuisances to a polity that was striding purposefully ahead in the practice of what was increasingly turning out to be a rambunctious democracy. Furthermore, with the advent of democracy it was only to be expected that there would be a babel of dissenting voices, even threatening ones such as that raised by the Magarat Mukti Morcha, which had warned that it would fight for separation if the government did not take steps towards creating a state of Magarat (a state for Magars).[4] In fact, in the first years of the 1990s, given the stridency of janjati activism, an ethnic conflict seemed more of a possibility than anything else.

All of these factors perhaps help explain why there were differences of opinion within the government as to how to tackle the Maoist issue from the very beginning. While Deuba made it clear that he was willing to talk to the Maoists and find a political answer, his home minister, Khum Bahadur Khadka, was for total suppression.[5] The latter even went so far as to suggest that the government would be able to suppress the Maoists in a matter of days.[6] There were also views like the one expressed by law and justice minister, Bhim Bahadur Tamang, who wondered how it would be possible to find a political solution by negotiating with a group that did not believe in the constitution in the first place.[7]

Prime Minister Deuba convened an all-party meeting to examine the Maoist issue a month after the first attacks, but the meeting ended without any resolution primarily because the ruling Nepali Congress party itself was not represented at the meeting. The participants accused the government of calling the meeting only for the sake of formality.[8] Ad hocism such as this marked the state's response to the Maoist crisis over the years. This, and the transient nature of the governments over the following years, makes it easier to understand how the

Maoists were able to reach their position of strength by the end of 2002.

Centre in disarray

One of the tragedies of post-1990 Nepal has been the unstable politics at the centre which saw twelve changes of government between 1991 and late 2002. These frequent changes have meant that there has been no consistency in government policy in dealing with the rebels, while the kind of politicking that went on in Kathmandu bolstered the Maoists' argument that parliamentary democracy was a sham that could not work for the benefit of the people.

The seeds of instability and unprincipled opportunism were sown early on when Girija Prasad Koirala became prime minister in 1991, and the subsequent infighting that broke out within the Nepali Congress over government appointments. As discussed earlier, dissension within the ruling party led to a mid-term election in 1994, resulting in a hung parliament. Neither of the major parties in the 1994 parliament, the CPN (UML) or the Nepali Congress, could muster a majority, and were thus at the mercy of the Rastriya Prajatantra Party (RPP), the party of the former panchas, which had the numbers to swing the balance either way.

As the largest party in parliament, the CPN (UML) was given the opportunity to form the government. But the minority communist government lasted just nine months before a coalition led by the Nepali Congress, with the RPP and the Nepal Sadbhavana Party as junior partners, took over in September 1995. Through this alignment, the Nepali Congress accorded respectability to the RPP, a party that had until then been shunned because of its association with the Panchayat regime. Not to be outdone in the numbers game, the CPN (UML) went a step further a year later when the Congress-led coalition was ousted and propped up a government under the leadership of the RPP itself. Thus, Nepal saw Lokendra Bahadur Chand back as prime minister in March 1997. The irony was that it had been Chand's appointment to the high office in April 1990 that had provoked massive rioting in the streets of Kathmandu and ultimately the collapse of the Panchayat system.

The Chand government lasted only up to October 1997, when the Nepali Congress made its move and effected a split in the RPP with the understanding that it would support the faction led by Surya Bahadur Thapa in forming the new government. The Nepal

Sadbhavana Party once again joined the alliance. However, the RPP's second stint proved equally abortive when the Nepali Congress withdrew its support in April 1998. A minority government took office under Girija Prasad Koirala with the backing of the CPN (Marxist-Leninist), which had been formed a month earlier by a splinter group from the CPN (UML). The CPN (ML) joined the Nepali Congress-led government in August that year. But in another surprise move, in December, Koirala ejected the CPN (ML) to make room for the CPN (UML) and the Nepal Sadbhavana Party; the understanding being that fresh polls would be called as soon as possible.

In May 1999, the third general elections were held and the Nepali Congress won an outright majority once again. Krishna Prasad Bhattarai, who had been projected as the prime ministerial candidate of the Nepali Congress, headed the new Congress government. Less than a year later, in March 2000, Koirala removed his old friend-cum-foe as leader of the parliamentary party and eased himself back into the prime minister's chair. But he did not last long either in the face of renewed Maoist attacks, and the open battle that had ensued in the Nepali Congress since his ouster of Bhattarai. Sher Bahadur Deuba, who had by now become firmly identified as Bhattarai's blue-eyed boy, came back to power in July 2001 sporting a peace agenda to pull the country out of the morass it was sinking into ever deeper.

This state of disarray is all that faced a very determined CPN (Maoist) as it built up its insurgency.

Tackling the Maoists

There has always been a strong lobby in the government that favoured using brute force against the Maoists, despite the far-from-desired effect of Operation Romeo. Since the 'people's war' was viewed as a mere irritant compared to the very real threat to the longevity of his government, Deuba was more preoccupied with the minutiae of ensuring his survival than holding the Maoist bull by the horns.

A section of the intelligentsia as well as some political parties called for a negotiated end to the fighting from the very beginning.[9] But the mainstream Left remained ambivalent. It could not overtly support the Deuba government's resort to police methods, and neither could it root for the Maoists. There was, however, a noticeable trace of wishful thinking in their formal stance. '[T]he present violent acts committed in the name of a People's War can only impact negatively on the real People's War...', commented the Nepali-language weekly *Chhalphal*.[10] That a newspaper known to speak for the CPN (UML), a party already committed to 'multi-party people's democracy', should refer to a 'real people's war' indicated the dilemma the Left found itself in.[11] Not much different was the position of the UPFN led by Niranjan Govinda Vaidya, which simply stated that it did not agree with the nature and objectives of the 'people's war'.[12] All in all, this was implicit recognition by the Left that a 'people's war' was certainly called for, and the only divergence was on when and how.

After the CPN (UML) came back into government in 1997 (albeit under the leadership of Chand of the RPP), there was a let up in the violence on both sides and a feeble attempt was made to resolve the issue politically.[13] But the unofficial détente came to an end around the time of the May 1997 local elections, which were boycotted by the Maoists. In some village development committees, Maoist threats led to not a single person standing for election, and even those who filed their candidacy papers later withdrew. Eight people were killed during the boycott campaign.[14] Polls could not be held in 87 village development committees and as a result, district development committees could not be formed in 15 districts in western Nepal.[15]

The government's response was an attempt in July to introduce a law entitled the Terrorist and Destructive Activities (Control and Punishment) Act at the active initiative of the deputy prime minister and home minister, Bamdev Gautam, who was also the deputy general secretary of the CPN (UML). Partly an attempt to address the police complaint that the Maoists they captured were being released by the courts in the absence of proof, the law would have given the police wide-ranging powers against 'terrorists'. The Maoists denounced the government attempt to pass the anti-terrorist law as 'the unmasking of the seemingly bourgeois democratic state to reveal its fascist nature'.[16] The government was forced to backtrack on the law even before it was placed before parliament owing to massive protests from the civil society, the media, and international organisations.

But in the face of renewed attacks, the government was forced to abandon its conciliatory attitude towards the Maoists even though it had earlier tried to articulate a 'political solution' to the Maoist problem by forming a taskforce to look into 'Maoist Activities and a Search for Solutions' in April 1997 under CPN (UML) MP, Prem Singh Dhami. The voluminous Dhami Commission report (it ran to 169 pages) was presented to the government in August the same year, but because the situation was quite inopportune at the time due to continued Maoist belligerence, it was shelved.

The Dhami report, which has formed the basis of many subsequent reports, was noteworthy for the following reasons: 1) it provided a comprehensive analysis of the growth of the Maoists, their organisation, battle strategies, and future plans; 2) it made recommendations that were pretty much along the lines of the socio-economic reforms demanded by the Maoists; 3) it admitted that the police actions were brutal and many innocents had been targeted; and finally, 4) it emphasised the need to bring the CPN (Maoist) into the constitutional process and to make a formal offer of talks to the UPFN [Bhattarai]. Failing this, the report suggested that 'their intentions should be laid bare before the people'.[17]

The political scenario changed a couple of months later when, in October 1997, Surya Bahadur Thapa ousted his party colleague Chand, and formed another minority government. The new government declared that it would not try to pass the 'Black Law', as the anti-terrorist bill had become known; but it did little else to counter the Maoists.

Kilo Sierra Two

Emboldened by its success in disrupting the local elections, the Maoists set about consolidating their hold in their strongholds in western Nepal. In 1999, Prachanda wrote in his 'Third Turbulent Year of People's War: A General Review':

> Practice of people's power started openly after overpowering principally the enemy's local agents and police force by people's guerrillas in the areas where [a] political vacuum was created because of mass boycotting of reactionary local election[s]. People's co-operatives, collective labour and farming, construction of rural tracks, bridges, memorials for martyrs, registration, purchase and sale of land, people's security, people's culture, people's court and running of schools etc. became preliminary daily exercises of new

people's power. People in those areas felt themselves for the first time the master[s] of their own destiny. For the first four months of the third year [from 13 February 1998] the main areas of Western Nepal experienced a de-facto liberated area. With some differences in degree, many areas in Eastern and Central hills also exercised preliminary people's power.[18]

This was the beginning of the taking over of government functions by the rebels (See news report in Box 4).

Box 4. Expansion of Maoist control

More than half of the 51 Village Development Committees in Rolpa district in west central Nepal, are said to be run or controlled by Maoists... [The Maoists are] operating an administration parallel to the official one. The latter has not been effective because of lack of money and personnel. Maoists have prevented elections and terrorised officials, and the national government has held back funds for fear they will fall into the hands of the Maoists. The district has been left without important health and development services. People thus go to the unofficial government with their problems. Almost all cases, including land transactions and other legal problems, are said to be handled in the People's Court.

—The Kathmandu Post, *14 May, 1998*

But the euphoria of the experiment was to be marred by the ferocity with which the government responded. In April 1998, Girija Prasad Koirala took over as prime minister and he took the increasing influence of the Maoists in the west as a serious challenge to the state's authority. The Maoists had announced the existence of a Central Military Commission under Prachanda on the second anniversary of the 'people's war' on 13 February 1998. There was also the question of conducting local elections in the areas where it had not been possible earlier, and parliamentary elections were in the offing within a year. Two things happened around that time. Koirala went on a tour of areas under Maoist influence and realised that the situation was getting out of hand. The second was a severe attack on Kalikatar of Tanahu, the home district of Govinda Raj Joshi, the home minister,[19] an attack that Prachanda characterised as one that 'symbolised the pinnacle of [the] Third Plan'.[20] (The 'Third Plan' was one of a series developed by the Maoists. See below for details). Pinnacle it may have been for the rebels but the state moved swiftly and in May 1998 launched the infamous

Operation 'Kilo Sierra Two'.

This was a 'search and kill' operation that was meant to prevent the Maoist movement from gaining strength. Although the police then, and to this day, have always denied the existence of such an operation, the police chief of the western region admitted that a campaign was on and that they were taking extreme measures. How extreme those measures were was made clear by his statement: 'If they [the Maoists] don't respect the Constitution, we don't have to stick to the Constitution and take them to court.'[21]

From mid-1998 onwards, the killing of Maoists and their supporters—as well as civilians caught in the middle—escalated to unprecedented heights. And unlike, Operation Romeo that had concentrated on a particular area in the western hills, 'Kilo Sierra Two' was spread out across all the 'Maoist-affected' regions of the country. It has to be noted that this police operation was launched at a time when the Koirala government was dependent on the external support of the CPN (ML); continued even after the latter joined the government; and did not end even after the CPN (UML) had replaced the CPN (ML) in December 1998.

Around 500 people were killed during 'Kilo Sierra Two', and although many of them may have been Maoists or their supporters, some of the casualties were definitely innocents. The pain and suffering of the peasantry due to the police action seems to have boomeranged on the political establishment and the police, as new recruits flocked to the Maoist side. 'In the main areas of struggle when massacres in dozens were carried out in one village after another, the poor peasants inspired the Party continuously asserting "let the Party continue [the] People's War for which they were ready to sacrifice everything",' wrote Prachanda. 'Hundreds of women victims of barbaric rape by the reactionary [state] joined the People's War with hatred...'[22] The case study in Box 5 illustrates the depths of feeling that swelled the ranks of Maoist fighters.

Police brutality clearly provided the long-lasting motive energy for the Maoist insurgency throughout the country. Public perception in the mid- and far-western parts of Nepal also seems to hold this view, as was evident in a nationwide opinion poll conducted in early 2001, in which 30 per cent of respondents believed police violence was to blame for the increase in Maoist activity (as opposed to the national average of 19 per cent). (The factor identified on the national level as being number one for the growth

---

Box 5. Desire for vengeance

Sita Kumari Pun was 11 years old when her 23-year-old brother was killed by the police while he was on the upper slopes harvesting potatoes. A passer-by brought the news that a man and a woman had been gunned down by the police and buried. She never saw the body. Afterwards, the police came and beat up the family. Her father suffered a paralytic stroke. Sita had to leave school and at 13 manages the house and the fields while her 14-year-old brother tends to the livestock. Sita blames Mane Karne, the former village chief's son, for setting the police on to her brother. He had nothing to do with the Maoists, she insists. Sita vows to revenge the killing of her brother, a 'simple, ordinary man'. 'It doesn't matter whether we have to use a *khukuri* or a gun, we will avenge ourselves against our enemies, and the police, in league with them.' Two years after her brother was killed, Sita, choking back her sobs, ended her story on a note of defiance resonating with Maoist rhetoric. 'Yes, my brother has been killed. But we have another 1000 brothers of the same kind. We will all come together and take revenge. We will not spare those responsible for our grief,' she said.

From Gautam, Shobha, Amrit Baskota, and Rita Manchanda. 'Where there are no men: Women in the Maoist insurgency in Nepal'. Women War and Peace in South Asia: Beyond Victimhood to Agency, edited by Rita Manchanda, 2001. p. 232.

---

of the Maoists—poverty/unemployment/corruption—came second at 28 per cent in that region.)[23] Even a police chief has conceded that the cavalier actions of his force had provided a boost to the Maoists.[24]

Whatever the case, the government was successful in conducting the parliamentary general elections in May 1999. Unlike the 1997 local elections, which had been heavily disrupted by the Maoists, this time the Maoists settled for a simple boycott call. Analysts believe that this quiescence could have been the result of the just concluded 'Kilo Sierra Two' operation since the Maoists may have been quite unprepared to handle another bout of repression.[25]

In the end, however, these efforts by successive governments to bring the Maoists to heel by using police force failed thoroughly. Sending in the police with the single-point brief to crush the insurgency without considering the possible fallout was one mistake. The other was not to realise the extent to which a police force trained to handle civilian law-and-order situations would be able to take on a highly motivated group. Ultimately, it only served to strengthen the rebels' hold on a population terrorised by police high-handedness.

It can also be argued that it was a general failure of the

Kathmandu-based leaders of civil society that they were not very alert to the goings-on in the hinterland. Rishikesh Shaha had written back in 1996, a few months after the insurgency began, 'It is just possible that the insurgency would never have acquired the intensity it did over the years if these elite categories had been more active when the situation was getting out of hand in the hills of the mid-west. With the elite classes in the capital either unknowing or deliberately looking the other way, the police operation succeeded in thoroughly alienating the local population of Rolpa.'[26]

The experience with the successful discrediting of the 'Black Law' in 1997 demonstrated that public opinion did count, and is heeded as well, if it comes across forcefully. But, whereas, with the anti-terrorist law there was great possibility of its misuse even in Kathmandu, police atrocities happening far away failed to rouse those who could have made a difference. This was true for Operation Romeo as it was for what took place later.

Nepali Congress in power again

Public hopes were generated when early parliamentary polls were announced for May 1999. After five years of instability and previously inconceivable cohabitations in government, there was a general sense of optimism that a fresh mandate would result in a majority government that could get down to the business of seriously dealing with the various problems facing the nation. Even at that juncture the Maoist issue was not generally perceived to be the topmost crisis facing the nation. Respondents to an opinion poll held on the eve of the election placed development (28.6 per cent) as the biggest challenge for the next government. Next in line came inflation (27.6 per cent), followed by unemployment (18.4 per cent), corruption (7.1 per cent), while only 4.7 per cent viewed the issue of peace and security to be of greatest importance.[27] Certainly all of these are linked to the questions raised by the Maoists, but the people did not consider the 'people's war' per se to be the number one cause for the sorry state of the country. (Unemployment, inflation, and corruption remained the three top concerns in yet another survey conducted in 2001.[28] It was only in 2002, that the Maoist problem shared top honours with corruption and unemployment as the most pressing problems facing the country.[29])

The biggest challenge, therefore, before the majority Nepali Congress government under Krishna Prasad Bhattarai that took

Box 6. **The Khara incident**

On 22 February 2000, 15 civilians were killed by police apparently in reprisal for the killing of 15 policemen during an attack by members of the CPN (Maoist) on a police station at Ghartigaun, Rolpa district three days before. Thirty police officers from Simrutu police station were sent to Kumcheri, in Khara village development committee, Rukum district, to search for Maoists believed to have participated in the attack on the police station. At around 5 am police spotted seven or eight Maoists hiding in the jungle. A group of police chased them and one policeman died in an exchange of fire. Reinforcements reportedly arrived by helicopter from Musikot police station (Rukum), Salyan, Nepalgunj and Jajarkot. Police started to burn houses in Khumcheri, Haiwang, Kural and Pokhari. In Pokhari, seven civilians were killed. A further seven were killed in Kural and one more in Daya. According to survivors, police dragged people out of their houses and shot them. All those killed were supporters of the Nepali Congress.

From Nepal: A Spiralling Human Rights Crisis, *Amnesty International, April 2002.*

office in May 1999 was the issue of governance and the related matter of engaging the Maoists. It was business as usual with regard to the first, but owing to overwhelming public opinion that was largely in favour of resolving the Maoist problem through talks, in December 1999 Bhattarai formed the ponderous-sounding 'High-Level Committee to Provide Suggestions to Solve the Maoist Problem' under Sher Bahadur Deuba, and two months later authorised it to hold talks with the CPN (Maoist).

Contact was established with the rebel leadership, and the response was positive. In a letter to a government intermediary in February 2000, Prachanda listed three demands and stated that 'should these minimum conditions be fulfilled, we are ready to send our representatives for high-level negotiations and we would like to inform you that we will cease all operations during the period of talks.' The demands were: 1) reveal the whereabouts of a central committee member of the CPN-Maoist along with others who had been 'disappeared'; 2) initiate moves to release arrested workers and sympathisers; and 3) end state terrorism and begin the process to investigate the incident of arson and killing in Rukum district (See Box 6), provide compensation, and take action against the guilty.[30] (When a group of eight prominent personalities had met Bhattarai in August 1999 to query the fate of the said CPN [Maoist] central committee member, Dandapani Neupane, and six others taken into custody by the police in May 1999, the prime minister's off-hand reply was: 'They are already dead.'[31] Prachanda's insistence on the matter seems to have only been seeking official confirmation of what the head of government had said in private.)

But Bhattarai was hamstrung by the lack of cooperation from his own party. Led by party president Girija Prasad Koirala, the Nepali Congress was extremely critical of Bhattarai's handling of the Maoists. They wanted firmer action, and, in March 2000, Koirala orchestrated the fall of Bhattarai. Upon becoming prime minister yet again, Koirala declared: 'The first priority of the government will be to restore law and order in the country to protect the lives of the people. Curbing corruption and ensuring good governance with administrative reforms are next on the government's agenda.'[32]

The Maoist response was swift. Terming Koirala a 'Nepali Hitler', the Maoists called on 'everyone' to fight against his leadership that, they claimed, would nurture 'fascism and anti-nationalism', and announced an 'Armed Nepal Bandh' for 6 April 2000.[33] Thereafter attacks on the police resumed, and the strategy this time was to remove all government presence from the countryside. The government received its biggest setback when the Maoists overran Dunai, the district headquarters of Dolpa in late September. Following the Dunai attack the army was mobilised for security duty in 16 district headquarters; but it was still not used in the fight against the Maoists because of the lack of understanding between the prime minister and the king, the supreme commander of the Nepali army.

Around the same time, with an as-yet-undisclosed western organisation acting as mediator, the Koirala government and the Maoists came into contact. As part of that effort, the deputy prime minister, Ram Chandra Poudel, met with a CPN (Maoist) central committee member as well, but what seemed to be a breakthrough came to naught after the government released a top Maoist leader after having him renounce his party at a press conference. The Maoists were furious at what they perceived to be double-dealing by the government and Prachanda decried the episode as a 'drama devoid of art'.[34]

In November the Deuba committee submitted its recommendations to the government. But the petty factionalism within the Congress party had reached such heights that the Koirala government simply ignored its suggestions. The Deuba committee had recommended continuing with police operations while trying to entice the Maoists for talks through the back door. In February 2001, the above-mentioned western mediator was almost successful in getting informal talks started between the two sides, but the Maoists backed out, asking for a postponement. Then on 26 February, the Maoists announced that they had just conducted their second national conference. Events began to move faster after this, as described in Chapter 5.

Maoist approach

While the political games at the centre were providing much cause for disenchantment with the state, the Maoists were rousing the masses with their slogans of the dawn of a new era. Take the following passage from the document adopted by the March 1995 plenum of the Central Committee of the CPN (Maoist), which provided the blueprint for the Maoists' struggle:

> [T]he target of armed struggle will be confiscating the lands of feudals and landlords and distributing them amongst the landless and poor peasants on the basis of land-to-the-tiller theory and to attack ... in order to cut the roots of imperialist exploitation the projects such as industries, banks, etc, in the hands of comprador and bureaucratic capitalists and projects run by government and non-government organisations.[35]

The same document also identified the various groups the 'revolution' hoped to motivate: 1) the proletariat—defined as the most revolutionary class of society despite its small numbers; 2) farm workers, bonded labourers, landless peasants, porters, poor peasants, urban service providers like cart pullers and transport and hotel workers—since they make up a large portion of the population 'the main motivating force' for the revolution; 3) middle peasants—ones who cannot live off the produce of their own land and have to hire out their services; 4) rich peasants—'a vacillating ally' for the 'New Democratic Revolution'; 5) petty-bourgeois—teachers of schools and colleges, students, doctors, engineers, lawyers, junior office workers, petty traders of towns, retail traders, craftsmen, etc, who 'can play an important auxiliary role'; and 6) the national bourgeoisie—capitalists who are involved in small handicraft and modern industries and trade but who fear competition from 'monopolist comprador and bureaucratic capitalists', also 'a vacillating ally'.

The areas of emphasis were also clearly mentioned as were the approach to be taken:

> [G]ive priority to rural work, but do not leave urban work; give priority to illegal struggle, but do not leave legal struggle too; give priority to specific strategic areas, but do not leave work related to mass movement too; give priority to class struggle in villages, but do not leave countrywide struggle too; give priority to guerrilla actions, but do not leave political exposure and propaganda too; give priority to propaganda work within the country but do not leave worldwide propaganda too; give priority to build army organisation, but do not leave to build [sic] front organisations too; give priority to rely on one's own organisation and force, but do not miss to forge [sic] unity in action, to take support and help from international arena; it is only by applying these policies carefully that the armed struggle can be initiated, presented and developed.

Military strategy

The Maoists borrowed their battle strategy (and lexicon) liberally from Mao Tse-tung. They have most effectively used Mao's military principle of replenishing their 'strength with all the arms ... captured from the enemy'.[36] This was the tactic used by the Maoists from the very beginning, and going by the rising intensity of their strikes against the security forces over the years it seems to have worked admirably. From a ragtag bunch of would-be guerillas, which started out with just two rifles (one of which did not work),[37] they graduated to self-loading rifles, machine guns, and even rocket launchers, most of it courtesy of government forces. In the September 2002 Arghakhanchi attack alone, the Maoists proudly claimed they were able to lay their hands on 173 assorted pieces of weaponry, including mortars, rocket launchers, light-machine guns and sub-machine guns.[38] (Box 10 gives an account of one of the most successful Maoists attacks. The firsthand reports from the surviving policemen gives an idea of the ferocity of these attacks.)

Another concept borrowed from Mao and which the rebels followed faithfully has been 'encircling the cities from the countryside', a strategy that also succeeded to a large extent. Before the emergency was imposed and the army called out in November 2001, the countryside over most of Nepal had been abandoned by the government in order to concentrate its forces in pockets of defensive formations. Even after the army mobilisation, apart from 'search operations' and regular patrols in a show of strength that took the security forces into the hinterland, the rural areas remained more or less in the control of the Maoists, whether they were physically present or not.

The third of Mao's military principles adopted by Nepal's Maoists was faithful adherence to the concept of 'protracted war', which consists of strategic defence, strategic stalemate, and strategic offence.[39] In Mao's words, 'The first stage covers the period of the enemy's strategic offensive and our strategic defensive. The second stage will be the period of the enemy's strategic consolidation and our preparation for the counter-offensive. The third stage will be the period of our strategic counter-offensive and the enemy's strategic retreat.'[40]

According to Mao, the first stage involves mobile warfare, supported by guerilla and positional warfare, and also sees the creation of a wide popular front. The gains of this stage are to set the basis for the fighting in the second stage. The second stage, which is 'the most trying period but also the pivotal one', is when the other side is reduced to protecting areas that remain under its control and concentrates on protecting the urban centres. That is from where attacks are launched against the rebels, and the fighting consists mainly of guerilla warfare. That is also when the united front is widened and consolidated. The third and final stage is when the rebels are on the offensive against a gradually retreating enemy. During this stage, guerilla tactics assume a supplementary role to the main thrust of mobile and positional warfare.[41] By the end of 2002, the Maoists believed they had reached the second stage of strategic stalemate and were apparently getting ready for an offensive.[42]

The six plans

In the years before the emergency various 'tactical stages' were identified as part of the overall military and political strategy. One such was the Final Preparation for Initiation of the 'people's war', which consisted of propaganda work among the people as in the Sija campaign (see Chapter 2). The 'war' itself was conducted through six sub-phases (their 'tactical stages' were called 'plans') from February 1996 through February 2001 as detailed below.

The main slogan for the First Plan was 'March Along the Path of People's War to Smash the Reactionary State and Establish a New Democratic State!' Its basic objectives 'were to make a practical leap into and establish amongst the masses of the people the politics of armed revolution for capturing political power and to initiate the process of making the people's army as the principal form of organisation and armed activities as the principal form of struggle...

Box 7: 'What had he done?'

A small thatched hut, walls covered with posters and slogans of the All Nepal National Free Students' Union (Revolutionary). In the small clearing in front is a woman of around 20 years of age dressed in the white of a widow, sobbing continuously. Nearby sleeps a two-month-old baby. Everyone gathered has tears in their eyes.

This is the scene from Tarigaun village in Dang district and the house belongs to Num Bahadur KC, the policeman killed at the Kotwadi police station by the Maoists.

'He had called about 10 to 12 days back asking how his two-month-old son was and said that he would come and see son's face when he comes home in February. But it was his dead body that arrived yesterday.' Num Bahadur's wife, Maya, can hardly speak the words. Maya, who is an SLC graduate, and Num Bahadur were married four years ago. They have a daughter who is 18 months old and it's only two months since the son was born.

Num Bahadur's father, Ghanshyam KC, 68, is presiding over his sons final rites. Num Bahadur was the second of Ghanshyam's three sons. 'When he left home last summer we told him to quit his job, but he didn't agree. 'My elder brother is in the force. My younger brother is in Malaysia. How can I feed my family?' he had asked. 'Everyone, his mother, father and mother-in-law, everybody were pressuring him to resign but he didn't agree...,' says the grieving father.

The mother of the dead policeman, Pima Devi, spoke in a voice breaking with grief: 'We have been cursed last year and this year. Last year our son-in-law died in a car crash when my daughter was two months' pregnant.'

Num Bahadur has four sisters. A younger sister says, 'Last Tihar we called him for Tika but he couldn't get leave and we called our elder brother, but as he too is in the police force he couldn't come either. Our youngest brother is in Malaysia, so there was no question of him coming. Our foreheads remained empty.'

The tragedy-stricken family has only one question in mind, 'What had he done that he had to be killed?'

Excerpted from 'What was his crime?', Nepali Times, 8-14 December, 2000. Published originally in Nepal Samacharpatra, 3 December, 2000

[T]he emphasis was placed on arousing the masses to rebel against the oppressive system and the state, and the selection of targets and the forms of actions were designed to give correct political message and derive maximum political propaganda rather than to make any material gain in the very beginning.'[43]

By end-June the central committee of the CPN (Maoist) had concluded that the First Plan had been successful and prepared the Second Plan, which lasted from October 1996 to August 1997.[44] This Plan called for the 'Planned Development of Guerrilla Warfare' to 'prepare grounds to convert specific areas into guerrilla zones in the near future'. Military actions such as the 'selected annihilation of local tyrants, police informers, and policemen' and the seizure of weapons from the local population went together with propaganda campaigns. Preparations were also made for the setting up of local governments.

'Develop Guerrilla Warfare to New Heights' was the slogan of the Third Plan, which lasted until October 1998. This stage was to be a transitional phase before the establishment of base areas. The latter were to be used by the Maoists to launch strikes against government forces. It was during this phase that the Maoists formed local people's committees to take over the functions of the village development committees that did not exist either because of the boycotted local elections or because the elected officials had been forced to resign. The formation of a Central Military Commission was also announced in February 1998.[45] The police operation 'Kilo Sierra Two', characterised as a 'fascist campaign' by Prachanda,[46] was undertaken by the government during this phase of the 'people's war'.

The Fourth Plan was decided upon during the fourth extended meeting of the central committee of the CPN (Maoist) in August 1998. The slogan for this plan was 'Advance in the great direction of creating base areas', and came at a time when the Maoists were receiving a severe battering at the hands of the police. A rally protesting the police action was held in front of the Nepali embassy in New Delhi under the banner of the 'Solidarity Forum to Support the People's War in Nepal'. This period saw the formation of three fighting units: a main force, a secondary force, and a base force. The main force was organised at the platoon level, which had a political commissar attached to it, the secondary force at the squad level, and the base force consisted of the armed militia. (A squad consists of nine to eleven fighters and a platoon is composed of three squads.) The militia was the stationary 'base force', while the other two were part of the mobile 'military force'. The plan was to increase the platoons to company strength. On the political arena, the principle of three-in-one committees (made up of representatives of the party, the fighting force, and the United Front, that is to say members of frontal organisations allied to the Maoists) was implemented.[47] (See section below for a discussion on three-in-one committees.) It was during this period that it was decided to replace the United People's Front with a Revolutionary United Front since the former was considered 'inadequate with the changing times and requirements'.[48]

The Fifth Plan began in October 1999. One notable incident during this period was the prosecution of Yan Prasad Gautam (Comrade Alok), an alternate member of the politbureau who was in charge of party activities in the eastern region. He was purged for committing 'serious crimes like ordering physical liquidation of opponents within the Party, indulgence in adultery, embezzlement, factionalism, etc'. The 'Alok tendency', so called after Alok, was described as 'the meanest form of right opportunism masquerading in a 'left' cloak', and has since been the term used to describe similar deviations in a supposedly puritanical organisation.[49]

The Sixth Plan began in June 2000 with a focus on guerrilla raids and ambushes, sabotage, annihilation, and propaganda, apart from continuing to strengthen the 'base areas'. The Maoists resorted to kidnapping and detention to retaliate for the 'disappearances' by the government.[50] Company-level formations were used in armed raids in the western region where the 'people's war' was assessed to have reached a relatively advanced stage.[51] It was perhaps this confidence that led to the surprise attack on Dunai, the district headquarters of Dolpa district, in September 2000 — the first time the Maoists were able to overrun a district centre (See Box 8). The Dunai attack was authorised by the Western Regional Bureau under Prachanda himself, who described the success as one of the 'high-level military actions of universal significance among the successes gained under the leadership of the Maoist revolutionaries after the restoration of capitalism in China'.[52]

The six sub-phases ended with the CPN (Maoist)'s Second National Conference in February 2001.

Three-in-One

According to the Maoists, 'the three magic instruments of the New Democratic Revolution are the Party, the revolutionary United Front and the People's Army', among which the party is the most important.[53]

The party

The 1997 Dhami Commission had provided a clear picture of the organisational structure of the CPN (Maoist), and it is believed not much had changed up to the time of writing apart from some modifications introduced during the Second National Conference. Following this change, the apex bodies at the central level of the CPN (Maoist) came to consist of a standing committee of the politbureau with about seven members; a politbureau of around 15, including alternate members; and a 40 to 50-member central committee. Operations were divided into five regional bureaus — Eastern, Central, Western, Kathmandu Valley and Abroad (mostly, India) — each under the command of a politbureau member. The Eastern Regional Bureau encompassed Mechi, Koshi, Sagarmatha and Janakpur zones and some eastern districts of Bagmati and Narayani zones. The Central Regional Bureau covered Narayani, Bagmati, Gandaki, Lumbini, and Dhaulagiri, while the Western Regional Bureau consisted of Rapti, Bheri, Karnali, Seti and Mahakali.[54]

Below the regional bureaus came the sub-regional bureaus of which there were three under each regional bureau. Further down were the district committees (which did not necessarily correspond with the district divisions of the government and could include two or three districts under one committee), the area committees, and finally the cell committees at the grassroots.[55]

All policies pertaining to the 'people's war' were designed by the central committee.

The army

Having begun the 'people's war' without even proper weapons, the Maoists had used irregular guerilla units to launch attacks for the first two years. The process of forming the 'people's army' began after the Central Military Commission was set up under Prachanda (the existence of which was announced in February 1998). Starting with platoons and progressing through company and battalion-level strengths, the Maoists declared they had begun experimenting with brigade formations by early 2001,[56] and by mid-2002 the Maoists claimed they had organised their fighting force at the brigade level. (Three platoons make a company and three or four companies form a batallion. It is not clear how many fighters the Maoist brigade represented, but going by Mao's concept a brigade would be more than 5000 people functioning as one

Box 8. Attack on Dunai

Around 1000 Maoist guerrillas stormed Dunai [the district headquarters of the northwestern district of Dolpa] early Monday morning [25 September, 2000]. The six-hour firefight left 14 policemen dead, 41 wounded, and 12 missing, presumed taken prisoner. Maoist leader Prachanda issued a statement several hours after the attack, blaming the government for not agreeing to peace talks even though his group was ready.

The attack itself was not a total surprise. Army personnel had notified headquarters of unusual activity in the mountains above Dunai of people with binoculars and guns. The chief district officer of Dolpa, Parsuram Aryal, had sent word to Kathmandu last week that a Maoist attack was imminent, and requested reinforcements. The government started mobilising backup support, and says it requested the Army, which has a company-level detachment 40 minutes away, for assistance. Army sources claimed they were 'not formally asked' for help by the home ministry.

On Sunday afternoon, a 48-strong police contingent was helicoptered into Dunai from the south. Within nine hours they were in action, trying to repel the attack that they were expecting. The fighting began with a bang soon after midnight with the guerrillas pounding the police station with pipe bombs, peppering sentry posts with gunfire, and demolishing the nearby jail to free prisoners.

Then they went to the house of the manager of Nepal Bank Limited and forced him to open the vaults and made off with more than Rs 50 million in cash and jewellery. The bank had received Rs 35 million in cash from Nepal Rastra Bank on Sunday afternoon on a flight from Nepalgunj to Jufal airfield, four hours' walk away. The Maoists had prior knowledge of this money transfer, and had apparently delayed their attack by three days because the Royal Nepal Airlines flight remained cancelled until Sunday due to bad weather. No one knows why such a big amount was sent to an insurgency area without major development projects. Another mystery is why the regional and zonal police chiefs were both out of station at the time of the attack and without notice. Both have since been suspended. Wounded police personnel who were airlifted to Kathmandu on Monday afternoon told reporters that they fought till they ran out of ammunition, and were waiting for the nearby soldiers to come to their rescue. One of the wounded told the *Kantipur* daily: 'We fought till dawn and they came only in the morning to pick up the corpses.'

Excerpted from 'Who's in charge?', Nepali Times, 27 September 2000.

independent unit.[57]) In September 2001, the 'people's army' was re-christened the 'people's liberation army' (PLA) and a central head-quarters set up complete with 'general staff, general political de-partment, and general logistics department'. The supreme command of the PLA was placed in Prachanda's hands.[58]

The PLA consisted of the bulk of the Maoist guerilla fighting force, which was variously estimated to be anything between 5000 and 10,000-strong. Along with the guerillas, the Maoists also have the militia, which has mainly been assigned guard duty in the vil-lages, and sometimes called upon to support the fighting units. And unlike the guerillas, the militia do not wear uniforms.

The united front

The concept of the united front has been a very important part of the Maoists' scheme of things. The idea, of course, was that the party would lead and the army would follow, since without broad-based mass support, the battle against the state was not believed to be possible. '[T]he importance of the united front is, on the one hand, as an instrument of struggle crucial for the whole future of the People's War and, on the other, to develop it practically from the local level as an instrument of the state power,' stated the party organ.[59] It was in pursuit of this goal that the United People's Front Nepal was disbanded, and preparations begun for the creation of a 'revolutionary united front'.

Since the objective was to propagate the importance of such a front 'amongst the workers, peasants, different nationalities, op-pressed castes and the people of the oppressed regions', it followed that various frontal organisations representing the ethnic and other marginalised population groups would be set up. In a 1998 article Prachanda explained how that was happening:

> Along with the development of the People's War a new conscious-ness for fighting for their own rights and liberation is spreading amongst many oppressed nationalities of the country such as Magars, Gurungs, Tamangs, Newars, Tharus, Rais, Limbus and Madhises [sic]. The People's War has speeded up the process of formation of various national liberation fronts and expansion of nationality organisations. Similarly, today along with the devel-opment of People's War, a wave of organisation and struggle has been created among Dalit castes at a greater speed and a wider

scale. The Dalits are today rebelling against inhuman tyranny per-petrated upon them by the feudal state of high caste Hindus.[60]

Thus, ethnic fronts such as the Tharuwan Liberation Front, the Magarat Liberation Front, the Limbuwan National Liberation Front, and Nepal Dalit Liberation Front, and region-based ones like the Karnali Regional Liberation Front and the Madhesi National Lib-eration Front were formed during various stages of the 'people's war'. Class organisations like the All Nepal National Intellectuals' Organisation, the All Nepal Transport Workers' Organisation, the All Nepal Women's Organisation, and the All Nepal National Free Students' Union had also been set up. The Maoists demonstrated that these bodies could be almost as effective in undermining the state as armed conflict. This became most evident during the anti-alcohol campaign led by the All Nepal Women's Organisation (Revo-lutionary) in 2001, and the periodic school closures enforced by the All Nepal National Free Students' Union (Revolutionary) campaign-ing against the 'commercialisation' of education. Pro-Maoist outfits were also active in India, most notably the All-India Nepali Unity Society,[61] the All India Nepali Students' Association (of which Baburam Bhattarai was once the president), and the All India Nepali Youth Association.

People's government
A power vacuum was created in the countryside in mid-2000 due to the strategic decision by the Nepal Police to withdraw their far-flung village outposts in the face of increasingly daring attacks by the Maoists and to concentrate them in a few well-manned posi-tions in larger police stations. This meant that police presence al-most ceased in most rural areas. For instance, in Rolpa the earlier 39 posts was reduced to just eight, while in Rukum it went down from 23 to eight, and in Jajarkot, from 15 to six.[62] So total was the hold of the Maoists on the countryside that a journalist who toured this area extensively at the time wrote: 'The Maoist presence is much stronger than the government's (which is limited to district capitals alone...). The chief district officers and the deputy superintendents of police (these are the district police chiefs) who are posted to these district headquarters can be viewed as "ambassadors" of the Kathmandu government to the "Maoist nation".'[63]

In the absence of the state, the Maoists began holding massive rallies. And realising the propaganda value of getting these events covered by the media, they began inviting selected journalists to these meetings. Although it was clear that the Maoists would sweep up entire villages for participation at these mass gatherings, the fact that these could be held at all demonstrated the helplessness of the government (still debating the use of the army) to do anything about it.

A journalist for a Kathmandu daily described one of these assemblies which was held in Korchabang, just a three-hour-walk from Libang, the headquarters of Rolpa district.

> To take part in the first mass meeting organised by the CPN (Maoist) Rolpa district committee, people had come from as far away as Gam, five days' walk away in the eastern part of the district... People carrying flags, staves, khukuri and people's militia and people's guerillas armed with weapons began arriving from around 12.30 till 4 in the afternoon to participate in the procession. In this mass meeting which had more women than men, the militia and guerillas performed a march past, martyrs were remembered, the Internationale was sung and families of the raped, wounded, martyred and imprisoned were felicitated...
>
> ...a little way off the organising party and the various people's fronts had set up seven messes. Food was available at these messes for Rs 25 per head...
>
> ...among the 8000-strong crowd, many gun-wielding militia and guerillas could be seen. Maoist guerillas were on sentry duty in far-off places while army and police helicopters hovered in the sky.[64]

The rebels had a free run of the countryside. The Maoists had established 'people's governments' after a fashion since local governments were non-existent in many of the villages in western Nepal due to the election boycott in 1998. Later, as a step towards 'new democratic governments', 'village united people's committees' began springing up in various places and taking over the functions of the local government as part of the objective of creating base areas. The formation of these committees was important to the Maoists' overall strategy because, as stated in their party organ, '...one of the important questions in differentiating the guerrilla zone and base area is the question relating to the exercise of people's political power. In reality people's political power cannot be maintained in a guerrilla zone.'[65]

Representation in these 'people's committees', which were set up quite extensively in Rolpa, Rukum, Jajarkot and Salyan districts, again followed the three-in-one principle, whereby 40 per cent of the seats were reserved for the party, 20 per cent for the army, and 40 per cent for the front organisations.[66] When the exercise first began, the committees were chosen at mass meetings, but subsequently elections were held. Everyone was forced to participate in the selection, including workers of parliamentary parties such as the Nepali Congress, the CPN (UML), and the RPP. Efforts were made to include all sections of society. However, people identified as 'feudalists' and 'comprador and bureaucratic capitalists' were not allowed either to be elected or elect the 'people's committees'.[67]

The 'people's committees' were run under the 'Directives for Local New People's Government', which envisaged four tiers of government at the sub-regional, district, village and ward levels. (The establishment of 'united people's committees' at the district level began in December 2000, with the first one formed in Rukum district.[68]) These committees took up most of the functions of local government covering administrative, economic, social and cultural, and educational matters.[69] On the administrative side, issues related to local litigations, land transactions and affairs of the 'people's court' were dealt with. Land captured from 'feudal lords and bureaucrats' were handed over to people to work on as collectives.

On the economic front, emphasis was placed on self-reliance. Goods leaving the committee areas were taxed and efforts made to establish cottage industries. The Maoists destroyed all kinds of legal and illegal loan documents and freed local people from debts owed to village moneylenders, government-owned banks like the Agriculture Development Bank, and landlords where the loans appeared to be excessive and exploitative.[70] Even a financial institution called the Jaljala Financial Co-operative Fund was set up in Rolpa in 1999 to provide banking services, with 8 per cent interest rates on deposits and 15 per cent on loans.[71]

In some cases, the tiller's rights were established and land belonging to those identified as landlords was captured in order to be run as communes. Several village people's committees issued land registration papers and collected taxes from everyone. This explains why government tax collection in Maoist-affected areas dropped to virtually nil.[72] The Maoists introduced a number of 'development' projects and activities in the areas under their control. This was strongly linked to Mao's idea of local self-reliance and limiting the import of goods from outside. The Maoists were also believed to have established small-scale industrial enterprises and initiated development projects such as collective livestock and poultry raising, running shops, establishing a people's fund, loan distribution through cooperatives, relief programmes to households affected by natural disasters, and the distribution of food at low prices to those families facing severe food insecurity.[73]

In the social sphere, the marriage of widows, inter-caste marriage, and so on were encouraged while the strict taboos during the menstrual period that are particularly strong in western Nepal were revoked. 'Superstitious' religious festivals were not allowed to be celebrated. Gambling and alcohol was prohibited. Sanskrit was banned in schools, while private schools were shut down altogether. And, due to the vigilance of the 'people's committees', teacher absenteeism was no longer a problem.

Some development works were also carried out at the local level using local resources to build irrigation canals, trails, and short bridges. Most NGOs and INGOs were not allowed to implement their projects, and the few that were allowed in were monitored strictly in terms of the value of their work. For instance, programmes like UNICEF's Vitamin A project were allowed to function unhindered even during the most intense periods of fighting.

The process of forming 'people's governments' at the district level accelerated during the four-month-long ceasefire in 2001. By the time the talks broke down in November, there were more than 20 'district united people's committees' in place. But not all of those inducted into these committees were Maoist supporters, and they were among the first to 'resign' with the onset of the emergency.

There were thus effectively two states at work in parts of the country. Kathmandu was represented at the district headquarters, while outside it was Maoist country. The situation did not change even after the deployment of the army after November 2001. Within a matter of months the army had been forced into defensive positions and the countryside left wide open. However, the Maoists were not able to totally consolidate their 'base areas' either, since, much to their chagrin, government presence continued to exist in pockets here and there.

Right to left: Prachanda, Ram Bahadur Thapa, Hisila Yami, Baburam Bhattarai and Prachanda's son, Prakash Dahal, at a party conclave believed to have been held in Rolpa district in mid-2001. Photograph released by the army.

Two Momentous Years
2001 and 2002

The CPN (Maoist)'s Second National Conference

On the surface of it, by the time 2001 rolled around events were eddying around an endless cycle of Maoist attacks on the police and retaliation by the latter while the army watched from the sidelines. The police had begun retreating and consolidating their forces and the rebels were out in strength in areas under their control. Such was the situation in February 2001, when the CPN (Maoist) declared through a press release that their Second National Conference had been held. Unlike the First National Conference of May 1994 of which only the most tenacious political observer would have been aware, the 2001 conference was thoroughly debated, and criticised.

The Conference made provision for a chairman as the highest authority in the party instead of a general secretary and Prachanda was duly elected chairman of the CPN (Maoist). Furthermore, it was announced that 'the guiding thought of the Party will become henceforth "Marxism-Leninism-Maoism and Prachanda Path"'. Prachanda Path had been presented to the conference by Prachanda himself in a paper entitled 'A Great Leap Forward: The Inevitable Necessity of History', which 'provided detailed explanation of mass line based on the experiences of the People's War. This explanation has made clear the Party policy as regards various departments such as workers, peasant[s], women, student[s], oppressed nationality[-ies], [the] Madhesi community, people of Karnali region, intellectual[s] and publication.' The document also acknowledged 'the role of devotion and sacrifice of hundreds of thousands of peoples and thousands of great immortal martyrs' and of international and national figures, while emphasising '[t]he contribution of the team of senior leaders of the Party in the development of this set of ideas'. The naming of this 'set of ideas' after Prachanda was explained by virtue of 'the correct and continuous leadership given by Com Prachanda' in its development.[1]

The Maoists were roundly criticised for developing a personality cult around Prachanda. Nevertheless, much interest was generated by the conference proposal to begin a dialogue with sections of society calling for a 'conference of all political parties, organisations and representatives of mass organisations in the country; election of an interim government by such a conference; and guarantee of people's constitution under the leadership of the interim government'.[2] This proposal assumed importance given the

CPN (Maoist)'s declaration that it would never allow 'this struggle to become a mere instrument for introducing partial reforms' or end 'in a simple compromise by exerting pressure on the reactionary classes'.[3] Also, since one of the main obstacles in any negotiations was likely to have been their long-standing demand for a constituent assembly, the noted absence of the latter demand in the new proposal was believed to be a sign of the Maoists' willingness to eventually join the mainstream.

The government soon came under intense pressure to come up with a suitable response to what was perceived to be a softening in the Maoist posture. And it did so on 6 March 2001 by publishing the names of 294 individuals who were in police custody charged with being sympathisers or members of the CPN (Maoist). But, if the publication of the list was meant to assuage the Maoists, who had been demanding that the whereabouts of 73 of their leaders and activists be publicly revealed, it did not work. The Maoists claimed that only three of the 73 figured among the 294 the government acknowledged were under detention.[4]

Then in early April, without any warning the Maoists carried out devastating attacks on police posts in Rukum and Dailekh districts within a week of each other, killing 70 policemen. The Maoists seemed to be following a two-pronged strategy of keeping hopes of talks alive even as they moved ahead with the 'people's war', for which the February conference had already provided the direction: 'Consolidate and expand base areas and local people's power'.[5]

Prachanda's interview to *A World to Win*, the magazine of the Revolutionary Internationalist Movement, attests to that strategy. 'Our guiding principles on the question of negotiations are the experiences and summation of the Brest-Litovsk Treaty under Lenin's leadership and the Chunking negotiations under Mao's leadership,' he said. [6] (Brest-Litovsk was where Leon Trotsky worked out the pragmatic deal with Imperial Germany to allow Russia to withdraw from World War I, thus allowing the communists to consolidate their position within Russia. The Chunking agreement brought the Chinese Communist Party into Chiang Kai-Shek's nationalist government against Japan even though control over the Red Army remained with the CCP.)

The second slogan adopted by the conference was 'March forward to the direction of building central people's government'. Prachanda Path had reiterated the importance of the united front 'in order to play the role of people's power at the central level with a view to consolidate and expand local people's power and base areas'. This indicated that the Maoists were getting ready to turn their attention to Kathmandu. The capital had till then been spared any serious rebel activity apart from a few blasts aimed at the houses of politicians and government officials that had yielded more noise than any serious damage. The Maoists had probably realised the futility of holding on to the hinterland as long as Kathmandu remained firmly in the grip of the state.

Their priority at that time, however, seemed to be the ouster of Prime Minister Girija Prasad Koirala. They declared that there would be no talks with the government until Koirala stepped down.[7] Koirala was under attack from various quarters. Demanding the resignation of the prime minister over his alleged role in an aircraft lease deal, which was being investigated by the statutory Commission for the Investigation of Abuse of Authority, the left parties had boycotted parliament and were out in force on the streets.[8] To add to the pandemonium in Kathmandu, in May, the Maoists' student body, the All Nepal National Free Students' Union (Revolutionary), began an agitation against the government's education policy, and were able to enforce a week-long closure of 8000 private schools.

Within his own party, senior leaders like Krishna Prasad Bhattarai and Sher Bahadur Deuba wanted Koirala out. Deuba was in fact itching to become prime minister again since he believed he would be able to deal with the Maoists through talks (and the Maoists appeared to reciprocate the sentiment). To add to Koirala's discomfiture, there were differences of opinion between the government and the palace on mobilising the army. The government had been preparing its Integrated Internal Security and Development Plan (IISDP) for the districts most affected by the Maoist insurgency. It was to be implemented with security provided by the army. But even before it was launched, the army chief created flutters by demanding a consensus and a firm commitment from all political parties and a clear set of guidelines from the government before the army moved.[9] (According to the 1990 constitution, the army is to be mobilised by the king in his capacity as Supreme Commander of the army on the advice of the National Defence Council consisting of the prime minister, the defence minister and the commander-in-chief.[10] But, since the army views itself first and foremost as a royal army, the king has a much larger say in its affairs in actual practice.)

It was almost out of desperation that the government decided in early 2001 to create a paramilitary unit which would be better armed that the civilian police and which would also be provided with the requisite training to fight the Maoists. The Armed Police Force was designed as a sort of civilian government counterpoise to the royal army. But the time taken between deciding to raise a new fighting force and its being ready for deployment is quite long. The beleaguered Koirala did not have that kind of time, and the last straw for the prime minister proved to be the events that followed 1 June 2001, when almost the entire royal family was massacred by a love-crazed crown prince.

The palace massacre and its aftermath

If the killing of King Birendra and his family came as a shock to Nepalis, the manner in which the 'republican' Maoists reacted was dumbfounding. Even as the nation was trying to come to terms with what had happened, Baburam Bhattarai came out with a highly provocative article in the Nepali-lánguage daily, *Kantipur*, titled 'Naya "Kotparba" lai manyata dinu hunna' (The new 'Kot Massacre'[11] should not be accepted) in which he wrote:

> Why… were King Birendra and his entire family murdered at this moment? What then, was his main 'crime' in the eyes of imperialists and expansionists? Whatever ideology they may embrace, all patriotic and honest Nepalis must surely accept that in the eyes of imperialists and expansionists King Birendra's greatest 'weakness' or 'crime' was that, although a product of the feudal class he had a relatively patriotic spirit and liberal political character. Although even some 'priests' of Marxism have, on that basis, called us 'royalists', we can now unhesitatingly say that on some national questions we and King Birendra had similar views and that there was an undeclared working unity between King Birendra and us on some matters.[12]

This apparently new-found love for the just-dead King Birendra came as a surprise to most. But that was not all. Bhattarai's pronouncements clearly expressed the Maoist perception of the new king, Gyanendra:

The old Indian expansionist dream of turning Nepal into a 'Sikkim' has now changed into a new grand design: instead of making a 'Sikkim' all at once, to first make a 'Bhutan' and then a 'Sikkim'. With the agreement of the CIA (via the FBI branch opened in Delhi), RAW planned this strategy....[C]reating the spectre of the ISI, 'RAW' extended its reach even inside the palace and chose the new 'Jigme Singhe'[13] in order to carry out the 'Bhutanisation' of Nepal. Via that 'Jigme Singhe' this 'Kot Massacre' was staged from within the palace itself. No one should now doubt that 'RAW', which already had its 'Lendup Dorje'[14] in the form of Girija, has now implemented its grand strategy: after bringing about 'Bhutanisation' through the new coalition of 'Jigme Singhe' and 'Lendup Dorje', to ultimately achieve the 'Sikkimisation' of Nepal.[15]

Prachanda followed up with a press release some days later in which he detailed the conclusions reached by the party's politbureau.

It is now clear that this horrendous massacre in the royal palace has been enacted as part of a conspiracy of the imperialists to 'smash' the Maoist People's War, which has been advancing in the form of the Nepalese people's powerful patriotic and democratic movement. Behind this lies the strategy of the Americans, who want to tighten their hold on South Asia so as to encircle China, and that of the Indians, who want to 'consolidate' their expansionist interests. It is crystal clear that the reason behind the massacre of King Birendra's entire family was his reluctance to mobilise the royal army to crush the People's War and the other forms of the Nepalese people's patriotic movement, which was marching forward by challenging this colonial master plan of the imperialists and expansionists.[16]

The Maoist strategy evidently was to 'fish in muddy waters', as Nepali politicians are wont to put it. There was utter confusion following King Birendra's murder. In the absence of official word on the killings, rumours spread like wildfire. The situation was made worse by the inept handling of the crisis by a government that was caught flat-footed with 1) a dead king, 2) a near-dead new king, who had perpetrated the regicide, and 3) a newly appointed regent whose public image was one of a cold and distant personality, not to mention the handicap of having an extremely unpopular son.

The Maoists did make attempts to rouse the people and even attempted to entice the army into rebellion by calling upon the soldiers not to support 'the puppet of the expansionists born within the palace'.[17] The sporadic outbursts of rioting witnessed in Kathmandu could have been the handiwork of Maoist provocateurs. But, in the end, the institutional loyalty of the army towards the monarchy held firm and civic disturbances were quickly brought under control.

The Maoist attempt to drive a wedge between the new king and the masses did not have the desired results. So, the attacks on the hapless policemen soon resumed, while the Maoists continued to spew vituperation against King Gyanendra and Koirala. In another newspaper article, Baburam Bhattarai declared 'the birth of a republic', arguing that 'Birendra's whole family was wiped out and now it is the duty of all nationalist Nepalis to help in the establishment of a republic... If what has been said about Dipendra is true, it only proves that the monarchy is outdated and it is time to discard it.'[18]

Perhaps deliberately, they killed 41 policemen in three districts outside their 'base areas' (Gulmi Lamjung and Nuwakot) on the occasion of the new king's birthday on 7 July. Later that month, they attacked a police post in Rolpa and took 69 policemen hostage. The Koirala government immediately despatched the army on a rescue mission, but when the soldiers failed to engage the Maoists, Koirala resigned as prime minister. His replacement, the prime minister-in-waiting, Sher Bahadur Deuba took office, declaring that his first priority was to solve the Maoist issue. He immediately declared a ceasefire, a gesture that was straightaway reciprocated by Prachanda with a similar announcement from the Maoist side.

Koirala's exit and Deuba's ascension was precisely the change the Maoists had been looking forward to since Deuba had been making noises for a negotiated settlement to the Maoist issue. (Prachanda called Deuba a 'liberal' whose taking over as prime minister signalled a victory 'over the fascist Girija faction'.)[19] Public opinion was no doubt behind Deuba's peace overtures. A public opinion survey in early 2001 had shown than an overwhelming majority of Nepalis (76 per cent) wanted the matter resolved through talks. (Compare that with 16 per cent who were for an all-party government, 13 per cent for an amended constitution, and 5 and 4 per cent respectively for mobilisation of the army and the armed police).[20]

As a gesture of good faith, the government began releasing in batches those charged with association with the CPN (Maoist). Negotiating teams were announced on both sides and the ground was prepared for talks.

Overground revolutionaries

The ceasefire allowed Maoists some breathing space, and taking advantage of the peace, they began to hold political rallies all over Nepal. One was even organised in the heart of Kathmandu within a month of the ceasefire announcement. Given the optimism generated by the cessation of hostilities, and the possibility of talks in the near future, these demonstrations did not generate much alarm either. For the Maoists, however, it provided a wonderful opportunity to reach out to the public. From a party that could hardly muster a presence at its public meetings in the pre-'people's war' days, the CPN (Maoist) had now grown to a potent political force with the numbers to prove it (although it must be said that not everyone in the huge masses they gathered were there by choice).

But soon public sentiment began turning against them, mainly because of the fund-raising among businesses and ordinary people. Unlike before the truce, when these 'revolutionary taxes' were restricted to areas where the Maoists held sway, the target of the 'donations' were now the people of Kathmandu. Most worrisome for the capital's residents was a grand rally planned for 21 September 2001, for which the Maoists claimed they would marshal 200,000 people from outside the valley. As Maoist activists set about preparing for it, there were reports of extortion. Groceries were being asked to provide food supplies, bus owners to provide the vehicles to cart in the rallyists, while schools and even private houses were told to get ready to billet the hordes. The Kathmandu public was alarmed and 'resistance committees' sprang up in certain localities of the city, and a showdown seemed imminent. On the other side, security forces worried about the consequences of this huge population staying put in the city or, worse, if the crowds got unruly and like in 1990 made moves to attack the royal palace. Coincidentally, 11 September happened, and following the worldwide condemnation of terrorism, the Nepali government felt emboldened to ban all public meetings in Kathmandu. The Maoist leadership too seemed to have sensed that the public mood was not very encouraging for such a rally and backed out.

In the backdrop of this and the more important drama of the talks, the government continued picking up Maoist sympathisers under one pretext or another, while there was no let up in attacks against supporters of mainstream parties by the Maoists, although for the first time in six years, the police were able to enjoy a respite.

Direct negotiations and failure

Even as they continued to indulge in shows of strength, the Maoists were busy with their political manoeuvres. A meeting with Prachanda of top leaders of the mainstream communist parties was arranged by the CPN (Masal) in mid-August near Siliguri in the Indian state of West Bengal. Nothing of significance emerged from it since Prachanda's request for support on the Maoist call for a republic was turned down. But it did indicate that the Maoists hoped to create a grand left alliance against the monarchy.

Meanwhile, preparations were underway to begin talks. The government side was led by the number two in the cabinet, while the Maoists sent their central committee members. The first round of talks was held on 30 August 2001. This was a 'getting to know each other' meeting, so nothing substantial was expected out of it apart from a mutual commitment to keep talking. Two weeks later, the second round was held, this time in western Nepal in deference to the Maoists' wish. It was during this meeting that a full range of demands were placed on the table by the rebels. These were of three categories. The first was political and called for a constituent assembly (which was now revived after having apparently been put on the backburner at the February 2001 conference), an interim government, and a republic. The second part consisted of issues relevant to the people and dealt with treaties with India and other policies regarding India. The third related to what the government should do to create a 'conducive atmosphere' for talks — going public with details of arrested Maoists and a rollback of police operations. (See Annex IV for full details.)

Given the extreme positions held by the two sides, the public waited to see some sort of compromise mechanism worked out. Instead, what ensued was a slanging contest with each side publicly charging the other of trying to endanger the talks. The government warned that unless there was some progress in the dialogue, the situation of a stalemate where the security forces were kept under control even as the Maoists continued their attacks on ordinary citizens (who were mainly workers of political parties) would no longer be tolerated.[21] Despite these hiccups, talk of talks went on and the situation did not seem hopeless.

Confidence-building measures were taken as a prelude to the third round of peace talks. The government scrapped the Public Security Regulations and freed 68 prisoners, while the Maoists dropped their republic demand even though they continued to insist on a constituent assembly (which could, in theory, decide the future of the monarchy anyway) and the formation of an interim government before talks were to proceed further. The third round of talks held on 13 November proved inconclusive. The main stumbling block was the constituent assembly demand, which the government refused to consider, a position supported by the other political parties.[22]

Neither side claimed a breakdown. Soon, however, the tenor of the statements from the Maoist side suddenly stepped up. There were rumours that the head of the 'military wing', Ram Bahadur Thapa alias Badal, was insisting on walking out of the talks while Prachanda and Baburam Bhattarai were for continuing negotiations. And on 21 November came a statement from Prachanda which indicated that the talks were about to collapse. He declared that there was no further justification for either dialogue or the ceasefire. 'We make it clear with this statement that our bid to establish peace has been rendered unsuccessful by reactionary and fascist forces,' he said.[23]

Two days later, on 23 November, the Maoists struck against government and private sector installations all over the country (Box 9) that began a 14-month period of one bloody and destructive attack after another (Box 11). This time, they took on the army as well by attacking army garrisons. A second attack on the headquarters of the eastern Nepal district of Solukhumbu a day later was rebuffed, but the one on a barracks in west Nepal yielded a substantial booty of arms and ammunition. With that one surprise move, the Maoists were able to enhance their arsenal from the World War II vintage .303s seized from the police to semi-automatic SLRs.[24] The raid also provided the rebels with sophisticated weapons such as machine guns and rocket launchers, both of which were later used against the army with devastating results.

On 24 November, the Maoists announced the formation of a

Box 9: Dang and Salleri

In a completely unanticipated move, the CPN (Maoist) ended the four-month-long ceasefire with attacks on various government installations on 23 November 2001. The largest attack was in Dang where the rebels briefly took control of the district headquarters, Ghorahi, and killed more than two dozen police and soldiers. Most of the government offices were blown up, and the three local banks were looted of Rs 64.8 million in cash and some gold and silver.

The Maoists abducted the chief district officer of Dang, Lok Bahadur Khatri, before releasing him the next day. The rebels also set free 37 prisoners from the local jail before they left.

The Dang raid coincided with attacks all over the country. The most serious was in Syangja district, where attacks on several police posts killed 14 policemen.

While all attention was focused on western Nepal, two days after Dang, the Maoists launched a full-scale attack on Salleri, the district head-quarters of Solukhumbu. This was the first large-scale Maoist attack in eastern Nepal, and it left 34 people dead, including the chief district officer and 11 soldiers. However, the eight-hour-long battle did not end in a total rout for the government due to the fight put up by the army. That did not stop the rebels from destroying government buildings as well as the nearby Phaplu airport. They also looted the local bank of cash and gold.

In all these attacks, it was suspected that a large number of Maoist guerillas were killed. But for the government, the most unsettling aspect of these attacks for the government was that the Maoists were able to make off with a large arsenal of weapons, especially from the army barracks in Dang. According to the CPN (Maoist) organ, The Worker, 'About 450 pieces of arms (including 99 SLRs [self-loading rifles], a dozen each of SMGs, and GPMs, several rocket launchers and mortars, etc.) and a heavy cache of ammunitions and a large quantity of grenades and bombs were captured. It may be interesting to note that a total twenty-two vehicles including twelve army trucks were used to transport the captured arms, ammunitions and other valuables.'[25] Home Minister Khum Bahadur Khadka confirmed the loss of 99 SLRs.[26]

37-member United Revolutionary People's Council of Nepal. The Council was called 'the revolutionary united front led by CPN (Maoist) and an embryonic Central People's Government Organising Committee'.[27] It was placed under the convenorship of Baburam Bhattarai, who had earlier headed the United People's Front Nepal, the political wing of the party, before going underground in 1996. In effect, it meant the Maoists had set up an alternative government.

In hindsight, it becomes pertinent to ask, did the Maoists do a

Brest-Litovsk and Chunking to Deuba by preparing for an armed offensive while talking peace and thus taking the heat off them (similar to the Bolshevik manoeuvre), and holding out the possibility that they would join an interim government while building up their strength (not unlike what Mao did to the Kuomintang)? There were indications that the CPN (Maoist) was preparing some form of precipitate action. A week before the third round of talks, a newspaper quoted a 'high-level' Maoist source as saying that the talks would not move beyond that stage. But the government seemed determined not to let the talks fail. After Prachanda's statement questioning the utility of the ceasefire, the prime minister even went to the extent of asking the Maoist strongman to reconsider his decision. 'I am surprised and shocked at his statement. I honestly urge him to sit for the fourth round of dialogue and not to jeopardise it,' Deuba had said and added that the Maoists were duty bound to ensure that the country was spared another round of bloodbaths.[28]

No one seemed more taken aback by the sudden Maoist withdrawal from the talks than Prime Minister Deuba. Just four days before the Maoist attacks, he had confidently asserted, 'I am hopeful that the Maoist problem will be solved from the coming round of talks. The government is committed to solving the problem through dialogue and I also personally pledge to solve the problem.'[29]

It was therefore not without reason that the prime minister himself now became the strongest proponent for using all possible force at the disposal of the state. Terming the Maoists' resumption of hostilities as a betrayal, Deuba imposed a state of emergency on 26 November, suspending all fundamental rights. Further, an antiterrorist ordinance was promulgated that labelled the CPN (Maoist) a 'terrorist' organisation. The party was banned along with all its fraternal organisations, and harsh penalties announced for anyone suspected of helping the rebels. Deuba also declared that there would be no further talking until the rebels disarmed.

What could have led to the Maoists' backing out of the talks? A letter dated 3 December 2001, marked for heads of diplomatic missions which was jointly signed by Prachanda and Bhattarai said:

As an immediate political solution, we proposed the formation of an interim government, drafting of a new constitution and proclamation of the republic. But when the idea of a republican form of state was not acceptable to the ruling side we put forward an alternative proposal of convening an elected constituent assembly so as to give the ultimate right of choosing between a monarchy or a republic to the sovereign people themselves. As this proposal, too, was summarily rejected and the fascist ruling gang mobilised the royal army throughout the country we had no other alternative than to return to the people and continue with the movement.

From the climb-down for the demand for a republican state soon after the second round of talks and the Maoist political leadership's insistence on the formation of an interim government, it seemed as if a breakthrough was in the offing. But days before the attacks, there was also speculation in the press that the Maoists' military wing was exerting severe pressure to break off talks, and the sudden attacks were even considered a sign that they had struck on their own. There is no way of verifying this at the time of writing and the Maoists were quick to point out that the supposed differences within the party were 'just the figment of imagination of the reactionaries, if not a deliberate disinformation campaign to confuse the masses.'[30] The rebels have proved adept at manipulating the Nepali press, with the latter's hunger for news on the Maoists amply fulfilled by 'sources' in Kathmandu, and the possibility of their having hoodwinked the media with stories of a rift in the leadership cannot be dismissed altogether. Given the steadfast refusal by parliamentary parties to even consider a constituent assembly, the Maoists could have been looking for a reason to begin fighting again in order to be able to bargain from a position of strength when negotiations began anew.

Interestingly, the *Far Eastern Economic Review* reported the following just days after the fighting had resumed: 'A large consignment of weapons seized by Burmese police near the northwestern border with India on November 2 may well have been headed for Maoist guerrillas in Nepal. India is battling its own insurgencies in the border area, but Asian intelligence officials believe neither the ethnic Nagas, Assamese or Manipuri rebel groups have the finances to order such a large number of weapons. They believe the haul of 200-400 assault rifles were bought by Nepal's Maoists.'[31]

The arms shipment may or may not have been headed for Nepal, but its significance has to be judged in the light of events taking place during the ceasefire. The restructuring of the formerly 'people's army' as the 'people's liberation army' (PLA) in September and the formulation of plans to form the United Revolutionary People's Council of Nepal could well have been in anticipation of all-out war even as the talks continued.

The emergency

The emergency that came into force on 26 November 2001, was the third in the country's history. The first was after the Raksha Dal revolt led by K.I. Singh in 1952, while the second came with the royal takeover of 1960. But these were events of two generations ago and had all but been erased from the nation's collective memory. And unlike the previous occasions, this time it was a democratic government that had imposed the emergency. That realisation seems to have been the reason behind Deuba's apologetic tone in his address to the nation the day after: 'I am fully convinced that all the Nepali people, political parties and the civic society is aware of the fact that a government accountable to the people won't take such a difficult decision if an unfavourable situation is not there.'[32]

It was not a particularly unpopular decision, and apart from the perfunctory naysaying from the opposition, the protest against the emergency was remarkably muted. Two reasons can be attributed for this. The first is that the ceasefire and the negotiations had brought hope that the killing season in Nepal was finally over after six years, and that by backing out for no obvious reason, the Maoists were proving to be unnecessarily provocative. But even more important seems to have been the manner in which the Maoists' public behaviour had affected the general population with their bullying tactics while collecting 'donations' and the intimidation of activists belonging to other political parties.

Daily newspapers that had been using various epithets to describe the Maoists, followed the government line in calling them 'terrorists' and limited their coverage of the fighting to government handouts. To be fair to the press though it was most likely a sense of being at a loss of how to react to the situation; some of the papers soon reverted to their old practice within a few weeks after having negotiated the space the government was likely to allow them. The government, for its part, did nothing to inspire the confidence of the press. One of the first post-emergency actions of the government was to take into custody journalists from newspapers considered Maoist mouthpieces. Then it came out with a controversial list of dos and don'ts for the press. And to prove that it meant to follow up on this, the government began arresting journalists for deviating from its injunction. By the middle of 2002, more than 100 journalists—most of whom were not even remotely connected to the Maoists—had been taken in for interrogation.

The political sphere

The government of Sher Bahadur Deuba, as the 'aggrieved party', quickly received the backing of foreign countries over the state of emergency. Even the US Secretary of State Colin Powell landed in Kathmandu in January 2002 in a gesture of encouragement. Support also came from the major political parties, most importantly, from the Nepali Congress party establishment controlled by Deuba's bête noire, Girija Prasad Koirala. As critical was the support from the main opposition, the CPN (UML), which could not resist taking some potshots at the Nepali Congress for bringing the situation to such a pass but could not lay the blame entirely on the government either.[33]

The political support was most crucial for Deuba since the emergency would have to be ratified by a two-third parliamentary majority after three months. He was adamant that he had been betrayed by the rebels who had used the talks as an excuse to build up their strength. He therefore took the position that there would be no talks before they disarmed,[34] and so had no choice but to go for an extension. When the time for the ratification came around in February, the ease with which the government proposal was pushed through made it look as if the parliamentary parties had finally forged unity against the Maoists. (For the record, the three small communist parties in parliament, the United People's Front, the National People's Front, and the Nepal Workers' and Peasants' Party, voted against the resolution.)

The CPN (UML) decided to side with the government despite the fact that many of their own supporters were being harassed by the army and the police which could hardly distinguish between the different shades of red sported by the various communist parties. The party probably calculated that with the decimation of the Maoists, workers who had strayed from the CPN (UML) into the Maoist fold would come back and it would regain its position as the premier left party of the country, a distinction it was being forced to share with the CPN (Maoist). Supporting the emergency, and, by implication, armed action against the Maoists was also a significant departure for the CPN (UML), which had for years been calling for a 'political solution' to the Maoist uprising—a form of 'ultra-leftist adventurism', to use its own phraseology, brought about by misguided (mainly Congress) government policies.

The other factor that helped the CPN (UML) make up its mind was the issue of amending the constitution. The reciprocal arrangement worked out for supporting the emergency was that the government would initiate steps to make changes in the so-far untouched constitution of 1990. Changing the constitution had been one of the main demands of the CPN (UML) since the 1999 election and it began to prepare in earnest to suggest the changes it desired. Given its 'revolutionary' background, and since the justification for constitutional amendment was to somehow bring the Maoist chapter to a close, there were expectations that the proposed changes would reflect a reformist agenda. But all it showed was the party's hurry to get into power. There certainly were references to issues such as curbing corruption and increasing decentralisation, but the number one priority was the idea of an all-party government to hold elections. The Nepali Congress was not far behind, coming up with its own wish list of amendments. It had many points in common with the CPN (UML), mainly to do with procedural matters, and some others with potentially long-term consequences for the country.[35]

Even as the manoeuvring at the policy level continued, actual politics went on in typical style. Having handed over the responsibility of dealing with the Maoists to the army, the government went back to business as usual. To illustrate that, the country was treated to the spectacle of the minister for forests and his junior colleague publicly accusing each other of irregularities over a deal. While no one would have been willing to bet on the innocence of either, it did not fail to titillate the public for days on end. Ultimately, both were forced to resign but not before further eroding what little integrity the government had. A second instalment came soon after with the information minister being chastised by the ruling party because the national television failed to show the hoary old faces of the party leadership at one of their regular meetings!

If things were not already bad enough, a real crisis blew up in May 2002 when the time came for another round of parliamentary approval for the extension of the emergency. This time, however, none of the parties, including the Nepali Congress represented by Koirala and his coterie, was in favour of extending the emergency further. (The ever-energetic Koirala was by then working on a pet idea of a 'grand democratic alliance' of political parties committed to multiparty democracy to work unitedly against the Maoists.) The argument was that the anti-terrorist ordinance gave enough authority to the security forces to tackle the Maoists. Prime Minister Deuba seemed to concur with this view.[36] But within a matter of days, he changed his tune, apparently at the insistence of the security forces,[37] and informed an all-party meeting that his government would be seeking a six-month extension. Accordingly, he called for a special parliamentary session to push through his proposal.

Deuba's move let to a direct confrontation with party president Koirala. Adding to the confusion was the position of the CPN (UML) since without its support, the government would not have been able to muster the required majority and the emergency would have automatically lapsed. But the main opposition now began to prevaricate. There is no knowing whether the government resolution would have passed had it been presented in parliament. But events took an unexpected turn when the party asked Deuba to furnish reasons for trying to prolong the state of emergency despite his party's wishes to the contrary. On 22 May, Deuba gave the party leadership his answer by dissolving the parliament and calling for fresh elections in November. He also re-imposed the emergency for a further three months through an ordinance two days after the earlier one expired on 25 May. A belligerent Koirala suspended Deuba from party membership, rendering him, in effect, a prime minister without a party. Deuba then convened a meeting of his supporters, claiming that they represented the 'real' Nepali Congress, and in turn expelled Koirala from the party.

Deuba's contention that he was invoking the prime minister's prerogative to seek a fresh mandate was decried in many quarters because of the virtual impossibility of holding elections while an insurgency raged across the country. But he characteristically insisted that the polls would be held in November, Maoist violence or not. Neither did the CPN (UML) protest; with the Congress divided, it expected the elections to provide easy pickings.

Everything seemed to be moving along smoothly as per Deuba's, and, by default, the CPN (UML)'s, plans. In July, Deuba was further buoyed by the Supreme Court's decision against the lawsuits challenging his dissolution of parliament. The Election Commission was yet to decide whether he could lay claim to the Nepali Congress flag and election symbol, but the CPN (UML) and, by all appearances, the king as well as the army were fully behind Deuba. When the emergency ended in late August, the government did not re-impose it. Defence ministry statements continued the daily litany of 'Maoist terrorists' killed. There were widespread reports of surrenders by Maoists and their sympathisers. Most importantly, by handing over to the Nepali authorities some Maoist militants who were undergoing treatment in border towns, India was seen to have taken some tentative steps to ensure that its territory could not be used as a safe haven. All these developments pointed to the likely fact that the Maoists were on the run.

But two major attacks on a police post in Sindhuli district in east Nepal and Sandikharka, the district headquarters of Arghakhanchi in the west (Box 10), in early September 2002 changed everything. Those strikes were totally unexpected by the political establishment in Kathmandu. Overnight, the parties did a re-think on the situation and began expressing doubts that elections could be held. Meanwhile, the Election Commission finally decided on the Nepali Congress row and, as most commentators had expected, decided in favour of Girija Prasad Koirala. Deuba promptly named his faction the Nepali Congress (Democratic).

A series of all-party meetings now took place to evaluate the situation even as the Election Commission announced that the polls would be held in six phases beginning 13 November. There was speculation that an all-party government would be formed to stave off the constitutional crisis that the country would face should the elections not be held, and that seemed to be the conventional wisdom. On 29 September, it was decided that Prime Minister Deuba would be given the authority to explore constitutional means to either defer the polls by six months or re-instate the parliament dissolved in May—the latter at the insistence mainly of the Nepali Congress.

On 3 October, Deuba met King Gyanendra to recommend deferring the elections for more than a year. The next day, the king, in a speech broadcast over the national media, removed the prime minister for his 'incompetence' to hold the elections as scheduled, and assumed the country's executive authority.

Box 10. The Arghakhanchi rout

The warring Maoist insurgents launched a second 'successful' attack in the last 24 hours, killing at least 65 security personnel, including soldiers, in Sandhikharka of Arghakhanchi district Sunday night [9 September 2002].

Forty-one other personnel were injured after thousands of armed Maoists launched a massive attack in the district headquarters of the western hill district.

The death toll on the security side could go up, as most of the security personnel are still missing and several others who sustained injuries are in critical condition, reports received here said.

Security officials said there were 70 soldiers, 200 members of the Nepal Police and over 40 Armed Police Force (APF) personnel posted in the district headquarters.

Though security forces have claimed that scores of Maoists too have been killed in the battle, the actual figure was not available.

A policeman who survived the deadliest battle claimed that at least 150 rebels were killed in the battle. He said that around 3,000 rebels encircled the army barracks, APF base, and District Police Office.

After making inroads into the security bases, the Maoists set almost all government facilities on fire except the district hospital. The district administration office, chief district officer's quarters, district forest office, district court, district development committee and offices of other development projects were set on fire by the rebels, according to the Defence Ministry.

The Maoists are also known to have abducted some government officials, including acting Chief District Officer Baburam Khatiwada, police Inspectors Rameshwor Khadka and Dambar Tamang.

*   *   *

The sounds of gunshots and bomb explosions continue to echo in their ears. For many policemen and soldiers, who are now receiving treatment at different hospitals in the capital, it is difficult to forget the nightmare of the battlefield.

They have regained consciousness, but the deep psychological trauma they have in their minds will perhaps remain forever. They fought bravely even though their colleague warriors fell on the ground in front of them.

They picked up the guns of their fallen brethren, refilling their stock of ammunition that was running low, and began aiming at the rebels, who were raining bullets and bombs from everywhere.

'Even when hit by a bullet on my arm, I fought till the last,' Deputy Superintendent of Police Madhu Prasad Pudasaini said from his bed in Birendra Police Hospital in Maharajgung. Deputy Superintendent Pudasaini was the commanding officer of the 200 policemen stationed in Sandhikharka, the district headquarters of Arghakhanchi that was attacked Sunday night.

Describing the harrowing incident of that fearful Sunday night he said, 'I fought the rebels till I was unconscious, I encouraged my colleagues to defend our position...I found myself lying amidst the bodies of my fellows. I had to carry on. I had to save other officers in spite of being injured.'

He said he now wants to send a message to the bereaved family members of all dead warriors that they fought fearlessly till their last breath for the sake of their nation and people.

'I tried my best to save them but I couldn't,' he added with an exasperated voice. 'All I can do now is share your sorrows and agonies.'

Inspector Ramdev Chapagain, who was also injured in the leg, added that the attack began all of a sudden from all sides. 'They began firing at 9:45 pm. They attacked both the army and police barracks. The firing stopped only in the morning,' Chapagain recalled.

However, [Deputy Superintendent of Police] Pudasaini said that he could not remember when the helicopter came to take him to Kathmandu as he was unconscious at that time.

When asked what was the most painstaking memory of Sunday, he answered slowly trying not to show the pain in his voice. 'An officer, ASI [assistant sub-inspector] Khanal came running to me with a blood drenched arm hit by a bullet,' he said. 'All I could do was rip my uniform and wrap it around his arm. I hear he is missing now. I worry about where he must be.'

Excerpted from 'Maoists kill 65 in Arghakhanchi: Toll could soar, as dozens reported missing', The Kathmandu Post, *10 September 2002; and 'First-hand accounts of massacre; Mental trauma of injured soldiers' by Suvecha Pant and Ujir Magar,* The Kathmandu Post, *11 September 2002.*

The Maoists

In the 2001 interview to RIM's *A World to Win*, Prachanda had declared: 'In establishing our form of actions, the first, second, third and fourth priorities have been accorded to: ambush and mining, raid and commando attack, various types of sabotage, and selective annihilation.' As the surprise attacks on the army (See Box 9) and subsequent actions demonstrated, the Maoists were true to their strategy. Except that the 'selective' annihilation became more indiscriminate, more frequent and more barbaric that it had been earlier.

The Maoists had shown what they were capable of even before the 2001 ceasefire. But with the onset of the emergency, their targeting led to many innocent deaths. Perhaps the most tragic was the burning alive of five passengers in an overnight bus on the eve of one of the shutdowns called in February 2002. Since then, the bombs used to terrorise the public have taken the lives of many ordinary people going about their daily business. Their vilest acts, however, were reserved for security personnel who were mutilated in the most inhumane manner before being killed (although such incidents went down after the first few months).

Even as the fighting went on, the Maoists continued with their denunciation of King Gyanendra and his son, Paras (the 'Gyanendra-Paras clique', according to the Maoists). The king presented an easy target, considering that his succession after the death of King Birendra was not the smoothest and there were still sections of the population that believed the new king was somehow involved in the palace massacre. His image was further tarnished by his son, the new crown prince, Paras, who had gained notoreity for his drunk and disorderly conduct in public in his earlier incarnation as the then Prince Gyanendra's son, and who had allegedly been involved in at least two hit-and-runs. The Maoists made it clear that their struggle was against the king, who, according to an April 2002 statement by Baburam Bhattarai, was trying to install a military dictatorship, and was 'preparing himself to wear the cloak of a puppet of the US like the one in Afghanistan to facilitate the US to establish a permanent base in Nepal to keep a close watch on China as well as the entire South Asia.'[38]

But despite of their military successes and rhetorical bravado, the Maoists continued to call for dialogue. Shortly after unilaterally breaking the ceasefire, Prachanda told an Indian newspaper that the Maoists were prepared to suspend their armed activities and talk if the 'right to determine their own political future is granted to the people'.[39] His statement on the sixth anniversary of the People's War in February 2002 was as indicative: 'Our party appeals to all parties within parliament and outside and pro-people forces to come together against the military dictatorship of the near-dead feudal autocracy. In this historic moment we are ready to be involved in talks, dialogue, fronts or show any kind of flexibility... We have never closed the door for talks to find a political solution and we will never do so in the future either.'

The Maoists continually stressed their readiness for dialogue through their periodic pronouncements:

> At the slightest positive sign we are ready to end the war and enter into dialogue.
> — Press statement by Prachanda, 10 May 2002

It is a matter of pleasure and pride for all of us that the entire country is in favour of talks and a political solution.
— Prachanda's note to the heads of political parties,
14 May 2002

[W]e would like to reassert our commitments towards seeking a
progressive political solution to the problem through negotiation
and dialogue and our willingness to present ourselves even more
responsively and flexibility [sic], and would pronounce our readiness for a ceasefire and withdrawal of this programme of struggle
if such a condition is created...
— Press statement from CPN (Maoist) and the United
Revolutionary People's Council, Nepal, signed
by Prachanda and Baburam Bhattarai, 21 September 2002

These sentiments notwithstanding, the rebels also declared that
they were ready to battle the forces of the state if need be. '[W]e
reiterate our commitment to fight till the end in case the feudal
autocrats continue with their foolish obstinacy,' warned the joint
statement by Prachanda and Bhattarai referred to above. And the
Maoists showed their ability to strike at will when they launched
the attacks in Sindhuli and Arghakhanchi. In a press release shortly
afterwards Prachanda lashed out at the 'feudal establishment',
which, he claimed, had 'rejected the repeated calls by our party to
end the present situation of civil war through a peaceful and positive political solution', and that since the attacks 'prove that the
terror campaign of the royal army will not affect the country or the
people, we will continue with our political and armed programmes'.

But it was, in all likelihood, becoming clear to the Maoist leadership that it would be difficult to maintain the high levels of support they had engendered across the country. The goodwill they
had gained through the social reforms they had initiated was not
going to last forever as people became more and more restless for
an end to the bloodletting. Both the army and the Maoists had
adopted a policy of starving out each other in certain parts of the
country; and it was ordinary folks who were caught between the
two conflicting decrees. Development work came to a complete
standstill in many parts of the country. The government slashed
the development budget and international aid agencies retreated
to the security of Kathmandu.

Box 11. Major Maoist attacks between 23 November 2001 and 29 January 2003

23 November 2001: Maoists end four-month old cease-fire with attacks in several districts. Major strikes on army and police posts in Dang and Syangja districts, killing 37.

26 November 2001: Attack on Salleri, the headquarters of Solukhumbu district. Total rout avoided, but 11 soldiers and chief district officer killed.

27 November 2001: Four policemen killed in encounter with Maoists in Darchula district, far-western Nepal.

3 December 2001: Bomb explosion in carpet factory in Kathmandu kills one.

8 December 2001: Attack on communication tower at Ratomate, Rolpa district. Attack repelled; four soldiers dead and 50-60 Maoists reported killed. Attack on communication tower in Kapurkot of Salyan district also repulsed.

15 December 2001: American embassy staffer shot dead.

23 December 2001: Three soldiers killed in Salang Khola of Lamjung in an ambush.

26 January 2002: The Khumbuwan Liberation Front, allied to the Maoists, destroys powerhouse of 250-kW micro-hydro project on Pikhuwa River in Bhojpur district. Ten million rupees worth of property damaged.

28 January 2002: Four policemen, including a superintendent of police, killed when their van is caught in a booby-trap in Syaule Bazar, Kailali district.

31 January 2002: Landmine kills police inspector and assistant sub-inspector on Prithvi Highway in Tanahun district.

5 February 2002: Attack on police station in Bhakundebesi of Kabhrepalanchowk district kills 16 policemen.

17 February 2002: Biggest setback to government as Maoists storm Mangalsen, headquarters of Achham district, and nearby Sanfebagar airport, killing 107 security personnel and chief district officer of Achham.

21 February 2002: Attack on police post at Shitalpati in Salyan district, killing at least 34 policemen, including two inspectors.

22 February 2002: On the first morning of a two-day bandh, Maoists petrol bomb overnight bus, killing five, including 8-year-old girl.

31 March 2002: Attack on 12-MW Jhimruk power plant in Pyuthan district destroys powerhouse.

6 April 2002: Five soldiers, including army major, killed in ambush in Bardiya district.

12 April 2002: Attack on Armed Police Force base in Satbariya and on police post in nearby Lamahi leaves 46 policemen dead, including a deputy superintendent of police and four police inspectors.

16 April 2002: Maoist attack on police station in Gorkha district kills nine policemen.

7 May 2002: Attack on army position in Gam in Rolpa district kills 70 security personnel.

12 May 2002: Offices of Mahendra Sanskrit University in Beljhundi of Dang district burnt down.

28 May 2002: Heavy assault on army post repelled in Khara, Rukum district.

8 September 2002: Attack on police post in Bhiman of Sindhuli district kills 49 policemen, including a police inspector.

9 September 2002: Attack on Sandhikharka, district headquarters of Arghakhanchi, kills 58 security personnel.

28 October 2002: Attack on Rumjatar airport foiled with only one loss of life among soldiers guarding airport.

15 November 2002: Attack on Khalanga, headquarters of Jumla district, kills 33 policemen and four soldiers.

19 December 2002: Six policemen killed in attack on border police post in Dang district.

26 January 2003: Inspector General of the Armed Police Force, Krishna Mohan Shrestha, his wife, and bodyguard shot dead in Kathmandu.

The most immediate concern for the Maoists, however, was finding willing volunteers to fill their ranks. During the first few days of the emergency in late November 2001, many people who had been inducted into the various 'people's governments' dissociated themselves from the militants. While these and others who 'surrendered' were generally only sympathisers and their actions could be interpreted as attempts to save their own skins, it also proved that when push came to shove, the Maoists would be left only with hardcore fighters willing to sacrifice their lives for the cause. Recruiting was going to be more difficult since the mountainsides of Nepal were being denuded of young people who were fleeing to escape both forced conscription into the Maoist force as well as harassment during the ongoing security operations. They were leaving the country in large numbers as was evident from the increasing demand for passports in remote districts following the onset of the emergency. Others either fled to India or sought shelter in the cities.

There is no doubt that despite their repeated calls for dialogue and the second ceasefire announced in January 2003, at the time of writing the Maoists still have a lot of fight left in them. So far, there has been no sign of the rebels using weapons that are more sophisticated than those captured from the army.[40] With their wide-ranging contacts in India and the active underground arms bazaar in the neighbouring Indian states of Bihar and Uttar Pradesh, it can be surmised that their arsenal is more sophisticated than what has been displayed. To back it all they have a significant treasury, accumulated through looting banks and 'levies' and 'donations' from all possible sources, including, it is believed, politicians, bureaucrats and police officials.

The army

The November 2001 attack in Dang took the army completely by surprise. At least a dozen soldiers were killed and the Maoists made off with an array of weaponry and ammunition. Nothing came of the reports that the search operations conducted immediately afterwards were about to strike a heavy blow to the Maoists. The army received a bigger setback in February 2002 when the rebels raided Mangalsen, the district headquarters of Achham district, and decimated both the army platoon stationed there and the district police force.

For six years the army had watched impassively as the civilian police force tried to fend off a dedicated revolutionary group. When the time came for the army itself to get active, it found the going very tough against a motivated force that had sharpened its fighting skills over the previous six years. The Nepali army found more than a match in the 'people's liberation army', which was now armed with automatic weapons courtesy of the army itself, and which consisted furthermore of fighters ready to sacrifice their lives for 'the cause'.

There was also the question of the battle-worthiness of the army. For more than a century the Royal Nepal Army's role had been limited to providing the pomp and pageantry in honour of the royalty in Kathmandu. During the two world wars, a few battalions were loaned to the British army, but they were mostly assigned to garrison duty in India. The last time it saw any real action was in the 1974 skirmishes against the CIA-backed Tibetan Khampa guerillas around the northwestern border of the country. Since then the only 'battle' experience the Nepali army had had was whilst serving as UN peacekeepers, most notably in Lebanon.

On the question of numbers also the odds were stacked against the army. When squared off, it did not look that bad: a 50,000-strong trained army pitted against a guerilla band consisting at most of a few thousand. But the actual numbers that could be deployed on the ground was pitifully small. This was something that even Prime Minister Deuba acknowledged as he waffled in reply to a CNN interviewer who had said: '[T]he majority of your army is involved in UN operations, in administration and also in protecting other cities, so the argument is that you really only have about 6,000 to 10,000 troops to fight about 2,000 Maoist guerrillas, but in the end, are not really effective at all, and you don't have that manpower or military capacity to really fight.'[41]

As the fighting dragged on for the whole of 2002, it became increasingly apparent that neither combatant was likely to gain outright victory. The best the army had going for it was that the Nepali state had not withered away and that time was on its side. It could probably have ultimately prevailed given that it would have access to more resources to make up for battle attrition. But it was equally clear that continued military action would be a costly, lengthy, and tragic solution to an issue with origins that lay in the injustice inherent in the socio-economic conditions of the country.

Eleven-year-old Dilli Biswokarma of Rukum district prepares a meal for his younger brother and sister. Both of Dilli's parents were killed by the police. February 2001.

Cost of
the Conflict

THE CPN (MAOIST) appeared to be taking the same course Peru's Shining Path had earlier traversed. From its beginnings in 1980, the conflict in Peru claimed 30,000 lives, turned one million people into internal refugees, and cost the country approximately US$25 billion in terms of infrastructure and production losses. The objective of the rebels was to gradually expand across the countryside while simultaneously increasing their military capacity with the ultimate goal of eventually encircling the cities. The rationale behind this was to cut the cities off from the countryside, provoking a reduction in the capacity of the economy to function, and leading to the collapse of the government. Symbolic actions against the representations of capitalism, imperialism and the 'establishment' were designed to demonstrate the capacity of the Shining Path and immobilise public as well as private authorities, and force their withdrawal. Indoctrination, food distribution, and establishment of a system of 'popular justice' were carried out simultaneously in order to gradually create a climate of disquiet and chaos that was believed to eventually lead to a 'progressive delegitimisation' of the state in the minds of the populace.[1]

Nepal's Maoists have been more or less succeeded in creating an environment of chaos by attacking the social classes identified as the 'people's enemies' (mainly local landowners and usurers), agents of the state (police, banks, government offices, foreign aid-supported projects) and other groups thought to be working against them (police informers, renegades, local representatives of what they see as the primary exploitative parties, the Nepali Congress and the Rastriya Prajatantra Party, and lately, the CPN [UML] as well). By the end of January 2003, when a fresh ceasefire was announced, the death toll of the 'people's war' had nearly reached the 7000 mark, of whom more than 5000 had been killed since the breakdown of peace talks in November 2001 and the subsequent deployment of the army.[2]

Macro perspective

As in conflicts elsewhere, the Nepali economy has been the primary victim of the insurgency. Even though the extent of the damage can only be guessed at,[3] it is obvious that the insurgency has weighed heavily on the already very fragile economy. Nepal's GDP contracted by 0.6 per cent in 2001/02 compared to the previous fiscal year when the growth rate had been 4.7 per cent. This was the worst performance in more than 20 years. The Ministry of Finance's Economic Survey 2001/02 showed that the per capita income of the Nepali population went down to US$ 226 from US$ 240 it had stood at the year before.

The bleak economic situation and reduction in growth has been attributed primarily to the decline of up to 70 per cent in business activities in Kathmandu alone and the decrease in agricultural output due to large tracts of land having been left fallow in western Nepal as a result of mass migrations from villages in conflict areas. Despite the government's target of achieving an annual growth rate of 4.3 per cent in its Tenth Five-Year Plan (2002/03 to 2007/08),[4] the declining trend in GDP growth is expected to continue should the overall security situation not improve.

With a view to weakening the already fragile economy and aggravating the crisis, the Maoists targeted industries, mainly foreign investments and joint-venture companies in the manufacturing sector such as the Coca Cola bottling plant, Colgate-Palmolive, Nepal Lever, and Surya Tobacco. Unofficial estimates suggested that the total toll on infrastructure in the first six months after the breakdown of the ceasefire (November 2001 to May 2002), may have surpassed Rs 2 billion,[5] while losses incurred by tourism, exports, business activities and transportation could have totalled nearly Rs 20 billion over roughly the same period.[6] As early as May 2002, the state-owned insurance company Rastriya Beema Sansthan alone had received claims amounting to almost Rs 380 million related to the loss of property caused by Maoist insurgency (Table 3).

More significant, but probably also more difficult to assess has been and will be the 'cost' of infrastructural projects delayed or stopped because of Maoist attacks. Officials say that the Maoists

Table 3. Example of cost of insurgency: in insurance claims

Claimant	Claim
Nepal Rastra Bank	Rs 80 million
Agriculture Development Bank	Rs 20 million
Nepal Bank Ltd	Rs 70 million
Nepal Telecommunication Corporation	Rs 80 million
Jhimruk Hydropower Plant	Rs 100 million
Shah Distillery	Rs 30 million
Total	**Rs 380 million**

Source: New Business Age, May 2002 (Yogi 2002).

had already destroyed telecom infrastructure worth more than Rs 200 million by mid-2002, resulting in an annual revenue loss of an equal amount of money. Moreover, because of 'insecurity', the roll-out of major projects such as DFID's Rural Access Programme, irrigation and other development programmes has proved problematic. Similarly, the Maoists' requisitioning of food-stocks such as those held by the World Food Programme has disrupted food-for-work schemes. These schemes are tied to a wide range of infrastructural development programmes such as road construction, repair and maintenance, and irrigation works.[7]

In addition to attacking industries — the claimed symbols of capitalism and imperialism — the Maoist rebels raided the rural branches of the government-owned Agricultural Development Bank and destroyed loan records in order to 'liberate' poor villagers from their loan commitments. They also destroyed more than a third of the country's 3913 village development committee (VDC) offices (the actual number of destroyed VDCs is probably higher as the government is still in the process of updating their records), thus directly hurting grassroots democracy. In monetary terms, this loss has been estimated at more than Rs 240 million (Table 4), and according to the Ministry of Local Development, a minimum of about Rs 400 million will be needed to rebuild the demolished VDC offices.[8]

Similarly, the tourism sector, one of Nepal's key industries has been badly affected by declining tourist arrivals. The dip actually began with the hijack of an Indian Airlines plane in December 1999, and continued with the Hrithik Roshan 'anti-India' street riots of December 2000, and the events following 11 September 2001 (not to mention Afghanistan and Iraq). But, it was the renewal of fighting in November 2001 that had the largest negative impact on tourist numbers. Tourist arrivals were down 17 per cent in 2001 and decreased by a further 28 per cent in 2002. That was a substantial loss considering that even as late as 2000 tourism had brought in more than US$ 160 million a year, and provided employment to more than 200,000 people.[9] To further aggravate the situation, the downturn in tourism put pressure on the banking sector as loans to hotels and other tourist facilities matured and redeeming them became problematic. The decline in tourism has been reflected in the negative growth rate of almost 7 per cent for the fiscal year 2001/02 in trade, restaurants, and hotels.[10]

Table 4. VDCs destroyed in the five development regions by Sept 2002		
Region	Estimated loss of VDC property *(in million NRs)*	VDC offices destroyed
Central	73.4	219
Far-western	66.6	307
Eastern	48.2	243
Western	32.2	219
Mid-western	24.9	119

Source: The Kathmandu Post, *27 September 2002.*

The Maoists used bandhs, or general strikes, as one of the main ways of demonstrating their political strength. These bandhs were very effective, not because of widespread support, especially in urban centres such as Kathmandu, but because individuals and businesses feared Maoist reprisals. It was estimated that a day's bandh costs the economy Rs 630 million, an amount that does not take into account the losses in the informal economic sector that consist of activities like sale of farm produce and load carrying.[11]

It is very likely that the loss of confidence, and real threats to profits due to political instability and a general sense of insecurity, has dissuaded both foreign companies and multinationals from investing in Nepal. Combined with bureaucratic hindrances and corruption-related problems that Nepal is notorious for, the conflict is believed to have caused a sharp decline in foreign direct investment and has led to a more rapid flight of (Indian and Nepali) capital out of the country.

Reports indicated that most business leaders of the 100-member Confederation of Nepalese Industries based in the capital have faced extortion threats and as a result have invested elsewhere. The effects of this were evident in fiscal year 2001/02 when the revenue growth rate was only 8 per cent compared to more than 18 per cent in the previous year.[12] In mid-2002 the governor of the Nepal Rastra Bank indicated that the inflow of foreign direct investment (FDI) was likely to go down, owing to non-economic factors affecting economic and business activities. The FDI inflow in Nepal stands at an insignificant 0.004 per cent of FDI movement worldwide and during 2000/01 it was less than a paltry $1 million.[13]

To manage the unplanned extra security expenditures, the

government introduced an ordinance in 2002 to change some of the clauses of the Financial Act 2058 BS (2001/02) and increased import tax on goods such as paddy and rice; excise duty on cigarettes, and liquor; export tax on certain goods; and tariffs on telecommunication services, diesel and petrol.[14] For an economy that is not only underdeveloped but also non-diversified with external investment limited to low-tech and low-value consumer goods besides its hydro energy potential, these economic pressures have made resolving the insurgency all the more imperative.

Human development perspective

During the Nepal Development Forum meeting in February 2002, the donor community pledged an annual assistance of US$ 500 million for the following two years. However, unless the security situation improves, the utility of such assistance is debatable even though the nation faces a spiralling socio-economic crisis which has been made worse by the government's diverting funds to meet counter-insurgency expenditures.

The 'people's war' has adversely affected almost every sector of national life. The delivery of whatever social services people had access to in remote areas have been severely disrupted. Health care centres, schools, community centres, and local government offices have been burnt down in more than 300 communities. The destruction of telephone and radio towers left more than 20 districts with limited or no communications with the outside world. Transportation within and between districts either slowed down or reduced significantly due to frequent checkpoints, curfews, and a general fear of being caught in booby-traps. Several urban centres experienced a significant increase in internally displaced persons after families and orphaned or abandoned children fled their villages following Maoist attacks.[15]

The Ministry of Finance's Economic Survey, 2001/02 reported that not a single hospital, health post, or health centre was added during the review period. The number of primary health centres only rose by 20 while the number of sub-health posts actually went down from 3171 to 3161. Anyway, most of the health posts were abandoned by health workers, fearful of both the Maoists and the security forces. The Maoists killed nearly five dozen school teachers and physically abused hundreds of others for failing to provide them with 'donations' or for not obeying their orders. As a result, teachers too have fled their posts. The ones most affected by this have been the women and children who depend the most on these facilities.[16]

The extension of drinking water and sewerage facilities has also been dismal. Only an additional 45,575 people benefited from new or repaired projects in fiscal year 2001/02. The total availability of water stood at only 1,400,000 litres per day, 80,000 litres less than in the previous twelve months. The expansion of modern sewerage systems was only 2 km against the previous year's 5 km.[17]

The significant obstacles to travel and transport throughout the conflict-affected areas had to a serious effect on food security. There is enough anecdotal evidence to suggest that the Maoists requisitioned food supplies from villagers and even forced them to provide lodging. For their part, the security forces are known to have punished people providing shelter to the Maoists by seizing food they believed could be used by the Maoists. People in the affected areas have only been allowed to bring in a limited supply of food grains from outside. This has proved particularly hard on the population in food-scarce districts where the majority of people have historically depended on imported rice and flour, mainly from the tarai.[18] Indeed, the general population has suffered most from these restrictions as the Maoists have continued to live off food collected from locals and looted from trucks.[19] The persistent food crisis, in addition to the rent hikes in the business hubs of the affected districts, have forced many hotel entrepreneurs to either close down or increase prices by 50 per cent or more.[20] The looting of a number of the food-for-work programme's storage godowns by the Maoists has also had a serious localised effect on food security.[21]

The destruction of bridges by the Maoists in the midhills that are criss-crossed by river valleys has increased walking distances. Aggravating this problem even further, the security forces have barred pack animal trains from carrying food supplies to the hills. Likewise, traditional livelihood opportunities such as going into the forests to collect non-timber forest produce has been disrupted because anyone found in the forest has been liable to be treated as a Maoist.[22] In the districts in the mid-west and far-west regions that face a food deficit even in normal circumstances, the scarcity also led to an increase in prices which in turn hit the subsistence-based remote areas.

Opportunity cost of increased security expenditure

In addition to the human costs, the opportunity costs of increased security have been huge as the government dedicated a growing share of its budget to security to the direct detriment of development allocations. Public expenditure on defence expanded far beyond its natural rate of increase and overtook other sectors irrespective of equity considerations in the social and economic sectors. Defence expenses increased approximately seven-fold from slightly over Rs 1 billion in 1990/91 to over Rs 7 billion in 2002/03. With the additional burden since November 2001 of providing for the armed police forces, expenses shot up further. The budget outlay for fiscal year 2002/2003 earmarked the total security expenditure (including Rs 7.54 billion under the home ministry) at Rs 14.82 billion (more than the Rs 14.13 billion for the social sector). This means that the army and police will together absorb 15.4 per cent of the total budget.[23] According to one estimate, the cost of deploying security forces during the most intense fighting—in the early part of the emergency—was at least US$ 100,000 per day.[24] This is a startling figure for a country where per capita annual income is around US$ 200.

The investment in security, euphemistically called 'Investment for Peace' in the 2002/03 budget, has become the government's primary agenda, and for the first time in over a decade, poverty reduction was nudged aside as the number one priority.[25] Experiences in other countries have shown that once built up, downsizing security spending is difficult.[26] And the trend is already visible in the case of Nepal. Although spending on social services went up four-fold nominally and 6.6 per cent in real terms from 1991 to 2000,[27] public expenditure on economic services grew by just 3.3 per cent nominally and declined by 3.9 per cent in real terms. This means that resources meant for economic growth and poverty reduction were redirected towards security during the decade.

As the government has tried to meet the escalating security expenses by cutting off up to 25 per cent of the allocated development budget, it is likely that the country will fall into a downward economic spiral, leading to growing unemployment. The cut in the development budget prompted the government to end 165 development projects.[28] Amongst the projects discarded was the army's Integrated Internal Security and Development Programme (IISDP) introduced in 2001.

Depending on how the conflict plays out, it might be necessary for the government to increase its security expenses by reallocating the current budget plans. After the declaration of the state of emergency, the army purchased 5000 M-16 guns from the US and 5500 machine guns from a Belgian manufacturer. But this is unlikely to satisfy an armed force that suddenly finds itself in a commanding position to purchase more modern weaponry.

In a country where illiteracy, lack of proper health services, and poverty are rampant, there is a strong debate about whether weapons will necessarily provide the country with security. Controversies have even arisen on the advisability of selling arms to a government with a poor human rights record. The opportunity costs of these military expenditures over the next five years has been estimated to equal thousands of primary schools, 50 new district hospitals and 5000 bridges.[29] Poverty alleviation programmes are stagnating due to inadequate social services and infrastructure. And the much-touted Poverty Alleviation Fund (PAF), an umbrella plan for various anti-poverty programmes, continues to remain only in rhetoric.

Aid agencies have been equally affected as their programmes and projects on the ground have been compromised by the insurgency and the surrounding conflict. During 2001, when talks were being held between the government and the Maoists, major bilateral and multilateral agencies discussed 'coordination' and 'concerted action'.[30] But increasingly, external agencies, even those concentrating on 'development' with poverty alleviation as a primary focus and goal, have begun directing their programmes more towards the issue of conflict and possible measures for conflict resolution.[31] This will certainly divert attention away from the major structural and long-term causes of worsening poverty indicators, gross inequalities, lack of social justice, and corruption and patronage in the political system. Even the basic principle of humanitarian aid – 'do no harm' – is proving difficult for development agencies (and programmes and projects) in practice, given the fact that DFID- and USAID-funded programmes are perceived to have lost a semblance of neutrality for the Maoists by virtue of the British and US government's whole-hearted endorsement of the Nepali government's war against the rebels. Even more worrying is the possibility that the attention of both the government and the most influential foreign powers will increasingly be diverted away from longer-term development issues, and towards more immediate military concerns.[32]

Nonetheless, the Nepali state has been quite fortunate in its fight against the Maoists as the breakdown of the 2001 ceasefire followed events of 11 September 2001 and the 'War against Terrorism'. The government thus found it rather convenient to label the Maoists 'terrorists'. Procuring foreign assistance (or assurances in some cases) to fight the insurgency has not been problematic. The Indian government quickly responded by donating two helicopters and an unknown quantity of arms immediately after the emergency was proclaimed. And, during his January 2002 visit, Colin Powell, the first US Secretary of the State to visit Nepal, declared, 'We fully acknowledge the government of Nepal's right to protect its citizens and institutions from terrorist attacks.'[33]

Consequently, the US promised $20 million for special equipment, like helicopters and night-vision apparatus, for the Royal Nepal Army (although the amount was subsequently reduced to $12 when the US government's priority shifted elsewhere). The British government was not far behind in trying to provide military assistance of two Russian-made MI-17 support helicopters (delivered in March 2003, after the ceasefire was in place), and other assistance aimed at improving the army's capability to conduct counter-insurgency operations.

While this type of foreign assistance is bound to help the government fight the Maoists, the growing military costs and fall in revenue are likely to drive the budget deficit up to 6 per cent of GDP in fiscal year 2002/03; up from 4.2 per cent the year before. As a corollary, foreign aid dependence will certainly rise in an economy where in 2001 itself, foreign loans and grants financed 58 per cent of development expenditure, compared to the average 47 per cent over the previous five years.

Human rights violations

On 27 December 2002, the army announced that 3500 people were confirmed dead and a further 1026 presumed dead as a result of the conflict since the emergency was imposed in November 2001. The human rights group INSEC provided a higher figure (Table 5). In any case, the death toll in the 14 months of emergency was nearly three times the total in the preceding six years of the 'people's war'.

Of those killed in the course of the seven years of conflict up to

2002, many have been either members of the security forces (police and soldiers) or people involved in the Maoist movement (the vast majority of whom come from similar socio-economic backgrounds as the police and soldiers). But a substantial number have been civilians from poor rural households who have been caught in the crossfire. On December 2002, Amnesty International condemned both the government and the Maoists for committing grave human rights violations. While it accused the Maoists of killing around 800 civilians, it maintained that half of the killings by security forces since November 2001 might have been unlawful.

The onset of the state of emergency in 2001 saw the CPN (Maoist) declared as a 'terrorist organisation' and the insurgents labelled as 'terrorists'. The army was called out and a Terrorist and Disruptive Activities (Control and Punishment) Ordinance (TADO), which granted the state wide powers to arrest people involved in 'terrorist' actions, was promulgated. The ordinance suspended key articles and clauses relating to rights to freedom of thought and expression, assembly and movement; the right not to be held in preventive detention without sufficient ground; and rights to information, property, privacy and constitutional remedy. In effect, the courts were rendered irrelevant.

These developments severely constricted human rights in Nepal, a fact noted by Amnesty International in its report 'Nepal:

Table 5. **Estimated casualties** (26 Nov. 2001-26 Dec. 2002)		
Groups	Killed by the state	Killed by the Maoists
Maoists	4132	1
Police	0	495
General population	65	149
Army	0	201
Political workers	12	131
Farmers	46	59
Teachers	5	34
Workers	23	10
Students	11	15
Civil servants	10	16
Others	2	16
Total	4306	1127

Source: INSEC, Human Rights Yearbook 2002. *2003.*

A spiralling human rights crisis', released a few months after the emergency was imposed. Security operations to 'encircle and kill' killed more innocent civilians than rebels. It did not help that initially human rights organisations, which over the previous decade had benefited from a surge of foreign aid meant to support democracy and pluralism in Nepal, generally kept silent, while the media too was compromised after a grouping of publishers and editors of influential newspapers undertook to support the government's fight against the rebels.[34]

The level of abuse in terms of executions, disappearances, torture, maiming and use of civilians and child soldiers in the combat can only be speculated on because human rights groups, the media, and others have hardly monitored the events on the ground. There is no comprehensive data to confirm the level of human rights abuses.[35]

Since the army was called out, there has been no institution or individual to hold the soldiers to any human rights standards. In some respects, the army's compliance to humanitarian principles has been lower than that of the police, since the police generally cohabit with the people in the areas they patrol. The army, since it usually enters an area and then quickly leaves after its operation, has been less accountable and has had less regard for human life. As Kanak Mani Dixit pointed out, the fact that the daily Defence Ministry news bulletins referred to dead insurgents, and rarely to the 'captured wounded', provides the evidence that the army has taken few prisoners.[36] The killings often took place during staged encounters, and many incidents have been reported where individuals rounded up from one village one day were said to have been killed in an 'encounter' in another village the next day. The number of innocent human lives sacrificed in the pursuit of the Maoists has been unacceptably high. For instance, soldiers in pursuit of Maoists who had attacked Mangalsen, the district headquarters of Achham, killed 35 labourers, most of them migrant workers, in Kotwara village in Kalikot in February 2002.[37] Similarly, six villagers in Thulo Sirubari, east of Kathmandu, were tricked by soldiers into replying with a Maoist greeting and then killed (Box 12).

Undoubtedly, the critical problem here has been the difficulty of distinguishing between an 'enemy' and an ordinary villager. It can be said with certainty that many villagers killed for being Maoists have been peasants with no ideological grounding, but were Maoist

Box 12. Sirubari victims

The Nepali Army arrived [in Thulo Sirubari] last Wednesday before dawn, about 4 am. They were dressed as Maoists, complete with the velcro red stars attached to their camouflage caps, and they greeted villagers with a pumped fist, called lal salaam, or red salute.

They said, 'lal salaam, comrade', but I knew they were army, so I didn't respond, otherwise I knew I would be dead,' says Guruprasad Chaulagai, a young farmer. Maoists wear their weapons openly, Chaulagai says, while these soldiers hid their weapons under their Maoist-style camouflage uniforms.

Chiring Tamang, a farmer from a neighbouring village, wasn't as observant. He returned the lal salaam and was promptly arrested. An hour later, he was marched about 10 minutes away to a piney knoll for interrogation. At 9 am, the villagers heard shots ring out. The bodies of six captives were later found in the woods where they were killed.

Spokesmen for the joint force of 70 soldiers and policemen say the six men killed were shot while trying to escape. The troops recovered a cache of weapons and crude pipe bombs from the suspects' homes. But villagers of Thulo Sirubari (which means 'big pasture' in Nepali) say Chiring Tamang and the others shot were just farmers, shopkeepers, and family men with no interest in either the Maoists or the government.

'We are in the crossfire and both sides are firing at us,' says Chaulagai, who was also beaten with rifle butts but later released. 'I don't believe in either side. If I trust the Maoists, that's foolish, because they are all hiding somewhere else. If I trust the government, they hate us too. We are the victims, and we don't have a way out.'

One prominent Nepali human rights activist who once spoke openly to the press and now requests anonymity, says that police and military forces can operate with impunity because of the current state of emergency declared by the government this past November.

'The government leaders, the prime minister and his cabinet, say that for us to comment against the military action may demoralise the military,' says the activist. But 'because of the emergency provisions, we are not as free to report the facts. So the information one gets is one-sided, with the government saying Maoists were killed by the military,' the activist continues. 'Although they say they are killed in encounters, we have no independent way to confirm whether encounters took place, or if these were simply killings in custody.'

In Thulo Sirubari, the trouble started back in October, while Maoists were observing a cease-fire and seemed to be moving toward re-entering mainstream politics. Maoist newspapers printed lists of towns where Maoist 'people's governments' had been established to bring Marxist style rule and services to the poor farmers.

Thulo Sirubari was one of those towns, and the six men shot by the army (Chiring Tamang, Shiva Hari Gautam, Ganesh Gautam, Jhalak Dulal, Tika Dutta Dulal, and Bhaktalal Dulal) were listed in Maoist newspapers as members of the village people's government. Even today, Maoist slogans, painted in red and blue, cover the walls of the stone buildings along the dirt road that runs through the village.

According to some villagers, the army and police returned to the village after the shooting and forced village elders to sign a document that verified that the six people were Maoists and that they were killed in an encounter. One villager, who refuses to give his name, says he signed the form.

'They made a document saying they were killed in an encounter, and they asked me to sign it,' says the middle-aged farmer. 'I didn't have any alternative. They said: "We have a list, and we kill those people who are on the list."'

Shiva Hari's wife, Kamala, is also wearing a white cloth, and she clutches her son, one of her three young children. She is mourning not only for her husband, but also for her father, Tika Dutta Dulal, a former legislator from the National Democratic Party who was killed.

When the army took Shiva Hari, Kamala followed them, pleading for his release. 'They chased me away, saying "Run away, or else you'll get the blood of your own husband on your clothes."'

'Shiva Hari was not involved in any of that kind of activity, so why was he killed?' She denies that the army took any weapons from her home.

'Terrorists are [in Nepal],' says Muktinath, Shiva Hari's father, 'but the army can't kill them, so they kill us.'

Government officials admit that the army and police killed Shiva Hari, Chiring, and the others, but they say they have firm evidence that the six were Maoists.

'Every father and mother says their children are not involved, but these were real Maoists,' says Kobiraj Khanal, the chief government official of Sindhupalchowk district, which includes this village.

Like the villagers, Mr Khanal says the police arrested the six villagers after they gave the pumped fist of a red salute. But the villagers made an escape attempt after the army had taken them up into the woods for questioning.

'These people wanted to escape and the army shot them,' says Khanal. 'They didn't have any alternative.'

Excerpted from 'In Nepal's Maoist hunt, villagers are hit hardest' by Scott Baldauf, The Christian Science Monitor, *8 May, 2002.*

supporters either through coercion, or because they saw in the Maoists a saviour where there had been none. They could also have turned to the Maoists only because the state had been absent for so long from their villages. It has also been reported that many village chiefs were forcibly declared heads of the 'people's government' at the village level by the rebels. There is also the accusation by the army that the Maoists have used peasants from nearby villages as 'human shields' during their assaults, making it impossible for the army to distinguish between rebels and civilians.

For its part, the government has been seen to be rather insensitive to the issues of human rights as was evident when it placed a bounty on the heads of the Maoist leaders caught 'dead or alive' — Rs 5 million for the top leaders, Rs 2.5 million for the field commanders, and so on down the line. The state minister for home even announced that people seeking the bounty could bring the head of a Maoist in a bag, and take back the cash in the same bag. According to Dixit, 'The fact that apart from a few murmurs of protest, the national human rights community did not vocally protest against such an outrageous pronouncement — in a country where the death penalty is actually illegal — shows both an exasperation with the Maoists as well as an ambivalence towards principles of civilised governance.'[38]

In a situation of dire security threats, some might argue that the desperate actions taken by the government and the collateral damage witnessed were permissible to try and finish off the Maoists and get the country back 'on track'. However, experience from across the world indicates that killing thousands of innocents creates many more disaffected, who are bound to rise up as different kinds of militants, a fact amply demonstrated in Nepal in the aftermath of Operation Romeo and 'Kilo Sierra Two'.

Human dislocations

The Maoist insurgency took a heavy toll on the countryside from where people were forced to migrate to safer urban areas. After 1997/98, when the police and army intensified their operations against the Maoists, it became increasingly difficult for able-bodied men to live in the villages. Caught between the army and the police, and the Maoists, these men, and some women, could no longer live in the villages and fled to safer areas within Nepal or went to India or abroad, seeking employment. In areas where government control has been weak, the Maoists are believed to have ordered some individuals and their families to leave. It has primarily been the Nepali Congress supporters who have been targeted by the Maoists. According to the Association for the Sufferers of Maoists, Nepal — an organisation of Maoist victims in Kathmandu — 90 per cent of the 900 people associated with the organisation were aligned to the Nepali Congress.[39]

While it is hard to put an exact figure on the internal displacement caused by the conflict, there is enough evidence to suggest that forced migration of people has taken place on a large scale. The mid-west's Regional Administration Office (RAO), Surkhet, recorded 14,181 people displaced by the insurgency from the beginning of 2002 until the ceasefire announcement in January 2003. Of these, around 2000 were estimated to be taking refuge in Surkhet.[40] Records at the border crossing at Gaddachauki in Kanchanpur district, western Nepal showed that in the 30 days between 14 December 2002 and 14 January 2003, 40,000 Nepalis crossed in to India. Across the border at Banbasa, India, the border police post recorded more than 100,000 Nepalis going over to India between mid-September 2002 and mid-January 2003.[41] Similarly, Indian embassy officials indicate that roughly 120,000 displaced Nepalis crossed into India during January 2003 alone.[42]

Kathmandu also witnessed an influx of people fleeing the fighting in the hinterland. This put pressure on house rents, which rose steadily as even those houses that had remained vacant in the past attracted new tenants. The government has no data or estimates on the number of people that have come to Kathmandu from rural areas, but the rent hikes suggest that the figure could be substantial.[43] As part of its relief efforts, the government has been providing a modest 'displacement allowance' of Rs 100 per day to displaced people living in the capital.

Amongst those who fled the villages, in general terms, it appears that the wealthier and higher status families and households were able to obtain access to better paying and more secure employment, which has also allowed them to send back substantial sums in remittances. As for the lower middle groups, only a minority of these have been able to secure the more desirable forms of employment, in East and Southeast Asia, but more often in India, and increasingly in the Gulf. As for the most disadvantaged groups, they have had the greatest difficulty in obtaining anything other than low-paid and insecure employment, if indeed they have risked attempting labour migration at all. In order to avoid being forcibly enlisted by the Maoists or killed or detained by the army or the police, these poor have been seeking work elsewhere in Nepal, mainly in other rural areas as agricultural workers and as casual wage labourers in the cities.

The rate of migration has showed a dramatic increase due to the crisis coupled with low rates of agricultural growth; declining per capita agricultural output (leading to serious food shortages in

155

some hill districts, and famine in the Karnali zone and adjoining districts); isolation from the mainstream; significant inequalities in the control of resources; and the lack of alternative income sources. An example of this happened at Kholagaun village, Rolpa district after the Maoists attacked a nearby police post in June 2002. Not long after, 700 people out of a total population of 1300 left for India in search for work.[44]

The predicament in Maoist-affected areas

The insurgency that began from three mid-western districts of Rolpa, Rukum and Jajarkot, the western district of Gorkha and the eastern one of Sindhuli, by January 2003 had spread to 68 of Nepal's 75 districts. Available data of those killed in clashes since 23 November 2001 suggests that by that time there were no longer any Maoist-free areas. By mid-January 2001, the Maoists had declared the formation of provisional revolutionary district governments in Rukum, Jajarkot, Salyan and Rolpa districts. Similarly, by the end of 2002, there were greater Maoist activity in the western and mid-western tarai as the rebels tried to take up the cause of the recently freed bonded labourers (ex-Kamaiyas) and landless squatters. As a result, it has been estimated that the insurgency has directly touched the lives of roughly two-thirds of Nepal's 24 million people.[45]

The retreat of the state's representation and thus the shrinking of the state and the resulting decrease in faith in the government facilitated the growth of the Maoists by allowing them to fill the void. In many villages in these districts where the government evacuated police posts and pulled back its forces, the Maoists established local structures to take over the functions of the state. These have been described in Chapter 4.

However, even as the Maoists began making new interventions designed to improve local livelihoods and access to social justice, so too did they begin categorically demanding 'taxes' from local inhabitants of their 'secure areas'. The Maoists simply argued that the resources needed for reform, development, and welfare have to be generated locally through land registration taxes; donations and contributions; party membership fees; levies; and funds confiscated from banks, local moneylenders, and 'feudal land-lords'. These funds collected through such 'contributions' have been quite significant, with some of it going to procure weapons and ordnance, but no one has dared to raise their voice in protest in those areas.

The general effectiveness of the Maoist campaign should also not obscure the fact that the Maoists have frequently employed brutal methods such as high-profile demonstration killings with the corpses left in public places as a way to spread fear and to intimidate. There are also reports to indicate that the 'people's liberation army' and the militia have not always been under control and their victims have sometimes been the very people who initially greeted the rebels as a welcome alternative to police excesses and whom the Maoists claimed to place at the centre of their agenda. In remote mid-western villages, where most people lead a hand-to-mouth existence, having to provide food and shelter to a dozen Maoist rebels has become an inordinately tough burden to bear. No one dares raise a voice in protest for fear of inviting 'people's action'.

Indeed, during the latter part of 2001 the press was full of reports of extortion by 'Maoists'. It was widely implied first that the Maoists were indulging in an unreasonable level of extortion, which was alienating even their supporters and sympathisers, and second that a significant proportion of those demanding these 'contributions' were in fact not even part of the guerrilla movement but 'freeloaders' and 'criminals' pretending to be operating on behalf of the movement. As Dixit put it, 'Their original promise of social reform lies in tatters as hooliganism has overcome the movement, with commissars delivering gruesome punishment to local politicians, teachers and others.[46]

The number of deaths due to Maoist violence assumes another dimension when considering that for every individual killed or seriously injured, on average some five or six persons have been directly affected. The almost 7000 killed till February 2003, and probably twice as many injured, means that at least 100,000 people have been directly affected, with possibly as many as 1 million (5 per cent of the total population) affected in some way by the conflict as a result of death and serious injury over the period of seven years.

Women, children and the 'people's war'

There has been a higher involvement of women in the CPN (Maoist) than in other political parties because of the focus of the Maoists on fighting alcoholism, polygamy, and other social practices that have

157

a direct bearing on women.[47] It is believed that women make up almost a third of the Maoist fighting forces.[48]

The backdrop to the large participation of women in the 'people's war' is that Nepal is one of the few countries where gender discrimination persists unchecked despite its accession to the Convention on the Elimination of all forms of Discrimination Against Women (CEDAW) and other international instruments. The continuing violence against women such as their trafficking to India to work as sex workers is reflected in Nepal topping South Asia's gender inequality ratio at 1:6 (compared to India's 1:5 and Sri Lanka's 2:3). In Nepal, maternity deaths are the highest in South Asia and till recently the lifespan of women was shorter by two and a half years.[49] A study undertaken by the International Fund for Agricultural Development (IFAD) in 1999 found that women in the hill districts of Nepal had heavy workloads and a high level of physical vulnerability, albeit with class/caste differences. Women were found to work around 16 hours a day, compared to the 9-10 hours men put in by men. Apart from being overworked, many women go hungry as well and these two conditions often go together.[50] The literacy index for males is 54.3 per cent compared to 21.3 per cent for females.[51] Although the country's Gender-related Development Index (GDI), which currently stands at 0.452, is slowly moving towards equality, there is wide variation over different geographic regions (see Table 6).[52] And it is the mid-western and far western development regions that have significantly greater gender disparities compared to the other three regions.[53]

There has been a socio-political vacuum with women's political participation limited to voting and occasional candidacy in elections, and the victimisation of women has been the norm. Into this vacuum, the 'ideological thrust of the Maoist movement has emerged as a vehicle oriented towards expanding the rights base of the poor and the marginal, including women'.[54] The 'people's war' offered women a chance to escape a situation where their lives would be one of deprivation from education and one that would eventually lead to nothing more than marriage and devotion to the family. Joining the Maoists has also been seen as the answer for many women who have been abandoned by their husbands or who have felt the government 'will not and cannot do anything about the inequality women face'.[55] This has been evident when women, describing the

Table 6. Gender-related development indices by region, 2001	
Area	GRD Index score
Urban	0.605
Rural	0.426
Mountains	0.355
Hills	0.494
Tarai	0.456
Eastern Development Region	0.465
Central Development Region	0.476
Western Development Region	0.463
Mid-western Development Region	0.376
Far-western Development Region	0.356
Nepal	**0.452**

Source: Nepal Human Development Report, 2001. *2002.*

biggest hardship they had had to endure as a result of the 'people's war' have pointed to atrocities they have suffered at the hands of the police.[56]

On the other hand, radical actions taken by the Maoists in favour of women have been evident in the fact that in areas under Maoist control alcohol production and consumption have been strictly controlled. The Maoists declared a number of areas 'alcohol-free' in many districts, and prohibited the sale of alcohol. In general, this has been welcomed, particularly by local women's groups. The Maoist-affiliated All Nepal Women's Association (Revolutionary) took radical action in 2001 in an attempt to close all Nepal's breweries and distilleries and ban the sale of alcohol. This included burning down breweries, despite the importance of the brewing industry to Nepal's economy (constituting some 3 per cent of the GDP) and the fact that some 30,000 people (many of whom are women) earn a living from brewing alcohol. It is a source of income to many poor households. Parliament responded to this pressure by passing legislation to regulate alcohol sales,[57] but implementation is yet to be seen. Similarly, the Maoists consider child marriage and polygamy as 'social evils' and do their best to prevent them.

Another aspect of the 'people's war' has been what in development jargon is known as 'empowerment'. Because most men have either fled to India or into the jungles, women have had to take on the responsibility of running the households. Whether that means ploughing the fields, which would otherwise have had to remain

> ### Box 13. Waiting for justice
>
> Kalika Khatri of Kudu in Jagatipur village development committee, Jajarkot district, was widowed when her husband, Man Bahadur Khatri, was shot dead by the Maoists. A village development committee vice-chairman elected on a Nepali Congress ticket, Man Bahadur had been living away from his village fearing for his life. But after being told by the Maoists that he could return, he came back to his village. Two months later, on 26 January 2001, Man Bahadur came back at around 9 in the evening after a visit to the district headquarters of Khalanga. He asked if dinner was ready and upon being told it was being prepared he went out to the village. He was killed soon after. The villagers informed Kalika and her mother-in-law about what had happened, and they hurried to the scene where they saw Man Bahadur had been shot in the chest.
>
> Kalika is not aware if her husband had any enmity against the Maoists, but believes he was killed because he was an elected official. She considers them to be the enemy. 'What does it matter what they do? They are the enemy because they have hurt us,' she says.
>
> The government has promised an ex-gratia payment of Rs 150,000 to Man Bahadur's wife, but so far she has not received anything although she has been to the district administration office three times. The government officials have not rejected her claim, but neither have they given her the money. Her biggest concern is the future of her three children. 'How am I to educate these small children now that my husband is dead. It has become very difficult. How am I to grow crops? We had a house in Chaur Jhahari earlier. But when my husband was on the run from the Maoists and living in Kathmandu and Nepalgunj, we had to mortgage the house for his needs.'
>
> *Excerpted from Gautam, Shobha*. Janyuddhako Serophero bhitra Mahila ra Balbalika, *2058. pp. 61-62.*

fallow, or engaging in public life, women have become more vocal in community activities. In some cases, they have even stood in elections simply because there were no men in the villages to become candidates.[58]

But as in any other war, it has been women and children who have borne the brunt of the fighting. Whether this has been in the form of extortion; the loss of male heads of households who have died in the fighting, incarceration or migration; reduced health and education facilities; or displacement, the results have been the same. A field study conducted by a team of journalists found that women were being indirectly victimised by Maoist actions since male members often flee their houses to escape being killed by the Maoists, police, or the army. The Maoists then turned up at these women-headed and other households and threatened them by demanding free meals and forced donations. The women could not refuse the Maoists for fear of reprisals and also because they had no one to turn to due to the lack of police or government presence in the villages. But in a desperate call for peace, talking to a journalist, the women also expressed their consistent belief that there would be peace if the government stopped its oppression of the people.[59] (The plight of the widow of an insurgency victim is described in Box 13.)

In the absence of their elders who had either fled or been killed, the work burden on children increased considerably. One study has shown that the predicament of children has been equally horrific. In its *State of the Rights of the Child in Nepal – 2003*, Child Workers in Nepal Concerned Centre (CWIN), an organisation working for children's welfare, reported that the seven-year-old Maoist conflict had directly made victims of at least 322 children, cost the lives of at least 186 children, and severely injured 95, while another 4000 children had been displaced. In the year 2002 alone, 146 children were victimised in one way or another, out of whom 64 were killed and 49 injured. Amongst the hundreds of children reportedly kidnapped by Maoist rebels, 100 have been rescued by the police.[60] (Box 14 relates the feelings of a child orphaned by the insurgency.)

The insurgency has impacted heavily on the education system. An estimated 3000 teachers have been displaced from public schools in outlying districts, affecting an estimated 100,000 students. In Dang and Bardiya, the teacher-student ratio has gone up to 1:70 due to 'internal migration' of students leading to over-crowding of the few schools in district headquarters.[61] The study by Child Workers in Nepal reported that many children remarked that even though they wanted to study, the teachers fleeing their villages meant that there was no one to teach them.

It has been estimated that the insurgency has led to the closure of more than 700 private schools across the country, particularly in the districts of Gorkha, Baglung, Syangja, Tanahu, Dang, and Surkhet. Apart from permanently shutting down these schools, the Maoists through their student wing, the All-Nepal National Independent Free Student Union (Revolutionary), or ANNIFSU(R), disrupted school education across the country. In only the latest instance, on 9 December 2002, the ANNIFSU(R) enforced an indefinite strike on schools in the Kathmandu valley. This came after educational institutions had been forced to shut down for two days earlier in October in support of the student union's 13-point demands, including the end of privatisation and 'commercialisation' of schools, cutting the security budget by 75 per cent, using the money thus saved for education, and making education free up to high school level. In an attempt to pre-empt an indefinite strike, the government announced a reform package which included termination of compulsory Sanskrit education in grades six and seven and schemes to provide free secondary education to students from backward and oppressed groups. However, unsure about the effects of these government decisions, the Private and Boarding Schools Association of Nepal (PABSON) announced the closure of schools for two weeks.[62] There have been other similar disruptions and the impasse over private schools was continuing at the time of writing.

Apart from disrupting their studies, the Maoists have also been accused of using children as fighters. The Maoists have denied such accusations vehemently, but there is no doubt that children have been part of the war effort. Talking to journalists, some children who were found among the guerillas asserted that they were aware of their rights to get education, food, clothes, and healthcare, but because of the corruption in the state, they had been deprived of such opportunities; hence their decision to join the Maoists.[63] Children have been used as human shields, as porters to carry dead Maoist fighters, as housekeepers and cooks, and in some extreme cases, as sex slaves. CWIN has recorded five cases of the sexual abuse of girls after being forcibly recruited by Maoist rebels, one case of sexual harassment by security personnel, and at least one 14-year-old murdered by the rebels on charges of spying.[64] Many young children and pre-adolescents have been left to fend for themselves, either abandoned for their own safety by their parents who are on the run, or orphaned by killings. Often these children have found themselves totally isolated as community protection systems, both formal and informal, have broken down.

In terms of the psychological development of children, virtually every child in the Maoist-affected villages has seen a relative die in the conflict. Some have seen their teachers or classmates dragged from their classrooms and have witnessed people falling dead in front of them after being hit by police firing. Many of these children have become familiar with guns and other weapons as it became normal to find armed people roaming around. Children younger than ten can reel off the names of weaponry such as GPMG,

LMG, SLR and so on. But most alarming is that they have started to believe that revenge should be taken against enemies. They have been taught from an early age to look out for any new faces and to work for the revolution. As a result, some children have started showing increasingly violent behaviour, while others remain traumatised and locked up in fear and depression.[65]

Box 14. Orphans of the 'people's war'

Both of Dilli Biswokarma's parents were killed by the police. It has been a year since his two elder brothers left home to join the Maoist militia, leaving eleven-year-old Dilli to look after his younger brother and sister. This young child has taken up the role of his siblings' guardian, but it seems he is only waiting for the day that he can join his brothers.

Dilli Biswokarma, Garayala, Rukum: I feel like drinking the blood of their heart.

Interviewer: Why?

They killed my father and mother.

Do you know who killed them?

(Dilli nods)

Who?

The police.

With the brutal slaying of both parents these children have lost their childhood. Although the government has remained immune to their plight, within their own community they have earned respect and sympathy. The Communist Party of Nepal (Maoist) considers them to be children of martyrs and provides them with the necessary support for sustenance.

Transcript from the documentary The Killing Terraces, *2001,*
directed by Dhurba Basnet.

SAGAR SHRESTHA

The Maoist negotiating team sit down for the second round of talks, 9 May 2003: *(left to right, with position in party hierarchy given within parentheses)* Dev Gurung (member, politbureau), Ram Bahadur Thapa (member, standing committee of politbureau), Baburam Bhattarai (member, standing committee of politbureau), Krishna Bahadur Mahara (member, politbureau) and Matrika Yadav (alternate member, politbureau).

Ceasefire Again

ON 29 January 2003, fourteen months after the breakdown of talks in November 2001, the government and the Maoists agreed to another ceasefire. It was a move that was greeted with great relief although the announcement was totally unexpected, especially since it came just three days after the assassination of the chief of the Armed Police Force, Krishna Mohan Shrestha. In hindsight, however, evidence that the Maoists were keen to restart talks can be discerned.

The rebel leadership had always maintained that they were ready for dialogue, but having reiterated it for the umpteenth times, it had almost become part of their rhetoric. Until, that is, the 3 December 2002, press release from Prachanda, which stated that the CPN (Maoist)'s politbureau meeting had formed a 'central dialogue team' since it recognised that 'it is possible and necessary to talk to all political forces as well as the present manager of the ancient regime in order to find a peaceful, positive and forward-looking political solution to the crisis facing the country'.[1]

It is generally believed that the Maoists are more serious about settling their grievances through talks this time round. For one, it is they who announced the ceasefire, albeit only after the government had agreed to their immediate pre-conditions that the Interpol 'red corner' notice be called off; the term 'terrorist' that the government had tagged onto the Maoists be removed; and the bounty on the heads of top Maoist leaders withdrawn. The second reason to be hopeful is that the 'restructured central dialogue team' announced by the Maoists after the ceasefire is possibly the strongest possible — short of including party supremo Prachanda himself — and one that has a fair mix of ethnic and regional representatives. As it is led by none other than Baburam Bhattarai, nominally the number two in the party hierarchy and the convenor of the 'United Revolutionary People's Council of Nepal', which is the 'embryonic Central People's Government Organising Committee' of the Maoists, their offer for dialogue seems very credible.

Given this scenario, the following section examines the probable causes that led the Maoists and the government to agree to enter into negotiations rather than continue with a war — which had begun to be characterised as a 'civil war' by the rebels — that neither side was getting the better of. This is followed by a discussion of the present political scenario (until end-May 2003).

Compelling factors

For the Maoists

The Maoists have enough reason to feel smug about what they have been able to accomplish. That a small communist group should be able to achieve so much in seven years was something no one, not even the Maoist leadership itself, could have imagined in the first few heady years after the 1990 changeover. From hanging onto the coattails of RIM for a presence internationally and citing the experience of Peru's Shining Path to explain the relevance of a Maoist revolution in Nepal, the 'people's war' has become a beacon for would-be revolutionaries the world over. Prachanda Path has been internationalised through the RIM mouthpiece *A World to Win*, and it may only be a matter of time before ultra-leftists begin debating it, bringing it on to a par with the earlier 'Gonzalo Thought' of Peru's Abimael Guzman.

Nepal's Maoists can be proud that no other class-based revolutionary struggle in South Asia has reached as far as they have. Starting with Telangana in Andhra Pradesh in 1947 when the Communist Party of India initiated a peasant uprising to establish a 'new people's democracy' only to die out in a few years, Maoist movements have sprung up in various parts of the subcontinent. The Janata Vimukthi Peramuna (JVP) in Sri Lanka had a short revolutionary stint in 1971 before the government crushed it.[2] The most tenacious have been the Naxalites, whose first campaign from 1967 to 1972 ended without even reaching the second stage of a Maoist revolution — the formation of a People's Liberation Army.[3] Various factions of the Naxalites still operate in India, but none have been anywhere near as successful as the CPN (Maoist).

When they walked out of the talks in November 2001, the Maoists could have gambled on consolidating and extending their base areas in order to 'march on towards the direction of forming New People's Central Government' as exhorted by their slogan from the Second National Conference. The four-month ceasefire in 2001 certainly did help them consolidate their position since they were able to openly carry out propaganda work. That they chose to form the 'United People's Revolutionary Council' and restructure their 'People's Army' into a 'People's Liberation Army' even as negotiations were on suggests that they were preparing for a larger struggle. They made their intent clear by dragging the army into a conflict that, in their own words, turned into a 'civil war'.

Prachanda Path envisaged a significant change in the Maoists' strategy. While the earlier plan had followed the classic Maoist line of encircling the cities from the countryside, Prachanda Path acknowledged that although such a strategy may have been suitable for a particular period of history and situation, the conditions in Nepal were different. The new 'master plan' was to carry out propaganda work among various groups, including the bureaucracy and the army and in the cities with the intention of inciting a general insurrection to seize state power, even as the earlier tactics of attacking government forces, exploring the possibility of talks, and developing of a broad-based united front went on.[4]

But as the fighting progressed there was no sign of any uprising in urban areas. Rather a growing exasperation could be sensed in the towns and cities which began to feel the squeeze of the 'people's war' that had so far been limited to the countryside. Indiscriminate bombings, especially in the capital, certainly instilled a sense of terror, but did nothing to endear the Maoists to the population. A major setback was the disarray the party found itself in the Kathmandu Valley, not least because of the arrest of Rabindra Shrestha, the central committee member in charge of Maoist activities in the Valley, a day before the emergency was imposed in November 2001.

Disillusionment with the government and the political parties had swelled Maoist ranks in the earlier phase. This was true especially for people belonging to communist parties that were engaged in parliamentary politics.[5] The circumstances are now different. A significant number of sympathisers have given themselves up, and many others have simply left their villages to avoid being caught in the crossfire between the army and the rebels. The more immediate concern for the Maoists would have been finding volunteers to join the fight that was becoming increasingly violent.

On the fighting itself, there did seem to be no appreciable weakening in the Maoists' military strength. Since they carried the element of surprise, they often proved effective in catching the security forces unawares. They were also able to avoid direct confrontation with government troops, an important aspect of guerrilla warfare according to Mao. That was not very difficult because, although Nepal may be small in terms of geographical spread, given the terrain, the relatively small numbers the army was able

169

to deploy in the field, and the difficulty of maintaining lines of supplies, it proved large enough for the highly mobile Maoist fighters to move around. But the question of how long they could carry on without a denouement was looming large towards the end of 2002.

There was also the danger of rifts within Maoist ranks. Reports occasionally surfaced of differences between Prachanda and Baburam Bhattarai, and in the run-up to the end of the 2001 ceasefire there were rumours of dissension by the military wing on the question of further talks. The consequences of a split between hardliners and the moderates within the Maoist movement could be very grave for the country since the possibility of ending the violence would recede further. There was also the problem of keeping the fighters under a tight leash. Mao had said, 'A highly centralised command is in direct contradiction to the great flexibility of guerilla warfare and must not and cannot be applied to it.'[6] Given the conditions under which the 'people's war' was being conducted, following Mao's stricture is not only a requirement but a necessity as well. But it can also lead to the emergence of rogue elements with repercussions both for the Maoists and society at large. The fact that the Maoists had to coin the term 'Alok tendency' after Comrade Alok, one of their top leaders who abused his position for personal benefit, proves that such aberrations are entirely possible.

Before the 2003 ceasefire, the Maoists had claimed that they had reached the second stage of their 'protracted war', the stage of strategic stalemate. Going by this definition, it would mean they believed they had reached the phase where they were equal to the government not only militarily, but also politically and diplomatically.[7] However, that is also the stage during which, as Mao said, the fighting would be 'ruthless' and the country would 'suffer serious devastation'.[8]

The intensity of the violence has extracted a huge material loss for the country. The earlier attacks on telephone towers were justified by the Maoists on the grounds that they were meant to disrupt the government communication system (although it did not actually affect operations against the rebels since the security forces were equipped with their own communication network); but the spate of random attacks on infrastructure after November 2001 defied logic. These actions pushed the country's development back by decades, but it seems that this was the least of the Maoist leadership's worries. Back in 2000, the CPN (Maoist) organ, *The Worker*, proclaimed: '[I]t should be noted that although the question of new "construction" is often raised in the prospective base areas, the Party has resolutely cautioned the cadres and the masses that "destruction" of the old state (both militarily and non-militarily) would continue to be the principal aspect of the activities of the revolutionary forces for a long time.'[9]

There is no doubt they were faithfully following their vision of the destruction of the state. For all that, however, the possibility of the Maoists capturing state power was remote; the most they would be able to do was continue mobile warfare, attacking one installation after another in the countryside. A full-scale assault against any significant target seemed very unlikely despite statements that the war would be fought to the finish. It was also unlikely that the Maoists would be able to keep their supporters happy with the situation of 'strategic stalemate' without moving to the 'strategic offensive' phase. But as one of their former area commanders, Pushkar Gautam has pointed out, it is in the transition from 'strategic stalemate' to 'strategic offensive' that most revolutionary movements have floundered the world over.[10] The rebels could have realised that this fate could be coming true for them, and so had come to believe that the sooner the 'protracted war' ended, the better.

The official Maoist version of the need for the ceasefire is, of course, different. It is explained in the context of the 'ground reality', according to which, Baburam Bhattarai says

> It is easy to understand the spirit of the present ceasefire and of the dialogue process once you recognise the fact that the country is undergoing a direct confrontation between two states, two armies and two ideologies and at the political level a triangular contest between monarchist, parliamentary and people's revolutionary forces, while concurrently at the international level the triangular military interests of the US, India and China are being played out in Nepal.[11]

For the army

Until forced out of the barracks, the unknown factor in the present conflict had always been the army. It was the state's trump card, and the threat of its use had always been something that could be wielded against the Maoists. But the issue of its control that had been the subject of a tug-of-war between the palace and the interim government during the writing of the constitution was to prove a great obstacle over the years. Girija Prasad Koirala is believed to have had differences with King Birendra on this matter. The refusal of the army to take on the Maoists who had captured a group of policemen in July 2001 is often cited as a major reason behind his resignation then.

That the army had a fair bit of clout within the state apparatus, despite its not being party to the conflict, became clear after the Maoist attack on Dunai, the district headquarters of Dolpa district in September 2000. The home minister of the time, Govinda Raj Joshi, was forced to resign when he accused the army of failing to cut off the retreating Maoists.

After Dunai, Koirala broke with tradition and appointed a defence minister (the defence ministry is usually headed by the prime minister) in order to provide the civilian government with a majority on the National Security Council (NSC). (The NSC, consisting of the prime minister, the defence minister and the army chief, advises the Supreme Commander of the army, the king, on the question of mobilisation.) But throughout his tenure Koirala was not able to impress upon the king the need to use the army against the Maoists. There were two main reasons why the army and the government could not see eye to eye. One was the army's insistence that an emergency be imposed and the Maoists declared 'terrorists' before they were mobilised. This had partly to do with providing the legal basis for their actions and the army's wanting to be in complete charge of the situation in matters such as controlling the press. The other was their reluctance to serve under the district security committees headed by civil servants. The argument for the last being that since the civil service had been heavily politicised in favour of the Nepali Congress, they might end up assisting Nepali Congress politicians in their political vendettas—a not-very-unfounded argument given the manner in which the police operated against the Maoists, and others who were labelled as such.

All of the army's conditions were fulfilled when the government imposed the emergency. However, its record was rather dismal. Despite the army's claims of a daily average of so many 'Maoists' killed, this did not seem to make much of a dent in the Maoists' fighting strength or morale. It did not do too badly for itself though. Hardware such as the standard issue rifle that it had been asking the government to replace with a modern version suddenly appeared within reach. And it did gain importance in national affairs on a scale not accorded it, perhaps since the war with Tibet in 1856. But the brief it received when it was called out—disarming the Maoists—was far from achieved.

As for the police, having abandoned the countryside to the Maoists to be concentrated in a few strategic locations, they continued to be killed in large numbers. This had to do with both their lack of training to fight a war as well as their equipment. Armed with only .303 rifles, the police were fighting an unequal battle against the Maoists, who were equipped with weapons captured from the army. There has, as yet, been no attempt to upgrade the police's weaponry even as they continue to provide the frontline defence of the state. The armed police force which has been raised precisely to fight the Maoists as the 'civilian government's force' (as opposed to the 'king's army'), still does not have the numbers required to make a difference in the conflict.

In the end, the greatest difference has proved to be the level of motivation. Government forces after all are paid to do a job; and in a crunch they would fight as well as anyone else since it would be a matter of life and death. But the advantage has been with the Maoists in that they were ready to kill and be killed for their cause.

The India factor
It has been more or less established that Maoist leaders used India as a safe haven. Although there is no evidence that Delhi has been actively assisting the Maoists, it has in the past been lax in controlling their activities there. The meeting of communist leaders in West Bengal during the 2001 ceasefire period was only one such instance. Earlier, in 1998, a meeting was organised in Calcutta in support of the 'People's War' in Nepal, and in 1999, a rally and public meeting was held in New Delhi to commemorate the third anniversary of the insurgency in Nepal. The All Nepal Unity Centre, one of the front organisations of the Maoists in India, was operating openly and it was only banned in 2002.

After the emergency was imposed, India was one of the first countries to come out in support of the government, offering assistance in the fight against the Maoists (whom they had termed 'terrorists' in early 2001, long before the Nepali government did). India has its own reasons to see Nepal's Maoist movement kept in check since there exists a real danger of a physical tie-up with Indian Maoist groups spreading in an arc from Nepal, through Bihar, Jharkhand, parts of West Bengal, Chhattisgarh, Madhya Pradesh, all the way to Andhra Pradesh. Nepal's Maoists have received support from Indian ultra-leftists in terms of shelter and training and possibly assistance in gaining access to the underground arms bazaar in India.

Given these reasons, it was imperative for India to crack down on the Maoists, or at least make it difficult for them to operate out of Indian territory. But that is going to be easier said than done given the long and porous border between the two countries. There were positive signals when New Delhi handed over some suspected Maoists arrested in India and deployed personnel of the federal Special Services Bureau along the Nepal border (mainly to prevent infiltration by Pakistan-sponsored militants who India has long accused of using the open border with Nepal). That western governments sensitive to the potential of the Maoists to foment instability in the region leant on the Indian government to cooperate with Nepal on the matter of the Maoists cannot be discounted either.

Situation of flux

While removing Sher Bahadur Deuba, the king probably calculated on mass support for his action given the general disenchantment with politicians. And, to an extent he was correct since the reaction on the street was one of being relieved of the unscrupulous politicians who had (mis)ruled the country for 12 years. But booting out an unpopular prime minister is one thing and taming the Maoists quite another. Especially since King Gyanendra also had to deal with political parties that were in no mood to compromise. Calling the king's action unconstitutional, the parties threatened agitations against the royal takeover from day one. They refused to recognise the government led by Lokendra Bahadur Chand, a three-time former prime minister who was appointed by the king. Constitutional experts questioned the legality of his government since it was accountable to no one but the king, and murmurs renewed in political circles about the need to opt for a constituent assembly to draw up a new constitution.

One thing is clear though. Events beginning with the infighting in the Nepali Congress, which led to the dissolution of the parliament in May 2002 and ultimately the dismissal of Sher Bahadur

Deuba from the position of prime minister, have played out in favour of the Maoists. For one, the parliamentary parties forever pulling in different directions have not been able to present a united front vis-à-vis either the palace or the Maoists. This has led the latter two forces, both with standing armies, into a position where they can dictate the agenda. But more important has been that it created a rift between the palace and the parliamentary forces, especially since the latter can be considered a bulwark against a leftist swing for a republic. As a result, for the first time in seven years, the Maoists are facing an establishment deeply fissured at the centre.

The CPN (Maoist) began by calling the king's action a 'retro-gressive coup'.[12] But a later statement by Prachanda called for a 'political exit' to the present impasse through a dialogue between all political forces, including the king. And they wanted the king to make the first move.[13] That statement was remarkable for the ab-sence of anti-monarchy rhetoric that had been the norm since the June 2001 palace massacre. The government announced that it was taking steps to get in touch with the Maoists through a committee of human rights activists, and cabinet ministers went around say-ing that it was only a matter of time before a breakthrough was reached. And when such a breakthrough came on 29 January, the political parties were caught totally unawares and all they could do in reaction was complain that the secret negotiations leading up to the ceasefire had not been 'transparent'.

But there was nothing they could offer by way of an alterna-tive. That was because the seven parties represented in the last parliament had nothing in common apart from the real or imagined fear of the palace and the Maoists acting in concert. (The other par-ties, including those represented in the Chand cabinet, did not re-ally count since none had anything resembling a mass support base.) Of the big seven, the Rastriya Prajatantra Party was hamstrung by the fact that one of its leaders, Chand, agreed to accept the king's nomination and become prime minister. The Nepal Sadbhavana Party was similarly handicapped since their acting chairman unilat-erally accepted the king's offer to become deputy prime minister, even though a faction that split from the main party sided with the other parties. The Nepali Congress (Democratic) led by Deuba has been burdened by its role in the dissolution of the parliament (and for not extending the tenure of local governments), which paved the way for the royal takeover. Of the remaining four, the CPN

(Unity Centre-Masal) and the Nepal Workers' and Peasants' Party, have not renounced their long-term objective of establishing a communist republic; they are still waiting for the right moment to begin a mass uprising, whenever that may be.

The main problem initially was that the political parties could not agree on the matter of what the king should be compelled to do to bring the polity back on a 'constitutional track'. Deuba believed he should be back as prime minister since the recommendation to the king that precipitated his removal was done at the behest of an all-party agreement. The CPN (UML) has been showing itself in favour of an all-party government, presumably led by it by virtue of its having been the largest party in the last parliament. The Nepali Congress wants the parliament restored, and insists that any future government should be chosen by it.

Despite the apparent cross-purposes inherent in their objectives, the political parties were one in cold-shouldering Prime Minister Chand. The prime minister repeatedly called in vain for an understanding between the two sides. All three all-party meetings he called to discuss the Maoist issue were boycotted by the opposition. Initially, the political parties even expressed the view that there could be some secret understanding between the Maoists and the king. Not so, the Maoists have been saying, and in February 2003 even they had a couple of their leaders do the rounds in Kathmandu, meeting other parties' leaders to try and convince them that their proposed roundtable conference would not proceed without participation of the political parties. In his statement to the press on the eve of the 13 February anniversary, CPN (Maoist) chairman Prachanda reiterated: 'Rather than viewing the [upcoming] talks as between the establishment and our party, it should form part of the dialogue process among all political parties, the intelligentsia and the common people.' King Gyanendra also referred to this atmosphere of distrust in his message to the nation on 19 February, Democracy Day, when he called upon all to stop 'blaming and doubting each other'.

On the face of it, the king seems to have gambled heavily on the negotiations to succeed since only that would provide the much-needed justification for his drastic step of dismissing Deuba. For the Maoists, they could not have been presented with a more suitable opportunity in terms of bargaining from a 'position of strength'. The biggest hurdle is lack of trust between the three forces. The Maoists initiated some measures to build confidence by withdrawing their protest programme centred around 13 February, the seventh anniversary of the 'people's war'. And when the government reported that extortions were still taking place in the countryside, Prachanda came out with a statement instructing his cadre to desist from 'all forms of fund-raising except voluntary donations until further notice'. All in all, propitious signs that there would be meaningful talks.

In conclusion

Given the power balance that presently lies between the Maoists and the monarchy and the apparent sidelining of the political parties, it might seem that the latter have received their comeuppance for their years of misrule. Such a view, however, can well be extremely short-sighted. For there can be no alternative to democratic governance no matter when or how the country ultimately reverts to normalcy. And when peace returns it is these same political parties that will provide the backbone of a functioning democracy, especially at the grassroots. That is why any agreement without their involvement will not have the stamp of total legitimacy that such an accord would require. Much reviled though the parties are, collectively they still constitute the only political entity that represents the people's will expressed through an electoral system, howsoever flawed that may have been. That is where the 'people's movement' against the 'retrogressive royal takeover' launched by the alliance of five political parties in May 2003 becomes relevant. However, it should also be noted that peace is the need today as an embattled nation awaits relief from the perennial uncertainty of conflict. This fundamental truth should not be obscured by rhetorical posturing, and everyone has to work with each other to find a way out of the present impasse.

All the three sides in the new political equation are still circling each other warily and only when there is total commitment and understanding between them will the chance of lasting peace be a reality in Nepal. As Anup Pahari puts its, 'The first requirement for a resolution is for the monarchy, the political parties and the Maoists to realise that each can pursue and achieve their long-term basic goals with far greater assurance within a peacefully negotiated political order than it can under conditions of civil war or the unpredictable and unstable circumstance that will result if the conflict is fought to its bitter end, if at all an end is possible.'[14]

On the other hand, there is no denying that no matter how the conflict is resolved, it has shaken to the core the structures of the past — political, social and economic. The very fact that a practically unknown political force has reached the stage where it can force the agenda of the state proves that the issues raised by the Maoists have a deep resonance in Nepali society. There may be differences of opinion on the means adopted, but there can be no doubt that the level of support the rebels have garnered has happened not because people have been sold on the vague idea of a 'people's democracy', but rather it has been the promise of a more just and equitable society that has attracted them.

This is a realisation that has already sunk into the state establishment and the intelligentsia at large. Unlike during the period when the 1990 constitution was being framed when demands for greater representation and for a more inclusive state policy had prompted a backlash from the social elite, there is now an understanding that no matter how the present conflict ends, Nepali society has changed forever and there is no going back to the old days. The challenge for the future is to avoid the exclusionary policies the restoration of democracy should have ended. Compared to twelve years ago, there are greater demands for a participatory political system, and groups that have hitherto been at the margins have developed a larger sense of awareness that their marginalisation can be done away with, if need be, with violence. It is these aspirations that the Maoists have been able to build their movement on. As a former Nepali army officer wrote just months before he was killed by the Maoists: 'In the *kuna kapchas* (remote corners) of our country where the majority of the neglected, exploited and oppressed villagers are living, there is no lessening of support for the *maobadis*, there is no government, and there is no alternative for the people. They have nothing to lose. Keeping aside the morality and the methods of the *maobadis*, they seem to offer the only hope.'[15]

A corollary to this bit of home-grown wisdom would be what was aptly expressed by an adviser to President Lyndon Johnson at the height of the Vietnam War: 'The best way to fight a guerilla warfare is to prevent it from happening.'[16]

Therein lies the ultimate challenge to those who would rule Nepal.

Photograph released by the army shows display of arms and ammunition captured from the Maoists after an attack. The rifles in the foreground are all Royal Enfield .303s, the standard issue for the Nepal Police. In the background on the left can be seen a pile of 'socket bombs', an improvised explosive device that has been used by the Maoists with devastating effect.

Update

ON 27 August, 2003, Prachanda declared that the Maoists were walking out of negotiations. That was the upshot of the third round of peace talks between the government and the rebels held from 17 to 19 August. It was clear from the very first day that progress through dialogue was going to be difficult, but a population wearied after eight years of fighting had all its hopes pinned on the tenuous ceasefire somehow holding out. The announcement by the CPN (Maoist) chairman thus dashed the hopes of a whole country even as it plunged immediately into yet another round of bloodbath.

The death toll has continued to rise steadily; more than 10,000 people have lost their lives since that fateful day in February 1996 that signalled the beginning of the 'people's war'. Two ceasefires have ended without result even though there is agreement all round that there is no alternative to a negotiated solution to the conflict. The 2003 ceasefire did show some promise initially with both sides warming up to begin talking, and there was indeed some progress compared to the 2001 truce. But ultimately there were just too many variables active in the political arena for dialogue to yield peace so easily.

End of ceasefire

The end of the ceasefire was perhaps as predictable as its announcement in late January was unexpected. As a result of negotiations that had gone on in secret between the Maoists and the Chand government (apparently with the concurrence of the palace) the fighting suddenly came to an end. Events did not exactly move swiftly but there seemed some progress towards talks. The Maoists took the lead by announcing their negotiating team a few days after the ceasefire was declared. A code of conduct was drawn up, and by the end of the March the heavyweight Maoist team had surfaced, eager to begin parleys in earnest.

But talks were a long time in starting. Despite the government's claims, there was no doubt that King Gyanendra still called the shots and the monarch's travels first to India and then to western Nepal around that time caused much delay. Inexplicable as it was in the context of the urgency that peace talks had assumed, the king's absence added to the confusion in Kathmandu. Speaking for the government was Narayan Singh Pun, the minister who had brokered the ceasefire deal with the Maoists, but it was not clear whether he had the mandate to deal further with the rebels or alternative arrangements would be made.

The code of conduct was already under strain. The Maoists had initially asked for a pullback of the army from the field. The government, however, had been adamant that the army was necessary to ensure peace and security in the country. As a compromise, it was agreed that while the army would still be out, it would desist from acting against the Maoists, while the latter were not to hold rallies involving armed guerillas or engage in activities that could be perceived as threatening the peace such as extortions and kidnappings or announce strikes and shutdowns. Most importantly, it was agreed that neither side would back out of the agreement and that any misunderstanding would be resolved through dialogue. But with negotiations nowhere in sight, the Maoists accused the government of stalling and insisted on a 'conducive atmosphere' for talks to begin. While the waiting game continued, allegations of violations of the code of conduct began to surface from both sides. The government claimed extortions and kidnapping were still going on, while the Maoists were none too happy that their cadre was being re-arrested even as they were released by the courts.

The political parties were still reeling from the sudden announcement of the ceasefire. In order to assuage their doubts that no conspiracy was afoot, Maoist leaders did the rounds meeting leaders of political parties. To their credit, the Maoists consistently emphasised a role for the political parties in any future arrangement, claiming that the balance of power was now three-pronged with the Maoists, the parties, and the palace ranged against each other.

The 'core demands' of the Maoists—a constituent assembly to draw up a new constitution, an interim government, and a roundtable conference—remained unchanged though and this was underscored by the coordinator of the Maoist negotiating team, Baburam Bhattarai, at the group's first press conference on 29 March. The CPN (Maoist), he said, would not compromise on the issue of a constituent assembly and called on all parties 'to settle forever the political debate that has been going on for half a century in the country' by electing such an assembly. At the same time, there was reason to hope for a more fruitful dialogue given Bhattarai's assertion that 'we have come with the conviction that the talks will succeed'.[1]

Finally, on 17 April, the government announced its own five-member ministerial team led by the deputy prime minister, Badri Prasad Mandal. The first round of talks held 10 days later, on 27 April. The Maoist presented their proposals for consideration, which, as is usual with their demands, were both general and specific and included the release of prisoners (with some high-ranking leaders named), withdrawal of court cases, abrogation of the Terrorist and Disruptive Activities (Punishment and Control) Act, the return of the army to the barracks and the ultimate merger of the two armies into a 'national army' and so on. (See Annex V for full text of the Maoist demands.) There was no change either in their political demands that called for a roundtable conference to be 'organised with the concurrence of the revolutionary force and the country's major political forces and this should include democratic, patriotic and leftist forces which have a proved popular base'. The idea being that such a conference would draft an interim constitution to allow for the formation of an interim government under the leadership of the Maoists which would, in turn, conduct elections to a constituent assembly. During talks, the two sides agreed to set up a team to monitor the ceasefire while its other demand that a group of facilitators be appointed to smoothen the peace process was also acceded to. A four-member sub-committee from among the negotiators was formed to work out details of the venue and timing of future talks as well as to discuss the shape of the monitoring team. There were differences, however, on the pace and focus of negotiations; the rebels wanted to deal with political questions as speedily as possible while the government adopted a go-slow approach, arguing that the peace process was a complex process and many issues had to be taken into consideration for it to succeed.[2]

On 9 May, the second round of talks was held and a number of agreements reached. Speaking to the press jointly, the appointed spokespersons for the two sides said certain confidence-building measures had been agreed upon, including keeping the army tied to within five kilometres of the barracks. It had also been agreed that a national team to monitor the code of conduct would be formed and some top Maoist leaders in government custody released. The government was reported to have provided assurance that necessary steps were being taken to the rebel demand that the Terrorist and Disruptive Activities (Punishment and Control) Act be abrogated. Although political issues did not figure at that point either, both sides seemed satisfied with the progress thus far, and expressed confidence that these would be considered at the next round.[3]

If Round II seemed to augur progress, it was momentary. The army immediately made its displeasure unknown. *The Kathmandu Post* reported that a meeting was held at the prime minister's residence that same evening where army and other security officials took strong exception to the government's action on the grounds that any decision regarding the military could be taken only by the National Security Council.[4] Confrontation over the issue became inevitable with the army stating publicly that it would disregard the deal because the security concerns of the people in the countryside who could not be left at the mercy of the Maoists, while the Maoists demanded that the army recognise the political nature of the agreement. Given the opportunity provided, some of the political parties also spoke out against the government's decision. By then it appeared that the understanding on the army's movements had been only a verbal one and the government soon backtracked. The Maoists were furious, but there was little they could do apart from issuing warnings that dishonouring agreements in that manner could jeopardise the peace process.

Meanwhile, the parliamentary political parties which had been calling for the king to retract his 'retrogressive' action of October 2002 began a movement against the government, incidentally just a day before Round II of the government-Maoist talks. While demonstrations had been a routine feature since the very first day King Gyanendra removed Sher Bahadur Deuba, the difference this time was that an alliance had been created among five of the parties – the Nepali Congress, the CPN (UML), the People's Front, Nepal Workers' and Peasants' Party and Nepal Sadbhavana Party (Anandi Devi).[5] The various student groups, generally inert since the re-introduction of democracy in 1990 but in the midst of their own agitation against educational authorities, found an issue to rally around and entered the fray with gusto. The heat generated by the street protests was more than what Prime Minister Lokendra Bahadur Chand could handle, and he handed in his papers on 30 May.

Chand's departure seemed to pave the way for an entente between King Gyanendra and the political parties. But, in a completely unanticipated move, the king appointed Surya Bahadur Thapa as prime minister. This was a slap in the face of the agitating parties that had recommended CPN (UML) general secretary, Madhav Kumar Nepal, as their consensus candidate. The new prime minister, who belonged to the same party as Chand, the Rastriya Prajatantra Party, quickly announced that he had been appointed prime minister with full executive powers and since the handover of authority to the prime minister was a major demand of the parties, there was no rationale for the protests to continue. He also said that his priority would be to continue talking to the Maoists and he asked for cooperation from the political parties by inviting them to join his government.

Thapa's enthusiasm proved to be naively optimistic for let alone extend cooperation he immediately came under attack from the political parties. The Maoists, too, were irked with the change and made their displeasure known through the press. The biggest blow, however, came from his own party with detractors dissatisfied that the prime minister had filled the cabinet with only his close associates. It was clearly more than what even a seasoned politician like Thapa would be capable of handling, but his test would be in how he dealt with the Maoists.

A two-member team had been formed to talk to the Maoists after Surya Bahadur Thapa took office.[6] A number of 'unofficial' contacts took place although actual negotiations did not proceed further. It was only a month and a half later that the government sent a formal invitation to the Maoists to resume talks. By then the press was abuzz with rumours that the Maoist team had gone underground once again. To queer the pitch, the person in charge of the Kathmandu 'contact office' of the Maoists was picked up by security forces and grilled extensively on what the rebel leadership was planning to do. A few days later, the Maoists shut down the office, citing undue surveillance and fearing for the security of the negotiating team. A panicked government immediately sent out assurances guaranteeing safe passage to the Maoist team even if negotiations were to fail.

Baburam Bhattarai responded to the government's invitation with a long letter setting out their grievances and mentioning the conditions under which they would sit down for talks. The understanding supposedly reached during the second round on limiting the army's movements was expressly mentioned as were other clauses such as the release of three central committee members of the CPN (Maoist). The letter also came out strongly against the army's ties with the US military and demanded that all 'foreign army advisors and army experts' be 'expelled' immediately. A further demand was that the army 'declare a commitment to abide fully and unconditionally by all decisions' taken during negotiations. Bhattarai accused the government of indifference towards the rebel proposals presented at the first round of talks: '[E]ven after three months have passed, the old state has neither expressed any comment over that proposal nor has dared to present [a] separate political agenda.' Finally, the Maoists wanted some form of public commitment from the king, who, they said, was 'monitoring and guiding [the negotiations] from the back of the curtain'. The letter declared that 'in order to make [the] third round [of] negotiation[s] meaningful either the king himself should participate in the negotiation process or he has to make a public commitment through a clear and unambiguous statement, announcing that the negotiation team enjoys full rights to negotiate all necessary aspects ...and that he himself is fully committed to implementing any decisions reached.'[7]

The government replied two days later saying that the 'agreements' of the second round had only been subjects under discussion and nothing had actually been put down in writing. Further, claiming that it was a government fully empowered with executive authority, the Maoists were invited for talks by mid-August, with the offer that all their demands would be discussed under the framework of constitutional monarchy and multiparty democracy. The Maoists became even more aggressive in their response and, after deriding the government's claims to being one enjoying executive rights, reiterated the fulfilment of the demands mentioned above as a precondition for talks and announced that if those were not met within four days, i.e., the 31st of July, they would consider the ceasefire to have been broken unilaterally by the government.

The situation began to look pretty grim. Commentators expressed their misgivings about the future of the peace talks. The army and the police were placed on high alert and the roadside checkpoints that had been gradually phased out over the months, made a reappearance. Soldiers and policemen on leave were ordered back on duty. But there was also intense pressure, both domestic and international, for dialogue to continue. It was under such an atmosphere that the government released the three Maoist leaders and urged the rebels to engage in dialogue than resort to an exchange of letters. This time the response was favourable, and Prachanda called for negotiations to begin. He also requested the political parties to participate in the talks and asked the government to make that possible. The Maoist supremo need not have bothered since the political parties wanted no part in the negotiations.

The third round of talks began on 17 August in the western Nepal town of Nepalgunj. The government presented its response to the Maoist proposal of 27 April. (See Annexe VI for full text of the government paper.) The rebels immediately found the government paper wanting in a number of respects, especially with regard to the proposed power structure of the state. But the talks continued for a further two days in a village setting away from the media glare. The expected breakthrough, however, did not happen. The Maoists stayed resolute on their demand for a constituent assembly while the government conceded to a roundtable conference but continued to insist that constitutional amendments would suffice to effect the reforms sought by the rebels. Ultimately, this one issue spelt the breakdown of negotiations, and on 27 August came the press release from Prachanda declaring the 'irrelevance' of the ceasefire.

So, why did the peace process fail despite the more-than-promising start? A number of papers have probed this question in detail.[8] But even a superficial examination of the situation shows how and where things went wrong. For instance, the code of conduct that had been worked out was a fine piece of document, but was nevertheless doomed to failure because of what it attempted to achieve. One example is the clause related to the collection of 'donations' by the rebels. Although the code clearly stated that 'forcibly taking money or goods as donations' was to cease, extortion continued in various guises. Considering that the Maoists had an organisational structure to sustain through all the months on inaction, that was only to be expected. The government, meanwhile, continued to dilly-dally rather than begin a dialogue that could have provided some portents about the future of the peace process. But both the Chand and Thapa governments were hamstrung by both the struggle for legitimacy vis-à-vis the political parties and with having to keep the interests of the palace (and the military) uppermost in mind. It would have been pretty premature to expect anything substantial to emerge out of talks but had meaningful negotiations begun, the Maoists would have had more reason to persevere at the table rather than worry about their fighters turning soft and hasten a return to the battlefield.

The mobility of the army was the other major point of contention. The code of conduct did mention that 'Both parties will refrain from aggressive activities around high security areas.' But the army, which had lost a lot of ground since it was swept into the fighting in November 2001, was impelled to demonstrate a presence in areas generally under Maoist control. That it did by setting up temporary medical and relief camps in remote villages. The Maoists did not take kindly to this intrusion into their 'territory', and that was one of the main reasons why they had sought to limit the army's movement. Maoist suspicion was also fuelled by the reported presence of US military advisers in the army as well as Nepal's signing the Anti-Terrorism Assistance programme with the US before the two sides had even met for formal talks.

Despite the ceasefire, killings also continued from both sides. A total of 206 people were killed during the seven-month ceasefire, with the government side responsible for 124 lives and the Maoists 82.[9] The lack of trust was so deep that a proposal by the National Human Rights Commission to get both sides to agree to sign an accord on respecting human rights and humanitarian law came to naught.

The seemingly high expectations of the Maoists and the government's lack of preparation did not help matters either. At their first press conference, the Maoist negotiators sounded quite confident of a settlement and evinced hope that they would soon be part of the government, if not actually leading it, to oversee the coming transitional period. The government, for its part, took almost three months even to name a team and when the talks actually began, it could offer little of substance to the Maoists' specific demands. And the change of government introduced a whole new set of uncertainties since any undertaking granted by the previous government now remained invalid or would have to be negotiated anew. It was only after the talks seemed in danger of imminent collapse did the government come up with a response to the Maoist proposal. But perhaps what led to an actual crisis of confidence was that on the same day the two sides were beginning the third round of talks in Nepalgunj, an army team gunned down 19 people, most of them Maoist cadre, in Doramba of Ramechhap District in eastern Nepal.[10]

The Doramba incident figured prominently in Prachanda's 27 August statement when he stated that 'both the "concept paper" of the old state presented at the third round of negotiation politically, and the massacres of the 19 people in Doramba by the Royal Army militarily, have declared the calling off of the negotiation process'. Prachanda also mentioned the agreement on restricting the army movement and accused the government of succumbing to pressure from the army to rescind it, which he said led to 'a serious crisis' on the 'possibility of peaceful and forward going political outlet.'[11] At a later date, he said

> After the old state refused to acknowledge the sovereign right of the people to decide on their own future, the country is once again going ahead with political and military confrontation. The serious effort by our Party and the people to arrive at a peaceful and forward-looking political solution has failed because of foreign imperialist intervention and the national capitulationist [sic] attitude of the old state. From this it has become clear that the genuine sovereignty, the freedom of the country and the aspiration for the peace and progress of the people cannot be achieved unless one fights [a] decisive battle against this reactionary feudal state which is being bred and fed by the imperialists.[12]

No matter what the Maoist excuse for breaking off the talks was, it is clear that they had just tired of waiting around for the power configuration to be sorted out between the king and the political parties. While there is no doubt that the government's proposal went far beyond what the Nepali state had hitherto been prepared to concede, and though it left many issues open to negotiation, it was too late in the day to entice the Maoists to any fruitful discussion. Instead, they resumed their chant for a constituent assembly and withdrew from the ceasefire.

The international response

At various rallies during the ceasefire, Maoist leaders had warned that the next stage of the fighting would be carried to the cities. As if on cue, the day after the ceasefire was declared over, Maoist hit squads shot dead one army colonel and injured another colonel in the capital, making them the highest-ranking military officials to fall casualty till that time. One day later, Devendra Raj Kandel, the deputy minister for home affairs during the Emergency, was shot and wounded.[13] Explosions rocked different parts of the Kathmandu Valley and if the Maoists wanted to prove that they were back to fighting with a vengeance, their message went straight to the hearts of Kathmandu residents.

But the resumption of hostilities proved to be a double-edged sword since it also allowed the government to blame the Maoists for yet again breaking the ceasefire unilaterally and seek external assistance, which was readily forthcoming from the US, the UK and India. Even as they called for the parliamentary forces and the monarchy unite against the Maoists, these three countries continued with the military aid that had begun with the end of the first ceasefire. While the US$ 20 million initially promised by the US was eventually whittled down to $17 million, in April 2004, the US announced a further US$ 14 million in military assistance for 2004.[14] The US had also provided a consignment of 5,000 US-made M-16 rifles in early 2003 in a separate procurement deal not related to the military assistance.[15] The UK granted £ 6.7 million from its conflict prevention fund. The funds were to be used to procure 'two Mi-17 support helicopters, explosive ordinance disposal equipment, logistical equipment, communications equipment and equipment in support of the military intelligence support group' which the UK was assisting the Nepali army in setting up.[16] India provided two helicopters soon after the emergency was proclaimed and followed up with two more helicopters, nearly 100 mine-protected vehicles, 25,000 Indian-made rifles, and a number of military transport vehicles, all at heavily discounted prices.[17] In total, Indian military assistance to Nepal has amounted to nearly US$ 70 million.[18]

The Maoists have long held that the US and India have a common interest in working together to the detriment of China even though they themselves have no love lost for what they consider the 'revisionist' Chinese leadership. Baburam Bhattarai has written about a 'tightening collusion between the ruling classes of USA and India with a strategic perspective of containing China.'[19] Whether there is actually some such nefarious design at work or not, there is little doubt that the Maoists can claim credit for the US, India and former colonial power of the region, the UK, cooperating actively in their policy towards Nepal's Maoists. And the interest of these three countries in helping the Nepali state counter the Maoist threat goes deeper than just the general ideological opposition to the possibility of a Maoist regime being installed in Kathmandu.

US strategic interest in Nepal, while always almost non-existent apart from the early years of trying to 'contain' communism personified by Mao Tse-tung's China, had been whetted in part by the routine anti-US statements of the Maoists and the attacks on Coke and Pepsi plants in Kathmandu. But the post-September 11 'war on terror' changed everything. First, the Nepali government tried to clamber into the American anti-terrorism bandwagon by offering its facilities to the US in the impending assault on Afghanistan soon after the New York attacks. It sought to further cement its standing with the US by declaring the Maoists to be 'terrorists' after the first ceasefire ended, a charge that seemed to be soon justified when the Maoists assassinated a Nepali guard employed with an American diplomatic establishment in December 2001.[20]

The Maoists' anti-American enthusiasm turned out to be a grave miscalculation. Besides providing military aid, which included sending in a number of US military advisers to train the Nepali army in counter-insurgency tactics,[21] the US undertook a series of measures designed to criminalise the CPN (Maoist) and its affiliates internationally: in April 2003, the Maoists figured in the 'Other Terrorist Groups' category in the report 'Patterns of Global Terrorism, 2002'; in November 2003, the US designated the CPN (Maoist) under Executive Order 13224 on terrorism financing for committing 'acts of terrorism that threaten the stability of a government friendly to the US' and for posing 'a terrorist threat to the security of US nationals and US national security and foreign policy interests;[22] and in April 2004, the Maoists were placed on the 'Terrorist Exclusion List'.[23]

The basis of US policy towards the Maoists was summed up by Donald Camp, Deputy Assistant Secretary for South Asian Affairs, in the following terms:

[T]he Maoists threaten US interests for other reasons as well. The leadership has made clear that it seeks to replace the constitutional monarchy with an absolutist communist regime — one that would be overtly hostile to the United States. Recent Maoist statements defending the Khmer Rouge give one indication of the kind of instability and humanitarian catastrophe that might follow a takeover. Such a development could destabilise the wider region, and Nepal could quite easily turn into a failed state, a potential haven for terrorists like that which we have transformed in Afghanistan.

This possibility is made more acute by Maoist statements expressing common cause with other South Asian extremist groups sharing similarly violent agendas.[24]

In the case of the UK, the Maoists oppose the recruitment of Nepalis into the British Army as have all the communist parties of Nepal since the days of the Malaya Emergency when Gurkhas formed an important part of the British fighting machine against communist insurgents there. But while the mainstream Left has come to accept this uniquely Nepali reality, the Maoists continue to cling to this old 'anti-imperialist' banner. However, this is a minor point with the UK and its interest is driven more by its old ties with the Nepali state as well as the lead role it has been handed by the US in Nepal. Underscoring the importance it has accorded to Nepal, in February 2003, the UK even appointed a special representative to coordinate international effort in seeking a resolution to the conflict.

India's role has by far been the most interesting. Although New Delhi was the first to call the CPN (Maoist) a 'terrorist' organisation,[25] for years it had turned a blind eye to Maoist activities within its borders.[26] As the Indian scholar, S.D. Muni, has noted:

> Law and order being treated as a state subject, the Central government in India absolved itself of any responsibility in restraining and containing the activities of the Maoists along the Indo-Nepal border. Even the June 2001 establishment of a coordination committee of the South Asian Maoists was just taken routine note of by the Indian intelligence agencies without any policy decision at the political level.[27]

India now seems determined to assist the Nepali state's war against the rebels, especially considering the battering the Nepali army received at the hands of the Maoists in the initial stages. It is not difficult to understand the alacrity with which India has appreciated the danger of a possible Maoist takeover given the threat to its own security through possible link-ups between the Maoists and the Indian radical left. In the words of the Indian ambassador to Nepal, Shyam Saran, 'The Maoist insurgency in Nepal is a threat to India's security as well. It is a problem that does not respect national boundary.'[28]

Apart from providing military aid, India had also arrested a number of Maoist leaders in 2002 and extradited them to Nepal. But those were small fry compared to whom the Indians have since netted: CPN (Maoist) politbureau member, C.P. Gajurel, in Madras; politbureau member, Matrika Prasad Yadav, arrested along with alternate member of the central committee, Suresh Ale Magar, in Lucknow; six central committee members among 11 Maoist leaders arrested in Patna; and the biggest catch of all—standing committee member and former general secretary of the party that eventually became the CPN (Maoist), Mohan Baidya (aka Kiran) in Siliguri of West Bengal.[29] That is an impressive haul that has had the Maoists scrambling for reactions such as this: 'Comrade Kiran was arrested with the active role of Indian rulers. It has bared the nexus between the neo-monarchy of the post-royal palace massacre and the reactionary rulers of India who believe in an indivisible India.'[30]

The Maoists, however, may be far off the mark in their assessment of the said 'nexus'. India's stated preference has been for Nepal to remain a constitutional monarchy and multiparty democracy. King Gyanendra's royal takeover has made things uncomfortable for the Indians and New Delhi, along with other countries, have been calling for reconciliation between the palace and the political parties. But, as things stand now, India seems to have no choice but to continue to support the royal government in its fight against the Maoists.

Nepal's other neighbour, China, although leery of greater US involvement, has more or less left the government to deal with the insurgency on its own. In fact, the Chinese have had to more often disavow any perceived links between the land of Mao and Nepal's Maoists while expressing support for the Nepali government's position.

The European Union, on the other hand, has been quite critical of the state's disregard of its international human rights commitments and its refusal to sign the human rights accord drawn up by the National Human Rights Commission. And though the criticism has not resulted in any substantial improvement in the behaviour of the security forces, it has forced the government to take note. Thus, on the eve of the meeting of the UN Commission on Human Rights in Geneva in April 2004, the government came up with what it termed its 'commitment' to 'implement human rights and international humanitarian laws'. This document did take the heat off Nepal at the Geneva meeting where a Swiss-sponsored motion indicting Nepal was scuttled, reportedly by the US,[31] but the EU was able to persevere in forcing the government to agree to technical assistance to the National Human Rights Commission from the Office of the High Commissioner for Human Rights in order to carry out nationwide monitoring.

Similarly, during the meeting of the aid group consortium, the Nepal Development Forum, in May 2004, a group of ten donors threatened that future support would be contingent on the reactivation of the democratic process and an immediate ceasefire and resumption of negotiations with the Maoists.32 Particular emphasis was placed on the 'promotion and protection of human rights'.33 Although the statement also appealed to the CPN (Maoist) 'to renounce violence' and 'to commit to respect the human rights of all people', the thrust of the message was clearly aimed at the government.

Nepal's image has received a severe battering in the international human rights arena. A number of rights groups have been keeping tabs on the situation in the country. Amnesty International has periodically produced reports since the very beginning of the conflict censuring both the government and the Maoists. And after the Emergency was proclaimed, it warned that 'the human rights situation in Nepal is spiralling out of control amid the escalating fighting between the security forces and the Communist Party of Nepal (Maoist)'.[34]

Others have also taken note of the situation in Nepal, particularly the prevalent climate of impunity. In her 2000 report, the UN Special Rapporteur on extrajudicial, summary or arbitrary executions, Asma Jahangir, had expressed concern at the growing number of extrajudicial killings and disappearances.[35] The UN's Working Group on Enforced or Involuntary Disappearances recorded the highest number of disappearances worldwide in Nepal in 2003.[36] The International Bar Association's report stated that the government's treatment of detainees 'are *prima facie* a breach of Nepal's international human rights obligations.'[37] The International Commission of Jurists was more explicit when it said, 'There is near total impunity for officials of the Army, armed police forces and police who engage in serious human rights violations including torture, unlawful killings and war crimes.'[38]

The increased scrutiny has forced the government to adopt a few measures such as the establishment of 'human rights cells' within the army and the armed police force. The army has also reported conducting internal investigations on some reports of abuses by its men although the penalties announced seem highly incommensurate with the gravity of the crimes.[39]

Despite pressure from the diplomatic community, the government continues with its face of foot-dragging with regards to reining in the security forces or forcing the army to prosecute the guilty for cases like the Doramba massacre.[40] Instead security forces continue to disregard the National Human Rights Commission even as they ignore the numerous court orders meant to provide legal redress to those in custody.

Street politics

It is a characteristic of Nepal's political scenario that in the backdrop of the high drama of the Maoist ceasefire and its subsequent demise, the sideshow of 'anti-retrogression' protests by Nepal's political parties continued unabated. Always deeply suspicious of being left on the sidelines by a possible rapprochement between the king-appointed government and the Maoists, the political opposition was able to force Lokendra Bahadur Chand out of office through street protests. But if the political parties had expected the king to be chastened by Chand's ouster and cooperate with them, they had miscalculated the king's disdain for them when he chose Surya Bahadur Thapa to head a new government.

There was no letup in the agitation that had drawn the hitherto bitterly opposed parties closer together. As part of their protests the five parties even held public sessions of the parliament's upper house as well as of the dissolved lower house and cautioned the government against making major decisions in the absence of an elected parliament. And in a rare display of consensus, in July, they came up with an 18-point reform agenda they claimed was an answer to the multiple crises facing the country. It was remarkable that such a disparate grouping could even agree to anything. A compromise document that expressed more vague-sounding promises than concrete ones, it was, however, clear on one thing—clipping the powers of the king.

The 18-point charter provided a position around which to rally the party faithful for some months, and the streets heated up with demonstrations on a daily basis. The Maoists proclaimed their support for the protests. But neither the government nor the king seemed impressed. The diplomatic community in Kathmandu tried its best to bring about an understanding between the political parties and the king, and while the former seemed willing to work out a deal, King Gyanendra proved recalcitrant. Instead, the king went around the country to be publicly felicitated by royalist supporters and made a whistle-stop tour of conflict-affected areas in a decidedly defiant gesture aimed at the political parties.

The opposition protests continued along what seemed to be a routine but meaningless effort. Some commotion was created in November 2003 when the general secretary of the CPN (UML), Madhav Kumar Nepal, met the Maoist leadership in the Indian city of Lucknow. But nothing substantial emerged from their talks apart from a 'roadmap' that the CPN (UML) presented as the way out of the political impasse. The 'roadmap' failed to elicit much interest with the other parties since they maintained that the commonly agreed upon 18 points remained their goal. However, a major protest programme launched on 1 April, 2004, gained sudden momentum with various non-political organisations also joining in. Pitched battles took place daily between the police and protestors in downtown Kathmandu for over a month. Inflammatory slogans targeted explicitly at King Gyanendra and his son, Paras, became the staple on the streets, while student organisations became more and more vocal in their calls to convert Nepal into a republic. Even Thapa's own party, the RPP, took to the streets. Surya Bahadur Thapa had no choice but to resign.

Thapa's ouster provided yet another opportunity for the king and the opposition parties to work together. But despite the nearly month-long discussions the king held with various political leaders, Gyanendra remained unyielding. And, in a surprise move, 20 months after sacking him, the king reappointed Sher Bahadur Deuba.

As prime minister Deuba, who had been leading his own, albeit less confrontational, protests focusing on his reinstatement, declared that his priority would be to hold elections to the parliament by establishing peace through talks with the Maoists, and, like his predecessor, sought cooperation from other political parties. He was rewarded when the CPN (UML) quit the five-party opposition alliance shortly and joined the Deuba government, promising to hold talks with the Maoists soon. The Rastriya Prajatantra Party and the Nepal Sadbhavana Party also entered the coalition. In a sense, the situation had reverted back to the pre-October 2002 period with Deuba at the helm pushing for an election which seemed as improbable as back then.

No end in sight

The end of each ceasefire has seen a rise in the intensity of the fighting. Before November 2001, fewer than 2,000 people had lost their lives in the nearly five years since the insurgency had begun; in the following three and a half years, more than 8,000 have been killed. Even though fierce battles have been fought, there is general consensus that this is not a war winnable by either side. Both the Thapa and Deuba governments have time and again proclaimed that the door to negotiations is open, a sentiment repeatedly expressed by the Maoists as well. But given no signs of talks taking place, it all seems like nothing more than empty posturing.

Meanwhile, the government, along with the army, seems determined to weaken the Maoists substantially before forcing them back to the table. Part of its strategy was the announcement of an amnesty in December 2003 to entice Maoist cadres to surrender. The relatively generous terms of the promise of employment opportunities and cash rewards for those handing in weapons, however, did not actually lead to a flood of deserters from the Maoist ranks. The government also tried to put in place a scheme to raise village militias — euphemistically called 'volunteer security groups' and 'peace management committees' — in the hope that villagers armed with rudimentary weapons would be able to take on the Maoists. Concerns raised both domestically and internationally about armed groups accountable to no one running loose in the countryside seem to have interrupted the plans for now, but it goes to highlight the government's desperation to expand its sphere of influence beyond the security of the barracks.[41]

The Maoists, on the other hand, have been at pains to prove their democratic credentials, perhaps in a bid to win the support of the parliamentary parties. Baburam Bhattarai wrote soon after the second ceasefire ended that the CPN (Maoist) is 'committed to multi-party democracy and other prerequisites of basic political, economic, social and cultural transformation, which we have outlined in the political agenda submitted during the recent peace negotiations'.[42] Similarly, Prachanda has outlined his party's political agenda as:

Full sovereignty to the people; secular state; elected house of representatives as the highest representative body of the people; reorganisation of a unified national army; provision of national and regional autonomy along with rights of self-determination; provision of constitutional changes or refinement according to the wishes of the people; guarantee of multi-party competition, periodic elections, adult franchise, rule of law and fundamental rights including freedom of speech and press; provision of special rights for women and dalits (i.e. oppressed caste); etc.[43] (See Annexe VII for the full text of Prachanda's 'A Brief Introduction to the Policies of the CPN [Maoist]'.)

The main obstacle, of course, is the question of a constituent assembly. To mollify opponents to such an assembly, Bhattarai has clarified that 'different political forces would be free to put forward their separate agenda on varied questions like the fate of the monarchy, but should abide by the decision of the constituent assembly.'[44] But, as the International Crisis Group has noted, 'An open-ended process [such as the above] poses existential threats to each actor: the parties fear they could be squeezed out as armed Maoists and armed government forces turn back the democratic rights secured in 1990; the king fears a republic could be established and end his reign; and the Maoists, who have not participated in elections since the early 1990s, fear they could be far less popular than they imagine.'[45]

Given this undeniable reality, and recognising that the CPN (Maoist) was not a victorious power to insist on having everything their own way, perhaps the best bet the rebels had of forcing their agenda on the Nepali state without further bloodshed was to discuss the government's 'concept paper' laid before them before the talks collapsed. The Maoists took issue with the fact that the government proposal presupposed only amendments to the present constitution, which, according to Bhattarai, has granted only 'partial sovereignty' to the people. But since Bhattarai is also pragmatic enough to concede that 'if the particular historical condition and the prevailing balance of forces so demand, there can be common understanding on certain issues during and after the election [to a constituent assembly]',[46] an obvious reference to the continuance of the monarchy in some form or the other, that certainly leaves space for the palace, the parties and the Maoists to come to some sort of compromise on the idea of a constituent assembly.

The 'concept paper' itself is a rather appealing statement of principles and is one that could certainly be built on through negotiations, particularly since the government had stated that it could 'be revised, clarified and readjusted on the basis of mutual understanding'. Surya Bahadur Thapa failed to honour his public proclamations to implement it and neither have Sher Bahadur Deuba and his main alliance partner, the CPN (UML), shown any enthusiasm for it, which certainly casts suspicion on the ruling class's innate desire to deal with the 'root causes' attributed to the rise and spread of the Maoist insurgency. But by dismissing the proposal outright and focusing solely on the one intractable issue of a constituent assembly, the Maoists may have missed out on the opportunity to enforce the socio-economic reforms they have advocated. Unless, of course, one accepts the cynical observation that the Maoists 'are not fighting for minority rights, they are fighting for power'.[47]

The Maoists are now eager for some form of international involvement, preferably the UN, in seeking a resolution to the conflict. Given the failure of two ceasefires to make any headway towards an agreement, external mediation is certainly looking much more attractive. However, that is not likely to happen anytime soon given India's strong aversion to mediation by an outside party in Nepal,[48] and its insistence that the Maoist issue can be resolved internally.[49] And neither is the government likely to pursue the matter without India's concurrence.

As things stand, the country continues to suffer from a conflict that is dragging on in its ninth year, and there seems little possibility of the Maoists entering into talks with the government anytime soon. Beginning in January of 2004, the Maoists announced the formation of a number of 'autonomous region people's governments' as part of the CPN (Maoist)'s 'known policy of granting autonomous rule along with rights of self-determination to the oppressed nationalities and regions'.[50] While this may have of little more than symbolic value, it does challenge the legitimacy of the state in the eyes of the people who are being forced to pay taxes to these 'governments'. At the same time, schools in the countryside are now being forced to set aside a period every day for a course on 'people-oriented education', and groups of students and teachers are regularly abducted all over the country to be provided indoctrination in the Maoist ideology.

On the political front, Sher Bahadur Deuba may have cobbled together a coalition, but the remaining four parties are still a formidable force on the streets. Politics has come to a standstill in most parts of the country. The previous government had sought to fill the political vacuum in local governments through arbitrary nominations, but these appointees only proved fair game for the Maoists who assassinated a number of them.

The financial burden of the conflict has grown immense. Besides the opportunity cost of the regular strikes affecting, among others, industrial production and tourist arrivals, Nepal has had to bear a sharp increase in direct military expenses as well. Defence expenditure rose nearly three-fold from Rs 6 billion in 1999/2000 to Rs 15 billion in 2002/2003.[51] The expenditures indicate not only the cost of arming the military with modern weapons but also an increase in the number of personnel in the army and the armed police force. From a force of only 50,000 three years ago, the army has grown by 50 per cent to reach a strength of 75,000, while the newly formed armed police force is now 20,000-strong. If the insurgency continues more troops will be needed just to secure government installations and check Maoist activities. The army itself thinks it will require battalion-level forces in each of the country's 75 districts instead of the company-strength troops stationed in the majority of the districts.[52] Should the conflict continue, such a possibility is very likely, and it will be a price that an impoverished Nepal can little afford.

In an interview to *Time* magazine in early 2004, King Gyanendra said, 'I personally believe there is nothing that cannot be solved by dialogue and there is no issue that cannot be addressed within the ambit of the constitution.'[53] The position of the political parties so far seems to be in consonance with the king's views. However, his refusal to work with the constitutional forces may be driving them more and more to consider the option of Nepal as a republic. That is a situation that would suit the Maoists perfectly, but, unfortunately for the country, it would also make the present crisis even more intractable.

Photograph released by the army of the Maoist dead after the unsuccessful rebel attack on Khara, Rukum district. May 2002.

Annexes

Major political developments related to the CPN (Maoist) and the insurgency

1949	Communist Party of Nepal (CPN) established under leadership of Pushpa Lal Shrestha.
1952	CPN banned. Manmohan Adhikari replaces Pushpa Lal as general secretary of CPN.
1954	First Congress of CPN held. Adhikari confirmed as general secretary.
1956	Ban on CPN removed.
1957	Second Congress of CPN held. Keshar Jung Rayamajhi elected general secretary.
1959	Country's first general election held. CPN wins only four of 47 seats contested in 109-member parliament.
1960	King Mahendra takes over. CPN banned along with all political parties.
1961	CPN plenum held in Darbhanga, India.
1962	CPN splits into pro-Moscow Rayamajhi and pro-Beijing Tulsi Lal Amatya factions. Panchayat system introduced.
1968	Pushpa Lal breaks with Tulsi Lal and starts his own party.
1971	Failed uprising by group of young communists in Jhapa district.

1974	Mohan Bikram Singh, Nirmal Lama, and others organised 'Fourth Congress' of CPN and announce formation of CPN (Fourth Congress).
1978	CPN (Marxist-Leninist) established.
1980	National referendum held. Communist parties support multiparty system, but Panchayat system wins.
1983	CPN (Fourth Congress) splits into CPN (Fourth Congress) and CPN (Masal).
1985	CPN (Masal) splits into CPN (Masal) and CPN (Mashal).
1987	Pushpa Lal and Man Mohan's factions merge to form CPN (Marxist).
1989	Pushpa Kamal Dahal (Prachanda) takes over as secretary general of CPN (Mashal).
1990	Movement for the Restoration of Democracy. Communist parties take part in it as United Left Front and United National People's Movement. Fourth Congress and Mashal form CPN (Unity Centre) with Prachanda as general secretary.
1991	CPN (M) and CPN (ML) unite to form CPN (Unified Marxist-Leninist). After Masal decides to boycott elections, Baburam Bhattarai leads breakaway faction to join Unity Centre. United People's Front projected as Unity Centre's political wing, and wins nine seats. Nepali Congress forms majority government under Girija Prasad Koirala.
1994	Unity Centre and United People's Front splits into pro-Nirmal Lama and pro-Prachanda factions. Pro-United People's Front is led by Baburam Bhattarai. Latter boycotts November 1994 mid-term polls.

	CPN (UML) forms minority government under Manmohan Adhikari.
September 1995	Sher Bahadur Deuba of Nepali Congress forms coalition government with Rastriya Prajatantra Party (RPP) and Nepal Sadbhavana Party (NSP).
4 February 1996	Baburam Bhattarai present 40-point demand to Prime Minister Sher Bahadur Deuba, warning of armed uprising if ignored.
13 February 1996	'People's War' begins.
March 1997	Lokendra Bahadur Chand of RPP heads coalition government supported by CPN (UML).
October 1997	RPP splits and Surya Bahadur Thapa heads faction to form coalition government with Nepali Congress and NSP.
March 1998	CPN (UML) splits into CPN (UML) and CPN (ML). Girija Prasad Koirala takes over to lead minority government.
August 1998	CPN (ML) joins Koirala government.
December 1998	CPN (UML) replaces CPN (ML) in Koirala government. Coalition joined by NSP.
May 1999	Third general elections. Krishna Prasad Bhattarai heads majority Nepali Congress government.
December 1999	Government sets up High-Level Committee to Provide Suggestions to Solve the Maoist Problem under Sher Bahadur Deuba.
March 2000	Krishna Prasad Bhattarai ousted by Girija Prasad Koirala.
25 September 2000	Maoists overrun Dunai, headquarters of Dolpa district; the first such attack.
27 October 2000	One-on-one contact between government and Maoists as Deputy Prime Minister Ram

	Chandra Poudel meets Maoist central committee member, Rabindra Shrestha.
25 February 2001	Maoists announce new doctrine 'Prachanda Path' adopted at party's Second National Conference.
2-7 April 2001	In separate attacks in Rukumkot, Rukum, and Naumule, Dailekh, Maoists kill 70 policemen.
1 June 2001	Massacre in royal palace; King Birendra and entire family wiped out.
12 July 2001	Maoists abduct 69 police from Holeri, Rolpa. Army fails to move in.
19 July 2001	Girija Prasad Koirala resigns.
22 July 2001	Sher Bahadur Deuba elected prime minister. Declares ceasefire.
30 August 2001	First round of peace talks between government and Maoists.
14-15 September 2001	Second round of peace talks.
13 November 2001	Third round of peace talks held.
21 November 2001	Maoists signal dissatisfaction with peace talks; Deuba urges patience.
23 November 2001	Four-month-long ceasefire comes to an end with resumption of Maoist attacks.
26 November 2001	State of Emergency proclaimed. Fundamental rights curtailed and CPN (Maoists) declared 'terrorist organisation'.
21 February 2002	Parliament ratifies emergency.
4 April 2002	Parliament passes Terrorist and Disruptive Activities (Control and Punishment) Bill.
23 April 2002	Government announces bounties on heads of Maoist leaders ranging from Rs 1 million to Rs 5 million.
17 May 2002	Parliament summoned to endorse six-month extension of emergency.
22 May 2002	Prime Minister Sher Bahadur Deuba dis-

	solves parliament and calls for fresh elections in November.
23 May 2002	Deuba suspended from primary membership of Nepali Congress and three days later expelled.
8 July 2002	New budget announced security receives Rs 14.81 billion—44 per cent higher than previous year.
5 August 2002	Supreme Court endorses dissolution of parliament.
12 August 2002	Interpol issues Red Corner Notice against top Maoists leaders.
15 August 2002	Local bodies' term ends and government decides against extension.
27 August 2002	Emergency ends.
4 October 2002	Deuba recommends postponing elections. King Gyanendra sacks him, postpones elections indefinitely, and assumes executive authority.
11 October 2002	Lokendra Bahadur Chand appointed prime minister.
3 December 2002	Maoists announce formation of 'central dialogue team'
26 January 2003	Inspector General of the Armed Police Force, Krishna Mohan Shrestha together with wife and bodyguard shot dead in Kathmandu.
29 January 2003	Ceasefire declared.
2 February 2003	Maoists announce 'restructured' central dialogue team.
13 March 2003	22-point of conduct to be followed during the ceasefire agreed upon.
27 April 2003	First round of talks held between government and Maoists.
8 May 2003	Political parties begin agitation for resto-

	ration of parliament and formation of all-party government.
9 May 2003	Round II of peace talks held.
30 May 2003	Lokendra Bahadur Chand resigns.
4 June 2003	Surya Bahadur Thapa appointed prime minister.
17-19 August 2003	Round III of peace talks held. 19 Maoist supporters gunned down by the army in eastern Nepal on 17 August.
27 August 2003	Prachanda announces end of ceasefire.
1 April 2004	Political parties begin fresh round of agitation against king's 'retrogressive step' of October 2002.
7 May 2004	Surya Bahadur Thapa resigns.
2 June 2004	Sher Bahadur Deuba appointed prime minister. Deuba government joined by the CPN (UML), the RPP and the NSP.

The 14-point charter

The 14-point charter of demands presented to Prime Minister Girija Prasad Koirala by Nirmal Lama on behalf of the Communist Party of Nepal (Unity Centre) on 5 March, 1992.

1. Control prices of fertiliser, electricity, water, telephone and goods of daily necessity. Stop black marketeering, smuggling and corruption.

2. End congressisation of the administration, education, communications and other fields.

3. End government terror, killing, firing, suppression and hooliganism.

4. Abrogate unequal treaties, agreements and understandings, including the 1950 Treaty [with India], and cancel the understanding that hands over rivers to India.

5. Provide settlement to squatters and stop displacing them without providing alternate areas of settlement.

6. End the expulsion and suspension of employees. Re-appoint employees who were sacked during the last agitation.

7. Determine the wages of industrial and agricultural labourers. Make arrangements to provide work and food for the unemployed.

8. End injustice and exploitation of farmers. Fix a reasonable market price for agricultural products.

9. End commercialisation of the education sector and provide education and study materials at a reasonable price.

10. End discrimination against oppressed people and the Dalits. Provide equal opportunity in the media, including radio and TV, for all languages.

11. End all kinds of discrimination against women, including their sale in the market. End discrimination in the distribution of citizenship papers. Ensure that daughters have equal rights to property.

12. End discrimination towards people living in the tarai and remote areas.

13. Take action against the corrupt people of the Panchayat regime.

14. End the conspiracy between the king and reactionary forces, helped by the Congress government, in ending the gains of the People's Movement of 1990.

Source: Pancha Narayan Maharjan, 'Role of the Extra-Parliamentary Political Party in Multi-party Democracy: A Study of the CPN–Unity Centre'. Contributions to Nepalese Studies, *vol 20 no 2, 1993.*

The forty demands

The 40-point charter of demands and covering letter presented to Prime Minister Sher Bahadur Deuba by Dr Baburam Bhattarai on behalf of the United People's Front Nepal on 4 February, 1996.

4 February, 1996

Right Honourable Prime Minister
Prime Minister's Office, Singha Durbar, Kathmandu

Subject: Memorandum

Sir,

It has been six years since the autocratic monarchical partyless Panchayat system was ended by the 1990 People's Movement and a constitutional monarchical multiparty parliamentary system established. During this period state control has been exercised by the tripartite interim government, the single-party government of the Nepali Congress, the minority government of UML and the present Nepali Congress-RPP-Sadbhavana coalition. That, instead of making progress, the situation of the country and the people is going downhill is evident from the facts that Nepal has slid to being the second poorest country in the world; people living below the absolute poverty line has gone up to 71 per cent; the number of unemployed has reached more than 10 per cent while the number of people who are semi-employed or in disguised employment has crossed 60 per cent; the country is on the verge of bankruptcy due to soaring foreign loans and deficit trade; economic and cultural encroachment within the country by foreign, and especially Indian, expansionists is increasing by the day; the gap between the rich and the poor and between towns and villages is growing wider. On the other hand, parliamentary parties that have formed the government by various means have shown that they are more interested in remaining in power with the blessings of foreign imperialist and expansionist master than in the welfare of the country and the people. This is clear from their blindly adopting the so-called privatisation and liberalisation to fulfil the interests of all imperialists and from the recent 'national consensus' reached in handing over the rights over Nepal's water resources to Indian expansionists. Since 6 April, 1992, the United People's Front has been involved in various struggles to fulfil relevant demands related to nationalism, democracy and livelihood either on its own or with others. But rather than fulfil those demands, the governments formed at different times have violently suppressed the agitators and taken the lives of hundreds; the most recent example of this is the armed police operation in Rolpa a few months back. In this context, we would like to once again present to the current coalition government the demands related to nationalism, democracy and livelihood, many of which have been raised in the past and many which have become relevant in the present context.

Our demands:

Concerning nationality

1 All discriminatory treaties, including the 1950 Nepal-India Treaty, should be abrogated.

2 The so-called Integrated Mahakali Treaty concluded on 29 January 1996 should be repealed immediately, as it is designed to conceal the disastrous Tanakpur Treaty and allows Indian imperialist monopoly over Nepal's water resources.

3 The open border between Nepal and India should be

regulated, controlled and systematised. All vehicles with Indian licence plates should be banned from Nepal.

4 The Gurkha/Gorkha Recruitment Centres should be closed. Nepali citizens should be provided dignified employment in the country.

5 Nepali workers should be given priority in different sectors. A 'work permit' system should be strictly implemented if foreign workers are required in the country.

6 The domination of foreign capital in Nepali industries, business and finance should be stopped.

7 An appropriate customs policy should be devised and implemented so that economic development helps the nation become self-reliant.

8 The invasion of imperialist and colonial culture should be banned. Vulgar Hindi films, videos and magazines should be immediately outlawed.

9 The invasion of colonial and imperial elements in the name of NGOs and INGOs should be stopped.

Concerning people's democracy

10 A new Constitution should be drafted by representatives elected for the establishment of a people's democratic system.

11 All special privileges of the king and the royal family should be abolished.

12 The army, the police and the bureaucracy should be completely under people's control.

13 All repressive acts, including the Security Act, should be repealed.

14 Everyone arrested extra-judicially for political reasons or revenge in Rukum, Rolpa, Jajarkot, Gorkha, Kavre, Sindhupalchowk, Sindhuli, Dhanusa, Ramechhap, and so on, should be immediately released. All false cases should be immediately withdrawn.

15 The operation of armed police, repression and State-sponsored terror should be immediately stopped.

16 The whereabouts of citizens who disappeared in police custody at different times, namely Dilip Chaudhary, Bhuwan Thapa Magar, Prabhakar Subedi and others, should be investigated and those responsible brought to justice. The families of victims should be duly compensated.

17 All those killed during the People's Movement should be declared martyrs. The families of the martyrs and those injured and deformed should be duly compensated, and the murderers brought to justice.

18 Nepal should be declared a secular nation.

19 Patriarchal exploitation and discrimination against women should be stopped. Daughters should be allowed access to paternal property.

20 All racial exploitation and suppression should be stopped. Where ethnic communities are in the majority, they should be allowed to form their own autonomous governments.

21 Discrimination against downtrodden and backward people should be stopped. The system of untouchability should be eliminated.

22 All languages and dialects should be given equal opportunities to prosper. The right to education in the mother tongue up to higher levels should be guaranteed.

23 The right to expression and freedom of press and publication should be guaranteed. The government mass media should be completely autonomous.

24 Academic and professional freedom of scholars, writers, artists and cultural workers should be guaranteed.

25 Regional discrimination between the hills and the tarai should be eliminated. Backward areas should be given regional autonomy. Rural and urban areas should be treated at par.

26 Local bodies should be empowered and appropriately equipped.

Concerning livelihood

27 Land should belong to 'tenants'. Land under the control of the feudal system should be confiscated and distributed to the landless and the homeless.

28 The property of middlemen and comprador capitalists should be confiscated and nationalised. Capital lying unproductive should be invested to promote industrialisation.

29 Employment should be guaranteed for all. Until such time as employment can be arranged, an unemployment allowance should be provided.

30 A minimum wage for workers in industries, agriculture and so on should be fixed and strictly implemented.

31 The homeless should be rehabilitated. No one should be relocated until alternative infrastructure is guaranteed.

32 Poor farmers should be exempt from loan repayments. Loans taken by small farmers from the Agricultural Development Bank should be written off. Appropriate provisions should be made to provide loans for small farmers.

33 Fertiliser and seed should be easily available and at a cheap rate. Farmers should be provided with appropriate prices and markets for their produce.

34 People in flood- and drought-affected areas should be provided with appropriate relief materials.

35 Free and scientific health services and education should be available to all. The commercialisation of education should be stopped.

36 Inflation should be checked. Wages should be increased proportionate to inflation. Essential goods should be cheaply and easily available to everyone.

37 Drinking water, roads and electricity should be provided to all villagers.

38 Domestic and cottage industries should be protected and promoted.

39 Corruption, smuggling, black marketeering, bribery, and the practices of middlemen and so on should be eliminated.

40 Orphans, the disabled, the elderly and children should be duly honoured and protected.

We would like to request the present coalition government to immediately initiate steps to fulfil these demands which are inextricably linked with the Nepali nation and the life of the people. If there are no positive indications towards this from the government by 17 February 1996, we would like to inform you that we will be forced to adopt the path of armed struggle against the existing state power.

Thank you.

Dr Baburam Bhattarai
Chairman
Central Committee, United People's Front, Nepal

Source: Nepalma Janayuddha, *Nepal Rastriya Buddhijibi Sangathan, Kathmandu, 2058 BS.*

Maoist agenda at second round of talks of 2001 ceasefire
(14-15 September 2001)

Principal political questions

1. The present constitution that is acting as an obstacle to finding a solution to the problems faced by the country and the people should be scrapped and the people given the right to frame a new constitution.

2. In order to introduce a new system the present parliament and government should be dissolved and an interim government formed.

3. Given the context that the traditional monarchy has come to an end and people have come to believe in the birth of a republic, steps should be taken to institutionalise the development of a republic.

Contemporary issues relevant to the people

1. All unequal treaties such as the 1950 Nepal-India treaty and the Integrated Mahakali Treaty should be scrapped, Indian troops should be removed from Kalapani and border

encroachments halted.

2. The open border between Nepal and India should be controlled and regulated.

3. A system of work permit should be introduced.

Proposals to create a conducive atmosphere at the talks

1. Reveal the whereabouts of Dandapani Neupane and others who have disappeared from police custody before and after the people's war began.

2. All prisoners, including CPN (Maoist) central committee member Matrika Yadav, should be released immediately.

3. All laws, including the Armed Police Force Act, targeted against the People's War, should be repealed.

4. The anti-people Integrated Internal Development and Security Programme that is being sought to be implemented should be rolled back.

5. The Royal Nepal Army that is terrorising the people on various pretexts should be sent back to the barracks.

Source: Kantipur, *15 September, 2001*

Summary of the CPN (Maoist) proposal presented for consideration during 2003 ceasefire
(27 April, 2003)

A. Preamble

Having ruled the country continuously for over 225 years, it is obvious that the old state is undergoing a serious crisis due to its internal and external retrogressive class relations. As a result of this, the inherent class, ethnic, regional and gender contradictions are looking for a progressive (forward-looking) solution and it is clear that it is necessary to re-structure the state in a progressive manner. Although the democratic movements of 1950-51 and 1990 tried to solve this crisis partially, those efforts were not adequate to solve the fundamental problems pertaining to nationality, democracy and people's daily life and this has been proved by the events of the last 52 years as well as the last 12 years in particular. Therefore, the oppressed classes, ethnicities, regions, sex and communities raised the flag of armed rebellion on 13 February 1996 under the leadership of CPN (Maoist) for total political, economic, social and cultural change and the formation of a progressive state to institutionalise the transformation. It is well known that the old state, facing a crisis due to seven years of civil war, and the rising new state have reached a stage of strategic equilibrium, and taking into account the distinct geo-political situation of the country, both parties agreed to a ceasefire in 29 January 2003 and entered into the process of dialogue, realising that it is appropriate to seek a peaceful and progressive political solution immediately. In this context, the official dialogue team of the CPN (Maoist) has proposed the following brief working list to find a progressive political solution through dialogue and which can be elaborated further and revised at the negotiating talks table.

B. Goals and objectives of dialogue

The goals and objectives of the dialogue between representatives of the old state and the new state should be as follows:

1. To end the present state of conflict through a progressive political solution and establish lasting peace in the country.
2. To eliminate existing class, racial, regional, sexual and other discriminations through political, economic and cultural changes. Resolve problems related to nationality, democracy and people's livelihood and create a democratic Nepal.
3. To establish a new, strong and people-oriented unity and defend national independence and sovereignty by embracing the integral, interdependent and inter-related elements of democracy and nationality.
4. To ensure the wide-ranging human and civic rights of everyone, especially minorities and underprivileged groups, and provide suitable compensation and rehabilitation to the victims of the civil war.

C. Implementation of ceasefire and code of conduct, and creating a conducive environment for dialogue

In the course of the seven-year-long people's war, control over most of the rural areas has been taken over by the People's Liberation Army, while the capital, big towns and district headquarters have remained in the control of the Royal Nepalese Army. It is well known that recognising this ground reality and based on the understanding that this status quo would be maintained and that neither party would launch armed invasions in the other's area, a ceasefire was declared on 29 January 2003 and a 22-point code of conduct agreed upon on 13 March 2003. In addition, only by taking immediate and effective steps to reveal the whereabouts of and release individuals captured or disappeared in the course of the war by both the parties and by repealing black laws against humanity like the Terrorist and Destructive Activities (Control and Punishment) Act 2058 and by withdrawing false cases can a conducive and credible environment for dialogue be created. In order to achieve this, the following has to be undertaken within a definite time frame.

1. The status of all prisoners of war, including CPN (Maoist) central committee member, Dandapani Neupane, disappeared by the police and the army, has to be made public by 15 May 2003.

2. All prisoners of war, including alternative politbureau member Rabindra Shrestha and alternative central committee members Bamdev Chettri and Mumaram Khanal, in army custody and in jail have to be released within 15 days.

3. All false cases have to be withdrawn and prisoners of conscience released within 15 days.

4. The so-called Terrorist and Destructive Activities (Control and Punishment) Act 2058 has to be immediately repealed.

5. The royal army has to be sent back to the barracks within a week and search and house arrests of ordinary people by the royal army has to end immediately.

6. In order to ensure that the code of conduct is adhered to and to monitor and investigate the status of the disappeared and of prisoners, a committee with full authority and comprising of representatives from national and international human rights organisations, major professional organisations and civil society has to be formed.

D. Dialogue process and time frame

In order to make the dialogue process transparent and result oriented, the following has to be done.

1. In order to make the dialogue transparent and [to create a] conducive [environment], a mutually agreed upon team of facilitators consisting of impartial and respected individuals has to be formed and this team has to involved in all phases of formal talks from the very beginning.

2. The facilitators have to set the date and venue of the talks with the consent of both parties.

3. Since the major issue of the present conflict is the question of the state, the political agenda has to be given priority in the talks and other matters can be dealt with gradually.

4. Since it is not only inappropriate but also risky to continue indefinitely with the present state of extreme flux in the country's political situation, efforts have to be made to reach a meaningful conclusion to the talks at the earliest.

E. The agenda at the talks

1. *Fundamental political agenda*

Since the overarching problem is the question of the state or politics, the main agenda of the talks must be political and it should receive the main focus. Given that a progressive state system and a constitution defining such a state have become necessary, and recognising the ground reality that the constitution drafted in 1990 following the People's Movement of 1990 is now all but dead and the country is in a situation without a constitution, the main agenda of the talks should be the process of drawing up a new constitution and the fundamental tenets of a new constitution. Although the 1990 constitution has enshrined some positive democratic issues (such as democratic competition, periodic elections, rule of law, freedom of speech and press), since the experience of the last 12 years has proved that it contained some major flaws and deficiencies (such as the so-called 'irrevocable' issues, the contradiction between sovereignty and state power, the disregard for 'true democracy' for oppressed classes, ethnic groups, regions, sex, etc, within the British 'formal democracy'), the new constitution has to be definitely more progressive than this. It is clear that in the present context of a new political power equation brought about by people's awareness of the 21st century and the seven years of civil war, the retrogressive idea of reverting to the pre-1990 system and the fixation of remaining wedded to the achievements of 1990 cannot fulfill the new requirements of the people or resolve the present crisis. That is why the process or procedure of drawing up the new constitution and its minimum progressive substance must be the following:

a. The process or procedure for the formulation of a new constitution

i.   A broad roundtable conference has to be organised with the concurrence of the revolutionary force and the country's major political forces and this should include democratic, patriotic and leftist forces which have a proved popular base.

ii. The roundtable conference has to formulate an interim constitution, reflecting the new power equation but without curtailing the democratic rights enshrined in the 1990 constitution, and an interim government has to be formed under the leadership of the revolutionary force.

iii. The interim government will hold elections to a constituent assembly which will have representation from different classes, caste/ethnic groups, regions, sex and communities, and the constituent assembly will draw up and promulgate a new constitution.

b. The minimum substance of the new constitution

i.   The people should be fully sovereign and state power has to be solely in the hands of people.

ii. A broad participatory people's parliament will be formed with representation from all classes, caste/ethnic groups, dalits, women, language, religion, region and noted personalities. All the bodies of the state will be accountable to this parliament. The government will also have proper representation of all groups.

iii. All provisions of the constitution will be amendable through either a two-third majority of parliament or a referendum.

iv. Suitable structural changes should be made to create a united national army by combining the Royal Army and the People's Liberation Army and such a national army has to be placed under the people's elected representatives.

v.   Universally accepted democratic and civic rights such as multiparty competition, periodic elections, universal franchise, rule of law, freedom of speech and press, and fundamental and human rights have to be guaranteed.

vi. All the country's oppressed caste/ethnic groups, madhesi community and marginalised regions have to be guaranteed the right to self-determination and to ethnic and regional autonomy.

vii. The country has to be made completely secular.

viii. Education, health and employment have to be made part of people's fundamental rights, and basic education and health services have to be provided to everyone free of cost and made easily accessible.

ix. New land relations have to be established on the basis of 'land to the tiller' and land distributed fairly and managed properly. A self-dependent national industrial policy has to be formulated and a policy to protect national capital and resources has to be followed.

x. All discriminatory treaties, including the 1950 Indo-Nepal treaty, have to be abrogated and an independent foreign policy based on panchsheel and nonalignment has to be followed in maintaining relations with others. All treaties and agreements with foreign countries have to be endorsed by a two-third majority of parliament.

c. It is our understanding that all political forces that seek a progressive political solution to the present crisis have to reach an agreement and understanding on the above minimum substance for a new, progressive constitution. But since a constituent assembly will formulate a new constitution without any conditions attached, it is inappropriate theoretically as well as practically to lay out all its features and provisions. It is obvious that the monarchy and other political forces should go to the people with their views and beliefs on the above minimum substance and let the people make the ultimate decision.

2. National and economic/social questions

i. All agreements, military assistance and presence and activities of external armed forces that have been resorted to in the name of counter-terrorism and which affect the nation gravely and prove counter-productive to the peace talks should immediately put to an end.

ii. The open Nepal-India border has to be controlled and regulated. All kinds of infiltrations and incursions along the border region have to be controlled. A work permit system has to be introduced for foreigners.

iii. The national blot of Gurkha recruitment centres has to be ended and honourable employment provided to Nepalis within the country itself.

iv. Foreign monopoly in the field of industry, commerce and finance has to be ended. National industries and business people have to be protected. The country should be made free of foreign loans within a given time frame.

v. Foreign infiltration and subversion in the name of NGOs/INGOs have to be stopped. Conditions imposed and to be imposed by international financial organisations that go against the country's interests have to be invalidated and declared unacceptable.

vi. An integrated national water policy has to be formulated to make use of the country's vast water resources. By according primacy to small and medium hydropower projects, the entire country has to be electrified within a given time frame.

vii. Landless and poor farmers have to be freed from all kinds of loans and employment has to be guaranteed.

viii. All bonded labourers have to be freed and employment and housing provided. Proper housing has to be provided to the landless.

ix. Fertilisers, seeds and other agricultural goods have to be made readily available and at a cheap price and proper irrigation has to be provided. Agricultural produce has to receive a proper price and markets provided accordingly.

x. The periodic price hike on petroleum products and other daily necessities has to be controlled. The wages of labourers and pay scales of employees have to be increased in proportion to price hikes.

xi. A proper mechanism has to be set up to immediately punish the corrupt, smugglers, middlemen and profiteers.

xii. A national and scientific education system has to be introduced. Education has to be made employment-oriented. The privatisation and commercialisation of education has to be stopped immediately.

xiii. Free health services have to be made easily available, especially in rural and other areas.

xiv. The rights of the blind, disabled, elderly, helpless and children have to be protected and special arrangements made for their care.

xv. All kinds of exploitation of women have to be stopped and women given equal rights in all areas, including right to parental property. Trafficking in women has to be stopped with firmness.

xvi. End all forms of oppression against dalits, including untouchability, and grant them complete equal rights.

xvii. A forty-hour week and provision of a minimum wage has to be instituted for workers, and it should be strictly implemented. Labourers have to be guaranteed involvement in the management of industries.

xviii. For the all-round development of the youth, concrete policies have to be formulated and implemented in stages.

xix. The academic freedom and professional protection of litterateurs, cultural artistes, intellectuals, doctors, lawyers, journalists, writers, engineers, teachers and so on have to be guaranteed in order to motivate them towards the service of the country and the people.

xx. The import and distribution of obscene films, videos and magazines have to be stopped in order to prevent retrogressive foreign cultural pollution and invasion.

xxi. A special plan to develop the infrastructure needed for drinking water, roads, bridges, electricity, etc, has to be made and implemented actively. A national plan for a balanced development that will eliminate the existing imbalances between villages and towns and various geographic regions has to be implemented.

xxii. The protection of the rights of Nepalis working abroad has to be guaranteed.

xxiii. Individuals who have died for the cause of the country and the liberation of the people in various people's movement as well as the people's war have to be declared martyrs and strict action taken against the guilty.

xiv. The just demands raised by the people and their organisations from all levels have to be fulfilled immediately.

3. Matters related to human rights and immediate compensation and rehabilitation

i.   In order to conduct an impartial investigation of the abuse of human rights in the course of the civil war, a high-level commission with full authority has to be formed with representatives from the human rights community and those responsible for human rights violations have to be punished.

ii. All the families of the martyrs have to be provided immediate relief and be suitably compensated.

iii. All the people wounded in the course of the civil war have to be provided with free treatment.

iv. All the people displaced by the war have to be re-settled either in their original homes or at a suitable alternative site.

F. Implementation and Monitoring

All matters agreed upon by the two sides have to be implemented with a given time frame and an impartial monitoring team formed to monitor the implementation.

27 April, 2003

Baburam Bhattarai
Coordinator, Dialogue Team
CPN (Maoist)

Source: www.cpnm.org

Government's agenda of reforms presented at the third round of talks with the CPN (Maoist) in response to the Maoist proposal of April 27.
(17 August, 2003)

Background

1. Gradual and continuous reform in substance, structure and values of the state authority together with the process of social development is a natural phenomenon. Historical developments and events in modern Nepal after the unification of the kingdom is also a testimony to these realities. The latest set of reforms and changes in the process were established by the People's Movement of 1990. Sovereignty vested in the people, constitutional monarchy and multiparty democracy are the fundamental achievements of 1990.

   The Constitution of the Kingdom of Nepal was formed in the course of institutionalising the political reforms of 1990. In spite of certain inconsistencies and obstacles in the implementation of some constitutional provisions, the constitution is alive and functional to date as an excellent document in view of democratic values and norms.

2. After the change of 1990, the state certainly has made important achievements in various areas. However, there has not been expected success in the process of achieving the objective of

political, economic and social transformation in accordance with the expectations of the people for change. After the re-establishment of multiparty democracy in the country, a big wave of hope and expectation had arisen among the people on the possibilities of economic and social progress. There was a belief among the people that the economic and social differences and traditions of exploitation institutionalised for centuries would fade out in the democratic environment and new aspects of progress would be open to indigenous people, ethnic groups and various cultural groups. But these potentialities could not be converted into reality during the course of the new exercise in democracy. A democratic constitution was formed. Structures were ready. General elections were held. But the fruit of democracy could not reach all the people in a manner to induce the desired change in the people's lifestyles in real terms. Though expectations against centuries of exploitation, discrimination, inequalities and deprivation in society could have an opportunity to be articulated in the democratic environment, these problems could not find an appropriate solution. Democracy was confined almost to formality alone.

The formation of governments through elections, constitutional checks and balances, and socio-economic transformations are factors mandatory for a democracy. These factors are complementary to each other. In the course of our democratic exercise, there could not be coherence and inter-relationship between electoral democracy, constitutional checks and balances and efforts at socio-economic transformation. As a result, many distortions and anomalies were created.

3. It is well known that there had been a recurring voicing of the need to introduce broad and forward-looking reforms in the existing constitutional system even from within constitutional forces for the creation of an environment in which the fruit of democracy could be shared by all Nepalis, correcting the mistakes and weaknesses in the way of conducting the business of the state in the past 13 years.

4. In the meantime, there has also been a fundamental change in the balance of equation between the political forces. There has been a basic change in the structure and balance of political power that had existed in 1990 and new political forces have been seen significantly in national politics.

Given the above background, it is necessary to bring about forward-looking changes in the state system in accordance with the popular will. Under the concept of the principle of sovereignty being vested in the people, multiparty electoral democracy, constitutional checks and balances, and forward-looking socio-economic transformation should be the mandatory factors of reforms in the state system.

Accepting the above-mentioned realities, an effort has been made to present a summary of the framework of reforms in the state system, rather than focusing only on the issues raised by the Maoists.

Objectives

The following should be the objectives of the forward-looking reforms in the existing state system:

a. Building a political system that can accommodate and ensure participation of the Nepali people.

b. Creating equal opportunities for self-development of all Nepalis.

c. Developing a political system on the basis of contemporary balance among the political forces.

d. Creating an egalitarian society bringing an end to all kinds of inequalities, discrimination and exploitation.

Mandatory bases

Sovereignty vested in the people, constitutional monarchy, multiparty democracy, and preservation of and promotion of the national integrity and unity shall remain the mandatory bases for the future course of development of the nation-state system of Nepal.

Fundamental policies and principles of forward-looking reforms

1. Promoting the national pride and identity of Nepal, preserving independence, national unity and territorial integrity of the country, and preventing a divisive tendency in the country.

2. Developing Nepal as a capable and developed nation-state by achieving the objective of social upliftment and modernisation.

3. Creating equal opportunity for self-development of all Nepalis by eliminating all kinds of discrimination on the basis of caste, gender, religion, and race.
4. Providing the benefits of the welfare state through a just and equitable system in all walks of national life.
5. Strengthening the national economy by adopting open market-oriented·economic policies.
6. Developing effective local autonomous governance system by increasing the participation and reach of the people in the governance system.

Main aspects of the forward-looking changes

The following shall be the main aspects of the forward-looking changes in the nation state system:

1. In accordance with the values that the people are the decision-makers in the conduct of the business of the state, the sovereignty of the nation should be vested in the people. A system for conducting the business of the state in accordance with popular will through representatives responsible to the people should be guaranteed. The Constitution should clearly define the procedure of the practice of sovereignty by the people.
2. The role and importance of the Nepali monarchy is irreplaceable for the continuity and preservation of the sanctity of national independence and territorial integrity of the country by uniting all Nepali people comprising of various languages, religions, ethnic groups and cultures. Therefore, the institution of monarchy shall continue to remain as a symbol of Nepali nationality and national unity. The changes of 1990 and the Constitution of the Kingdom of Nepal (1990) have already defined the position and esteem of the monarchy. The system of constitutional monarchy should be developed according to these very norms.
3. The essence of democracy is people's rule. In other words, democracy is the system of conducting the affairs of the state by the people through their representatives. As political parties established on the basis of various ideologies are the carriers of popular expectations and will, there is no dispute that a system based on competitive multiparty

democracy is the best system of governance. Therefore:

a. Multiparty democracy should continue to remain the backbone of the future state system of Nepal.

b. A constitutional guarantee should be put in place for making it impossible to ban the existence and activities of the political parties.

c. Appropriate legal bases should be prepared to make the structure, programmes and financial sources of the political parties continuously transparent, democratic and respectable.

4. The legitimate source of the conduct of business of the state is the popular verdict expressed by people through elections. Past experience has proved that distortions and anomalies can arise if the elections are not free and fair. Besides, the wider and more representative the verdict expressed elections in the parliament, the broader will be the basis of the legitimacy of the conduct of the business of state. Therefore:

a. The esteem, autonomy, jurisdiction and authority of the Election Commission should be strengthened so as to preserve free and fair elections.

b. In view of past experience, a system of a neutral caretaker government should be put in place three months before the polls to ensure free and fair elections.

c. Except in a few sectors, a system of proportional representation should be introduced in order to the create a basis for the expression of a broader popular will in a people-oriented manner in major elections.

5. The concept of a popularly elected government is an essential factor of democracy. A constitutional provision of vigilance should be maintained in order to prevent difficulties and breaks in the system of governance through popularly elected representatives. As the prime minister is the executive chief of the state in the parliamentary system the prime ministerial system should be strengthened in the reform of the state system giving continuity to the respectability and effectiveness of the office of the prime minister.

The inconsistency and discrepancy seen in the

authority of the prime minister in issues including the dissolution of the House of Representatives should be resolved. Besides, a provision for appointing ministers, including from outside the parliament, should be made in order to improve the effectiveness of the Council of Ministers.

6. Political parties are the carriers of the people's feelings and expectations and parliament is the place to reflect that. The parliament is the representative institution of the sovereign people and the people exercise the sovereignty vested in them through the parliament. As the effectiveness of the parliament shall ensure the sovereignty of the people, the following aspects should be taken care of in the course of making the parliament more effective:

   a. The structure and composition of the upper house should be totally reformed to include the representation of persons of high repute from various walks of life and the representation of ethnic groups, indigenous people and Dalits in proportion to their population.

   b. The effectiveness of both the houses should be improved and the system of government being responsible towards the parliament should be strengthened.

   c. The representation of at least 25 per cent women in both houses should be ensured.

7. In order to increase the reach of the people in the system of governance and to increase their participation, it is essential to strengthen the system of local self-governance. The closer the system of governance is brought to the people, the more effective is the state. Keeping in view this reality:

   a. The scope and authority of local bodies should be constitutionally ensured in accordance with the concept of local self-governance.

   b. There should be a complete revamping of the existing structure, regional divisions and number of local bodies in view of the ethnic composition, state of development and geographical conditions.

   c. Taking into account the economic potential, population and geographical conditions, new local governance structures should be created at the regional levels.

8. As the popular verdict is the main basis of the conduct of the business of the state and people are the main source of power, there should be a provision to allow a national referendum on decisions of the parliament on policy issues of national importance.

9. It is the responsibility of the state to create opportunities for every Nepali for self-development in a democratic environment. For that:
   a. The pluralistic society should be strengthened preserving and promoting all religions, ethnic groups, communities, languages and their beliefs. Local bodies should be given the option to use national languages as their second working language.
   b. A constitutional guarantee should be provided for the freedom of expression and organisation according to one's faith and beliefs in an unhindered manner.
   c. A situation should be created for the full commitment of the implementation of the rule of law in all aspects of national life.
   d. There should be a guarantee to ensure human rights, fundamental rights and humanitarian values even in difficult circumstances.

10. It is not possible to easily end the situation of ethnic and gender discrimination, exploitation and inequalities prevailing in Nepali society for centuries. The treatment of an extraordinary problem can only be found in extraordinary remedies. Therefore:
   a. For a certain period of time a system of reservations for indigenous, ethnic and Dalit people in representative institutions, education, health, administrative services and other employment sectors should be provided until they reach the national average on the basis of the Human Development Index.
   b. In order to remove all kinds of discrimination against women, at least 25 per cent of seats in all representative institutions should be reserved for women, and special reservations for them should be constitutionally ensured in education, health, administration and

other employment sectors.

c.   There should be an appropriate constitutional provision for a lasting resolution to the problem of citizenship.

11. Democracy cannot succeed without economic development and prosperity. Therefore, in the process of achieving economic development:

a.   The state should adopt a policy of free and liberal market-oriented economy in order to crate an environment for equal opportunity for each Nepali to benefit from the fruit of economic development in a democratic environment, and to discourage monopolistic tendencies.

b.   In order to end dual ownership over land and to make available land to the landless and marginal farmers and to increase the productivity of the land, a people-oriented land reforms policy should be implemented.

c.   The state should ensure raising the living standard of the people living under the poverty line on a time-bound basis and should fulfil their basic needs such as education, water supply, health and housing and provide social security for all.

d.   In order to end the regional disparity in development, the concept of equitable and balanced regional development should be practically implemented.

12. Separation of power and checks and balances are important characteristics of the modern state system. Taking these principles as the basis:

a.   The effectiveness of the related state organs should be improved through clear delineation of the authority and scope of the various organs of the state.

b.   Timely reforms should be made to improve the effectiveness of the judiciary.

c.   The role of the parliament should be established in appointments to constitutional bodies and a definite policy and standard should be developed for such appointments. The appointment process should be made transparent.

d.   Constitutional bodies should be given greater autonomy and authority.

13. Promotion of the ultimate national interest should be the guiding principle of the foreign policy of Nepal. The objective of the foreign policy should be to strengthen friendly relations with all countries of the world and to gradually institutionalise Nepal's aspirations for peace, while remaining committed to the principles of non-alignment, Panchasheel and the United Nations Charter.

Consensus on economic and social issues

Apart from the issues mentioned above, His Majesty's Government has no disagreement in principle regarding most of the social and economic issues presented by the Communist Party of Nepal (Maoist), which may be useful guidelines for future governments.

Method and process for implementation of the consensus

The main objective of talks is to arrive at a consensus on the objectives, policies and works of reforms and to decide the method and process of implementation. As it will be easier to arrive at a consensus on the method and process after a consensus is reached on the issue of reforms, it will be appropriate to concentrate the discussion on the issue of reforms. The method and process of reforms proposed by His Majesty's Government shall be implemented in the following stages:

Step A. Creating consensus between the government and the rebel side through negotiations on the objectives, policies and programmes of reforms.

Step B. Organising a roundtable conference with the participation including of the political parties in order to establish the agreement reached as the document of national consensus.

Step C. Formation of an interim electoral government including the rebel side as well.

Step D. Holding of the election to the House of Representatives.

Step E. Amending the constitution in accordance with the document of national consensus.

Objectives achievable from within the Constitution

After studying and analysing the proposals and agenda presented by the CPN (Maoist), the subjects mentioned in the proposals seem to be achievable through the amendment and rewriting of the Constitution of the Kingdom of Nepal (1991). However, His Majesty's Government is ready to discuss all subjects and alternatives with an open heart.

His Majesty's Government believes that a broader understanding can be reached during the process of negotiations on all aspects outlined in the preliminary concept papers presented by both sides, examining the merits and demerits of the issues.

Revisions of the concept
The issues mentioned in this concept paper on the forward-looking reforms presented by His Majesty's Government can be revised, clarified and readjusted on the basis of mutual understanding.

Ongoing implementation
As several issues agreed by the two sides can be implemented through the executive decision of the government, it will be appropriate to gradually implement such agreements by the government simultaneously.

Agenda setting and negotiations process

1. Considering the seriousness and sensitivity of the situation and the need to quickly resolve the existing uncertainly and confusion, His Majesty's Government is of the view that the peace negotiations should be concluded as soon as possible.
2. On the basis of this concept paper presented by His Majesty's Government and the proposal and agenda presented by the CPN (Maoist), the subject and agenda of the negotiations should be prepared in mutual agreement. The meetings for negotiations should be taken forward concentrating on the pre-determined agenda.
3. The discussions should be started giving priority to the political agenda as well as social, economic and humanitarian subjects. It is especially essential to give high priority to work related to the rehabilitation of the victims and people displaced during the 'people's war'.

Provisions for handing over arms
His Majesty's Government is fully convinced that a solution to the problem can be sought through peace negotiations if both sides are

fully committed to making sincere efforts. In order to create an environment for the implementation of the outcomes of the negotiations during the course of bringing the negotiations to a conclusion, the issue of handing over of the arms and ammunition lying with the Maoist should be one of the important items of the agenda of the negotiations.

Rehabilitation of victims and reconstruction of infrastructure

His Majesty's Government is of the view that high priority should be given to work related to the rehabilitation of the people displaced, disabled and victimised for various reasons during the 'people's war'. The reconstruction of damaged infrastructure because of the 'people's war' should also be included in the agenda of the talks.

Issues to be addressed for the success of negotiations

Realising that the tendency of imposing one's own perception and strategic interests against the other in the name of 'ground reality' can create difficult situation in negotiations, His Majesty's Government believes that it will be appropriate not to indulge in that kind of dispute. Instead, it is essential that both sides should be engaged in creating an environment of mutual trust and confidence, which is an essential factor for the success of negotiations. In this regard, His Majesty's Government wants to draw attention to the following subjects:

a. Both sides should sincerely implement and observe the agreed Code of Conduct to manage the ceasefire.
b. The Monitoring Committee established to monitor the Code of Conduct should be activated immediately. In case any dispute is seen in the implementation of the Code of Conduct, the responsibility for resolving that should be given to the Monitoring Committee.
c. In case of any dispute or difficulty in the implementation of the Code of Conduct, efforts should be made to resolve the issue through mutual consultations before making it an issue of public debate.
d. An environment should be created for the unhindered activities of the political parties and that of the government in all parts of the country.

Commitment not to break the ceasefire

Realising the fact that the nation will have to bear a big loss and the serious impact it will have on the very essence of democracy and nationality if there is a relapse to the situation of killings, violence and terror in the country due to the end of a ceasefire, both sides should make sincere efforts to seek resolution through peaceful negotiations. His Majesty's Government proposes that a commitment should be made from both sides for not breaking the ceasefire and for giving continuity to the negotiations under any circumstances, respecting the desire of the Nepali people for peace.

Source: The Rising Nepal, *18 August, 2003*

A brief introduction to the policies of the CPN (Maoist)

—Prachanda
Chairman, CPN (Maoist)
(12 January, 2004)

Ideology and ultimate goal

It is well known that the guiding principle of the CPN (Maoist), the political representative of the Nepalese proletariat, is Marxism-Leninism-Maoism (MLM), and its ultimate goal is socialism and communism. While firmly adhering to its principles and goals the Party has been developing its policies in a flexible manner on the basis of [a] concrete analysis of concrete conditions. The Party has been particularly stressing on [the] creative application and development of the principles with ceaseless struggles against dogmatism and empiricism in the realm of ideology. According to this scientific understanding, the Party has synthesised 'Prachanda Path' as a particular set of ideas of its own in the course of providing leadership to the anti-feudal and anti-imperialist democratic revolution of the Nepalese people. Prachanda Path has provided a new dimension of ingenuity and creativity to the communist movement with the proposed new idea of 'Development of Democracy in the 21st Century'. The CPN (Maoist) may not be cognigible [cognisable?] to those who fail to understand this ingenuity and creativity of the ideas and view it from the old perspective.

Political strategy

On the basis of [the] study of history of the Nepalese society and its economic, political and cultural specificities the Party has concluded that feudal production relations and imperialist exploitation and interventions are the main obstacles to the progress of Nepal. The Party is firm in its conviction that the development process of the productive forces would take a forward course and the progress of the Nepalese society would be ensured only when it is freed from the feudal production relations. Hence, the basic political strategy of the Party is to free the Nepalese society from feudalism and imperialism through the bourgeois democratic revolution. The military strategy of People's War (PW) is objectively based on the goal of achieving this political strategy.

Political tactics or immediate policy

In the light of the particularity of the total international situation and the prevailing balance of power within the country, the Party has been pursuing a very flexible political tactics [sic]. A roundtable conference, an interim government and election to a Constituent Assembly are the minimum political tactics proposed by the Party in this context. Only a new constitution made by a Constituent Assembly can in reality institutionalise the sovereign rights of the Nepalese people. There can be no reason for anybody to disagree with this supreme modality of democracy to let the Nepalese people determine their own destiny and future.

On the basis of this flexible tactical line the Party entered into negotiations with the old regime twice. However, both the times it was proved that the old regime was not in favour of a political solution but was in [on] the path of conspiracy and regression. Rejection of the supreme democratic method of Constituent Assembly to make a new constitution by the old regime merely proves that it does not rely on the people but on armaments, army and terror.

The past 53 years of political developments in Nepal have proved time and again that the feudal monarchy is the principal impediment to the democratic rights of the people. The eight years of PW, the infamous Narayanhiti palace massacre and the regressive step of October 4, 2002, have inflated the hatred and wrath of the Nepalese people against the King and the monarchy to its peak. Scared of the reality that republican consciousness has now become the consciousness of the general masses, the fake monarchy erected after the palace massacre has consistently opposed the proposal for a Constituent Assembly. Now it is making a vain attempt to perpetuate the rule of genocide and terror on Nepal and the Nepalese people by appeasing and kowtowing [to] mainly American imperialism.

As a conspiracy to hoodwink the international community and to perpetuate its feudal military dictatorship, the old regime has labeled the great and historic democratic movement of the Nepalese people as 'terrorism'. The Party has been cautioning the international community against the false and conspiratorial propaganda of the old feudal regime of Nepal that has degenerated into a pawn of American imperialism to maintain its hegemony in South Asia.

In this context, the Party once again reasserts its commitment to the following minimum policies and programmes:

- The Party still maintains the proposal of roundtable conference, an interim government and election to a Constituent Assembly to make a new constitution as its immediate minimum political proposal for a forward-looking political solution to the present crises in the country.
- The Party wants to institutionalise a republican form of state through the Constituent Assembly and believes that in a free and fair election the mandate of the Nepalese people would be in favour of a republic.
- In the given context of the existence of two ideologies, two armies and two states in the country, the Party is agreeable to demobilisation of both the armies and carrying out of elections to the Constituent Assembly under the supervision of United Nations Organisation and international human rights organisations.
- The content of the new constitution would be:

(a) Political

Full sovereignty to the people; secular state; elected house of representatives as the highest representative body of the people; reorganisation of a unified national army; provision of national and regional autonomy along with rights of self-determination; provision of constitutional changes or refinement according to the wishes of the people; guarantee of multi-party competition, periodic elections, adult franchise, rule of law and fundamental rights including freedom of speech and press; provision of special rights for women and dalits (i.e. oppressed caste); etc.

(b) Economic

Revolutionary land reforms for judicious redistribution of land on the principle of 'land to the tiller'; self-reliant and national industrial policy; promotion and development of national capital; formulation of an integrated national policy for proper utilisation of natural resources; etc.

(c) Social

Development of a mechanism for strict punishment to the corrupt, smugglers and profiteers; development of employment-oriented national and scientific education system; universal health service; provision of state care for the destitutes, the elderly and the children; end to all forms of exploitation, discrimination and dishonour to women and dalits; guarantee of minimum wages and worker's participation in industrial management; guarantee of intellectual and academic freedom and professional rights; promotion of democratic and scientific culture in place of feudal and imperialist reactionary culture; plan of integrated national infrastructure development; guarantee of full employment to all; fulfillment of demands of class and mass organisations; etc.

(d) Foreign policy

— Independent foreign policy of maintaining friendly relations with all on the basis of Panchasheel (i.e. five principles of peaceful coexistence) and non-alignment.

— Abrogation of all unequal treaties from the past and conclusion of new treaties and agreements on a new basis.

— Promotion of good neighbourly relations with neighbouring India and China with mutual cooperation in the fields of utilisation of natural resources, trade and transit, etc, for mutual benefit, keeping in view the particularity of economic, political, cultural, historical and geographical relations with them.

It is obvious that these immediate policies reflect the most flexible and democratic methods for peaceful and forward-looking political solution to the ongoing civil war in the country. However, the old feudal regime that has lost all support and confidence of the people is unleashing a naked military terror on the people relying on the military assistance of imperialism. In this context the Party highly values the solidarity of all the democratic forces inside and outside the country against the autocratic monarchy and in favour of the republican movement of the people. Hence the Party appeals to all concerned to lend their voices in favour of the democratic movement of the Nepalese people.

Source: Maoist Information Bulletin–8 (Occasional Bulletin of the Communist Party of Nepal [Maoist]), No 8, 20 January, 2004

Royal Nepal Army soldiers boarding a helicopter at the height of the emergency, Libang, Rolpa district. July 2002.

Notes

Chapter 1: Life and Death in the Time of War

1   Gautam, Shobha, Amrita Baskota and Rita Manchanda, 'Where there are no men: women in the Maoist insurgency in Nepal'. In *Women War and Peace in South Asia: Beyond Victimhood to Agency*, ed. Rita Manchanda, 2001. pp. 224-225.

2   Amnesty International. 'Nepal: A spiralling human rights crisis', 2002 (a). p. 37.

3   Shrestha, Manesh. 'Internal displacement in Nepal: A problem unprepared for' (forthcoming), 2003.

4   Pandey, J. and Rudra Khadka, 'Maoist terror: loot, burn & kill', *The Kathmandu Post*, 11 July 2002.

5   Amnesty International, 'Nepal: A deepening human rights crisis', 2002 (b). p. 8.

6   Thapa, Manjushree, 'The war in the west', *Himal South Asian*, January 2003.

7   Mainali, Mohan. 'Our descendants are doomed', *Nepali Times*, 6-12 December, 2002.

8   Informal Sector Service Centre (INSEC).

Chapter 2: Politics in Nepal (1768-1996)

1   Gyawali, S.P. *Jivan ra Kanoon*, 2038 BS (1981-82), p. 88.

2   See Pant, Shastra Dutta. *Comparative Constitutions of Nepal*, 1995. pp. 132-133.

3   A joint statement issued by the CPN, the Nepali Congress and a smaller party on 10 July 1957 had declared: 'So long as the country's resurgent-reactionary forces are getting stronger, all the democratic forces should unite and the basis of such a unity should be the election to a sovereign constituent assembly.' K.C., Surendra. *Nepalma Communist Andolan ko Itihas*, 1999. p. 111.

4   Joshi, B.L. and Leo Rose, *Democratic Innovations in Nepal: A Case Study of Political Acculturation*, 1966. Cited in Brown, T. Louise, *The Challenge to Democracy in Nepal*, 1996. p. 36

5   Brown 1996, p. 38.

6   Hoftun, Martin, William Raeper and John Whelpton. *People, Politics and Ideology: Democracy and Social Change in Nepal*, 1999. pp. 73-74.

7   Seddon, David. 'Democracy and Development in Nepal'. In Michael Hutt, *Nepal in the Nineties*, 2001. p. 132

8   The concept of 'satyagraha' (truth force) comes from the Indian independence movement where Mahatma Gandhi had used it as an effective civil disobedience strategy.

9   Ram Raja Prasad Singh was elected to the Rastriya Panchayat from the graduates' constituency in 1971, but was disqualified for professing faith in multi-party democracy. He had been imprisoned by the Panchayat administration, but released at the time of the referendum.

10 This was quite a considerable proportion in a house of 140, of whom only 112 were elected and the rest nominated by the king.

Politics in Nepal (1768-1996)

11   There is some dispute over the date of the founding of the CPN. Some sources put it as 22 April 1949, when Pushpa Lal and four others met and formed the central organising committee of the CPN.

12   Rawal, Bhim. *Nepal ma Samyabadi Andolan: Udbhav ra Bikas*, 2047 BS (1990-91). fn 8-9, p. 34.

13   Gupta, A. *Politics in Nepal, 1950-60*, 1993. p. 201. Gupta cites *May Divash ko Avasarma Kamyunist Party ko Ghosanapatra* (Manifesto of the Communist Party on the Occasion of May Day), 1951.

14   It is ironical that Acharya had been named president in absentia by the Nepali National Congress in 1946.

15   KC 1999, p. 92.

16   KC 1999, p. 172.

17   Baral, L, *Oppositional Politics in Nepal*, 1977. p. 82

18   Baral 1977, p. 82.

19   Gupta 1993, p. 204.

20   Baral 1977, p. 83.

21   Rawal 2047 BS, p. 51.

22   Baral 1977, p. 83.

23   Baral 1977, p. 84, cites *The Motherland*, 20 May 1961.

24   Interview with Shyam Shrestha, 18 April 2001. Shrestha, now the chief editor of the monthly magazine, *Mulyankan*, was originally with the Fourth Congress, and quit active politics after the Unity Conference of 1990.

25   Rawal 2047 BS. p. 73

26   Rawal 2047 BS. p. 73, quoting Krishna Ghimire 'Janmat Sangraha ra Samsamayik Bampanthi Rajniti' [The National Referendum and Contemporary Communist Politics], unpublished thesis, Tribhuvan University, 1980.

27   The key figures of the central nucleus were Man Mohan Adhikari, Mohan Bikram Singh, Nirmal Lama and Sambhu Ram Shrestha. The other members of the central nucleus are mentioned in Rawal 2047 BS, p. 73.

28   Interview with Shyam Shrestha. Mohan Bikram was to pen his famous monograph 'Gaddar Pushpa Lal' ('Traitor Pushpa Lal'), B.S. 2030 (1973/74), under the pseudonym Ananda Bahadur Chhetri, denouncing Pushpa Lal for advocating an alliance with the Nepali Congress.

29   Both Mohan Bikram and Nirmal Lama had begun their political careers with the Nepali Congress. As stalwarts of the CPN (Fourth Congress), they were referred to as Nepal's Mao (Tse-tung) and Chou (en-Lai), respectively. The Man Mohan group established its own party in 1979, but this too was riven with dissension. In 1987, it united with Pushpa Lal's rump CPN and emerged as the CPN (Marxist), which ultimately joined the CPN (ML) to become the CPN (UML) in 1990.

30   Interview with Shyam Shrestha.

31   Interviews with Amik Sherchan, 9 June 2001, and Shyam Shrestha. Hoftun et al., 1999, write that, although their demands were not met, the communist parties in general campaigned for the parliamentary system. (p. 92).

32   According to Amik Sherchan, Lama resigned under pressure from a section within the party, including Mohan Bikram, that was in favour of boycotting the referendum. The new leadership later realised that not voting at all meant indirectly supporting the Panchayat system, and ultimately it went along with what Lama had originally proposed. Shyam Shrestha's opinion is that Lama had to resign because he had advocated united action with the Nepali Congress, which Mohan Bikram described as a 'rightist view'.

Politics in Nepal (1768-1996)

33 Nirmal Lama himself contested elections to the Rastriya Panchayat, the national legislature, from Kathmandu, albeit unsuccessfully.

34 Interviews with Amik Sherchan and Shyam Shrestha. Shrestha also says that Mohan Bikram had a dictatorial attitude within the party. He would brook no dissent and would immediately see conspiracies behind differences of opinion. In the end, Mohan Bikram was just in a big hurry to split the party and would not listen to pleas for debate within the party.

35 Hachhethu, K, *Party Building in Nepal: Organisation, Leadership and People*, 2002. p. 70.

36 Hachhethu 2002, note 34 p. 37.

37 Hoftun et al 1999. p. 116, footnote 1. According to Shyam Shrestha the CPN (ML) was the main beneficiary of the splits within the Fourth Congress, because of the exodus of a large number of party workers into its ranks. Hoftun et al., pp. 91-2, describe the Fourth Congress and the CPN (Marxist-Leninist) that arose from the Jhapali movement as the two most radical communist groupings in the run-up to the 1980 referendum, and state that by 1986 the CPN (ML) had replaced the Fourth Congress as the most dynamic left force (p. 106) and by 1990 had become 'the Leftist group with the most effective network of cadres' (p. 116).

38 Prachanda, Baburam Bhattarai, and Mohan Baidya went with Mohan Bikram. The Nepal Rastriya Buddhjibi Sangathan 2054 BS (1997), p. 11, describes Lama's faction as 'rightist'.

39 Amik Sherchan told this writer that the reasons behind the split were 'technical' (he declined to elaborate on this) rather than ideological, while Shyam Shrestha says that it was a conspiracy hatched by Mohan Baidya and Prachanda since they knew that as long as Mohan Bikram remained in the party they would never be able to become its top leaders. For its part, the pro-Maoist, Nepal Rastriya Buddhijibi Sangathan says that the Fifth Congress (of Masal held in 1984) concluded that neither Mohan Bikram's viewpoint nor his character was proper. 2054 BS p. 11.

40 CPN (UML). 'Maobadi tatha rajyadwara hinsa ra atanka sambandha adhyayan karyadal prativedan, 2058' (Report of the working group to study violence and terror by the Maoists and the state, 2001), 2058 BS (a) (2001). The report says that Prachanda initially seemed disposed to conduct a struggle within the boundaries of the Panchayat constitution; but later emphasised people's war.

41 Upadhya, Sanjay. 'A dozen years of democracy: Games that parties play', Note 2, p. 60. In Kanak Mani Dixit and Shastri Ramachandaran (eds), *State of Nepal*, 2002.

42 Revolutionary Internationalist Movement. 'Declaration of the Revolutionary Internationalist Movement'. www.awtw/org/rim/declaration_eng.htm. In 1993, the declaration was changed and its ideology of 'Marxism-Leninism-Mao Tsetung Thought' was replaced by 'Marxism-Leninism-Maoism' 'in accordance with RIM's principles of functioning'. The difference between the two is that while 'Mao Tsetung Thought' is only considered a variation of Marxism-Leninism, Maoism implies its recognition as an ideology in itself.

43 Nickson, R.A., 'Democratisation and the Growth of Communism in Nepal: A Peruvian Scenario in the Making?', 1992. Endnote 20, p. 385.

44 Mohan Bikram Singh has devoted an entire book to the relations between RIM and the Maoists in which he also goes in detail to explain Masal's expulsion from RIM. See, Mohan Bikram Singh, *RIM ra Maobadiharuko Kathit Janayuddha* (RIM and the Maoists' So-called People's War), Kathmandu: Jana Sikshya Samuha, 2058 BS (2001-02).

45 *The Worker* no. 7 2002.

Politics in Nepal (1768-1996)

46   The CPN (Marxist) had been formed in 1987 though the merger of Pushpa Lal's group led by Sahana Pradhan and the Man Mohan group. The constituents of the United Left Front were: CPN (Marxist-Leninist), CPN (Marxist), Nepal Workers' and Peasants' Party, CPN (Fourth Congress), CPN (Amatya), CPN (Manandhar), and CPN (Varma).

47   Ogura, Kiyoko, *Kathmandu Spring: The People's Movement of 1990*, 2001. p. 90.

48   Hoftun et al. 1999, pp. 126-127.

49   Ogura 2001, p. 153.

50   Hoftun et al. 1999, p. 130.

51   Hutt, Michael. 'Drafting the 1990 constitution'. In Michael Hutt (ed). *Nepal in the Nineties*, 2001, p. 32.

52   Hutt 2001, p. 34.

53   Brown, 1996, says that the Congress leadership was afraid that the communists might succeed in getting an anti-monarchy constituent assembly elected. p. 151.

54   Bhattachan, Krishna, 'Public debate on development: Sociological perspectives on the public philosophy for the development of Nepal', unpublished PhD thesis, University of California at Berkeley, 1993, pp. 152-153. Cited in Devendra Raj Panday, *Nepal's Failed Development: Reflections on the Mission and the Maladies*, 2000. p. 86.

55   There is no mention of the multiplicity of Nepal's ethnic and caste groups in the 1962 constitution, while the status of official language to Nepali was given constitutional sanction for the first time in the same document.

56   Hutt 2001, p. 38.

57   Brown 1996, p. 154.

58   The others in the UNPM were the Proletarian Workers' Association, Nepal Marxist-Leninist Party and two other smaller parties. The view of the constituents of the UNPM towards the Nepali Congress-Left Front alliance was that the latter had a 'compromising attitude...towards Indian expansionists and various imperialist powers'. From the political resolution adopted by the Central Organising Committee of the CPN (Masal) in Asad, 2047 BS (i.e. after the People's Movement had ended). *Rato Tarwar*, 2059 BS (2002-03), p. 377.

59   Interview with Shyam Shrestha.

60   Hoftun et al. p. 147.

61   Whelpton, John. 'The general elections of May 1991'. In Michael Hutt (ed), *Nepal in the Nineties*, 2001. p. 50.

62   Nickson 1992, pp. 371-372.

63   Maharjan, Pancha. 'Role of the Extra-Parliamentary Political Party in Multi-party Democracy: A Study of the CPN–Unity Centre'. *Contributions to Nepalese Studies*, 1993. p. 221.

64   Whelpton, 2001. p. 59.

65   Maharjan, 1993. p. 221. According to the UPFN election manifesto, the party was going to make a 'revolutionary use' of the elections.

66   Brown 1996, p. 180.

67   It seemed to be a different matter that Singh's choices seemed to be equally partisan, chosen from amongst his own Newar community.

68   Nickson 1992, p. 384.

69   Maharjan, 1993, pp. 224-225.

70   Brown 1996, p. 178.

71   Hoftun et al. 1999, p. 189.

Politics in Nepal (1768-1996)

72　This was the first of a series of memoranda to various prime ministers by left parties. The most famous one, of course, was the 4 February 1996 one handed by Baburam Bhattarai to Sher Bahadur Deuba.

73　The 6th of April 1990 saw the massive demonstrations in the streets of Kathmandu, which proved to be the culmination of the People's Movement as two days later the king lifted the ban on political parties. The day has since been a day of protests and with perhaps a couple of exceptions has always been observed as a day of national strike.

74　Maharjan, 1993, p. 226.

75　Hoftun et al. 1999, p. 197.

76　Nepal Rastriya Buddhijibi Sangathan 2054 BS , p. 12.

77　*The Worker*, no. 3, 1997. According to Shyam Shrestha, who was also present at the meeting, the resolution was adopted without debate since the Prachanda faction were in a majority.

78　Shyam Shrestha says Nirmal Lama and the others were not permitted to have their say in the party, and quit as a result.

79　Amik Sherchan, who later became chairman of the UPF that split from Bhattarai and now heads the People's Front, was an MP in the 1991 parliament. He says that the main point of departure between the two factions of the Unity Centre and the UPF had been on whether or not to utilise the parliament as a forum to make people aware of its contradictions.

80　It is one of the quirks of fate that the petition Bhattarai had filed in the Supreme Court against the Election Commission's decision was ruled upon in June 1998, whereby the Supreme Court invalidated the Commission's decision. Of course, by that time it was too late.

81　Maharjan, Pancha. 'The Maoist Insurgency and Crisis of Governability in Nepal'. In Dhruba Kumar (ed) *Domestic Conflict and Crisis of Governability in Nepal*, 2000, p. 168.

82　Of the nine UPFN members of parliament in the 1991 House of Representatives, only three—Barman Budha and Krishna Bahadur Mahara (both from Rolpa district) and Khadga Bahadur Buda (from Rukum district)—sided with Bhattarai. But the fortunes of the Election Commission-sanctioned UPFN was to dip in the next two elections. From a 4.35 per cent share of the total vote by the undivided UPFN, the UPFN's vote went down to 1.32 per cent in 1994, and then 0.83 per cent in 1999. It won no seats in 1994 and managed to secure just one in 1999. The UPFN merged with the National People's Front, the political wing of CPN–Masal, in 2002 to create the People's Front, which had a total of six seats in the parliament that was dissolved in May 2002. The merger of the two fronts was followed by the unification between the Unity Centre and Masal. The new party, called the CPN–Unity Centre-Masal, chose Mohan Bikram Singh as its general secretary. This union, apart from ending years-long speculation that the Unity Centre was on the verge of uniting with the Maoists, has also led to the formation of a third left force in the country apart from the CPN (UML) and the CPN (Maoist).

83　Nepal Rastriya Buddhijibi Sangathan, 2054 BS, p. 13. Harka Gurung et al. state that the adoption of the new name happened during an underground conference in Chitwan, 30 May-4 June, 1994, in which 215 representatives from 60 districts participated. 'An overview of recent armed conflict in Nepal', 2001, pp. 18-19.

84　Interview with Shyam Shrestha. Narahari Acharya claims that RIM had objected to the Unity Centre's adherence to electoral politics. See Acharya, Narahari, 'Maobadi gatibidhi ko pristhabhumi' (Background to Maoist activities), paper outlining the Nepali Congress position and strategies for resolution at a seminar organised by the High-Level Committee to Solve the Maoist Problem, 2000.

Politics in Nepal (1768-1996)

    Shyam Shrestha also believes that the CPN (Maoist) foreswore elections at the insistence of RIM.

85   Nepal Rastriya Buddhijibi Sangathan, 2054 BS, pp. 12-13. It described the Jhapa movement as 'a historic revolt which encouraged all communist revolutionaries to understand the Maoist viewpoint on the question of power and struggle...But even though they were right in the main, they could not develop it into a people's war.' p. 10.

86   *The Worker* no. 3, 1997.

87   *The Worker* no. 2, 1996.

88   After the three Communist Internationals—1864-76; 1889-1914; and 1921-1943—the international umbrella organisation of communist parties worldwide.

89   The principle of mass line is a fundamental tenet of Mao's strategy of carrying the people with the revolution. In Mao's words: 'In all the practical work of our Party, all correct leadership is necessarily from the masses, to the masses. This means: take the ideas of the masses (scattered and unsystematic ideas) and concentrate them (through study turn them into concentrated and systematic ideas), then go to the masses and propagate and explain these ideas until the masses embrace them as their own, hold fast to them and translate them into action, and test the correctness of these ideas in such action. Then once again concentrate ideas from the masses and once again take them to the masses so that the ideas are persevered in and carried through. And so on, over and over again in an endless spiral, with the ideas becoming more correct, more vital and richer each time.' Selected Works, III. Cited in Schram, Stuart. *The Political Thought of Mao Tse-tung*, 1974, pp. 316-317.

90   *The Worker* 1997.

91   Onesto, Li, *Revolutionary Worker*, no. 1020, 1999.

92   *The Worker* 1997.

93   Interview with Narahari Acharya, 19 April, 2001.

Chapter 3: **Understanding the Causes of the 'People's War'**

1   *The Worker* 1997.

2   In the section titled 'Reasons behind the rise of the Maobadi problem', CPN (UML), 2058 BS (a), the UML does its utmost to prove that the Nepali Congress was largely responsible for the Maoist insurgency.

3   Acharya 2000.

4   Nickson 1992, pp. 358-386.

5   Mikesell, Stephen. 'The Paradoxical Support of Nepal's Left for Comrade Gonzalo', *Himal*, Mar/Apr 1993.

6   Gaige, Frederick. *Regionalism and National Unity in Nepal*, 1975. p. 189.

7   Blaikie, Piers, John Cameron, and David Seddon. *Nepal in Crisis: Growth and Stagnation at the Periphery*, 2001. p. 43.

8   Seddon 2001. p. 134.

9   The consumer price index had already more than doubled in the 1970s and doubled again during the 1980s, with an annual rate of inflation of over 10 per cent between 1980 and 1987.

10   Seddon 2001, pp. 135-136.

11   Seddon 2001, p. 139.

12   National Planning Commission, *Approach to the Eighth Five Year Plan, 1992-97*, 1991, p. 8.

Understanding the Causes of the 'People's War'

13 Shakya, Sujeev. 'The squandering of a promising economy'. In Dixit and Ramachandaran (eds), 2002, pp. 179-181.

14 The UNDP's Human Development Index measures achievements in terms of life expectancy, education, and adjusted real income.

15 The average annual growth in GDP is registered at 3.4 per cent for the 25-year period covering 1964-65 to 1989-90. See Ministry of Finance, *Economic Survey* (several years).

16 Panday 2000, pp. 48-53.

17 Tiwari, Chitra K. 'Maoist Insurgency in Nepal: Internal Dimensions', 2001. The year 2001/2002 had a negative growth rate of -0.6 per cent.

18 UNDP, *Human Development Report, 2001.* 2002.

19 Panday, 2000, pp. 316-347, and Seddon, David, Jagannath Adhikari and Ganesh Gurung. *The New Lahures,* 2001, pp. 72-81. For additional information on Nepal-India relations, see Majumdar, Kanhanmoy. *Nepal and the Indian Nationalist Movement.* Calcutta: K.L. Mukhopadhyay, 1975.

20 Rana, Pashupati S.J.B. and K.P. Malla. *Nepal in Perspective.* Kathmandu: CEDA, 1973, p. 20. Cited in Blaikie et al. 2001, p. 75.

21 The number of post-1990 governments has now reached 14 with the resignation of Lokendra Bahadur Chand and his replacement by Surya Bahadur Thapa in June 2003.

22 The incidence of poverty is highest in the mountain region and there is a higher level of poverty in the hills than in the tarai, while western Nepal is poorer than the regions to the east.

23 Hachhethu 2002, p. 74.

24 CPN (Masal), *Rato Tarwar,* 2059 BS, p. 59.

25 Sales, Anne de (2000). 'The Kham Magar country, Nepal: Between ethnic claims and Maoism', *European Bulletin of Himalayan Research,* no. 19, Autumn 2000.

26 Gautam, Shobha and Amrita Banskota. 'Maobadi janyuddhale mahila tatha bal-balikama pareko prabhavbareko adyayan prativedan', 2055 BS (1998-99), p. 17.

27 Nickson 1993, p. 376.

28 Nickson 1993, p. 376.

29 Hachhethu 2002. p. 61.

30 Hachhethu 2002. p. 61.

31 Interviews with Amik Sherchan, Hari Roka (30 April, 2001), Shyam Shrestha.

32 Hachhethu 2002. pp. 46-47.

33 Hachhethu 2002, pp. 97 and 102.

34 Hoftun et al. 1999, p. 169.

35 INSEC, *Human Rights Yearbook, 1992.* 1993, pp. 224-225.

36 INSEC 1993, p. 230.

37 INSEC, *Human Rights Yearbook, 1993,* 1994, p. 267.

38 INSEC 1994, p. 268.

39 Interview with Amik Sherchan.

40 Because of its nine-month-long spell in power, the CPN (UML) also came under severe attack from Baburam Bhattarai, who called it 'an extreme right revisionist party which has degenerated into an openly reactionary one after it vowed to serve and strengthen the existing constitutional multi-party system and formed its own government under this rotten reactionary system'. *The Independent,* 13-19 Dec. 1995.

Understanding the Causes of the 'People's War'

41 Khadka withdrew the case against himself when he became home minister.

42 *The Kathmandu Post*, 15 November 1995.

43 *Kantipur*, 16 November 1995.

44 *The Kathmandu Post*, 16 November 1995.

45 *Kantipur*, 16 November 1995.

46 *The Independent*, 13-19 December, 1995.

47 INSEC, *Human Rights Yearbook, 1995*. 1996, p. 12.

48 Onesto, Li. *Revolutionary Worker*, no. 1020, 1999.

49 Acharya 2000.

50 'Ekikrit antarik surakshya tatha bikas yojana' (Integrated Internal Security and Development Programme), 2057 BS (2000-01).

51 CPN (UML) 2058 BS (a).

52 See Blaikie et al. 2001, pp. 81-94, for an account of the centre's neglect.

53 Ahmad, Eqbal. 'Revolutionary warfare and counterinsurgency'. In Gerard Chaliand (ed), *Guerrilla Strategies: An Historical Anthology from the Long March to Afghanistan*, 1982. p. 247. Extracted from N. Miller and E. Aya (eds), *National Liberation and Revolution*, 1970.

54 In the hierarchy of the king's courtiers, the 'chautariya' were the highest and they all came from the royal family. Next in line came the 'kaji', which was the highest rank a commoner could aspire to. Regmi's survey of around 49 men who became kaji in the years 1768-1814 showed at least 10 were Magars and Gurungs, but after Rana Bahadur Shah's assassination in 1806, the representation of these two groups came almost to an end. (Regmi, Mahesh C. 1995. pp. 43- 46) Abhiman Singh Rana, a Magar general who was killed in the Kot Massacre of 1846, was the last ranking figure in the royal court from either of these two groups.

55 John Whelpton writes: 'In 1955, a landmark report on education planning conceded the need to use minority languages for oral communication with students just starting primary school, but advocated a switch to exclusive use of Nepali as soon as possible so that "other languages will gradually disappear and great national strength and unity will result".' From 'Political identity in Nepal: State, nation, and community'. In David N. Gellner, Joanna Pfaff-Czarnecka and John Whelpton (eds), *Nationalism and Ethnicity in a Hindu Kingdom: The Politics of Culture in Contemporary Nepal*, 1997, pp. 48-49.

56 'Langhali' means 'fellow-villager' in the Magar language.

57 Whelpton 2001, p. 36.

58 Enabling State Programme, *Pro-Poor Governance Assessment Nepal*, 2001. p. 13.

59 Dixit, Kanak Mani, 'Bahuns and the Nepali State', *Nepali Times*, 19-25 October 2001.

60 Pfaff-Czarnecka, Joanna. 'Debating the state of the nation: Ethnicisation of politics in Nepal—A position paper'. In Joanna Pfaff-Czarnecka, Darini Rajasingham-Senanayake, Ashis Nandy and Edmund Terence Gomes (eds). *Ethnic Futures: The State and Identity Politics in Asia*, 1999, p. 49.

61 Nickson 1992, p. 383.

62 The leadership of both parties is overwhelmingly Bahuns and Chhetris. To its credit, however, the Nepali Congress did begin new broadcasts over state radio in various other languages and set up the National Committee for the Development of Nationalities.

63 Lecomte-Tilouine, Marie, 'Ethnic claims within Maoism—The Magar dilemma between two regroupings: nationality and class', 2001.

Understanding the Causes of the 'People's War'

64 CPN (Masal) 2059 BS, p. 60.

65 *The Worker* 1996.

66 Bhattarai, Baburam (1998). *Politico-Economic Rationale of People's War in Nepal*. Kathmandu: Utprerak Publications. His last point appears as number 20 in the 1996, 40-point list of demands, stating: 'Where ethnic communities are in the majority, they should be allowed to form their own autonomous governments.'

67 For a first-hand description of mobilisation methods used by Maoists, see 'The Sija Campaign' in Onesto, Li, *Revolutionary Worker*, no. 1020, 1999.

68 Footnote 28 in Hoftun et al. 1999, quoting a letter to the editor by Marion Hughes in *Spotlight*, 25 December 1995.

69 Huntington, Samuel P. *Political Order in Changing Societies*, 1996 (1968), p. 5.

70 Lal, CK, Nepal's 'Nepal's Maobaadi', *Himal South Asian*, 2001.

71 Thapa, Deepak, 'Day of the Maoist', *Himal South Asia*, 2001.

72 Sales 2000.

73 *The Worker* 1996.

Chapter 4: The Growth of the Maoist Movement

1 *The Worker* 1996.

2 *Jana Awaj*, no. 29, 3 Oct 2002.

3 Nickson, 1992, p. 382. It should be noted here that Nickson believed it would be Masal, not Mashal (later, CPN-Maoist), that was likely to begin an armed struggle because of the former's then opposition to parliamentary politics. That ultimately it proved to be Mashal that took up arms does not detract from his overall analysis of the socio-economic conditions of the country.

4 Lecomte-Tilouine 2001.

5 *Janabhavana*, 26 February 1996. Cited in Nepal Rastriya Buddhijibi Sangathan, 2054 BS, p. 134.

6 *Deshantar*, 25 February 1996. Cited by Gurung et al. 2001.

7 *Lokpatra*, 3 March 1996. Cited in Nepal Rastriya Buddhijibi Sangathan, 2054 BS, p. 140.

8 *Shree Sagarmatha*, 6 March 1996. Cited in Nepal Rastriya Buddhijibi Sangathan, 2054 BS, p. 143.

9 See *Shree Sagarmatha*, 10 March, 1996, and *Mahima*, 11 March, 1996. Cited in Nepal Rastriya Buddhijibi Sangathan, 2054 BS, pp. 144 and 145.

10 *Chhalphal*, 15 February, 1996. Cited in Nepal Rastriya Buddhijibi Sangathan, 2054 BS, p. 132.

11 The CPN (UML), however, came out guns blazing at its Sixth Congress in January 1998. The document that was adopted by the congress had this to say of the CPN (Maoist): 'This party represents the petty bourgeois trend and dogmatist thinking existing within the communist movement of Nepal. This party, which refuses to move ahead taking constructive lesson from prevailing world situation, present state of the world communist movement, and the objective condition of the Nepalese society, has unleashed violent activities in the name of the "People's War" for the last one and a half years. This party is averse to Marxist method of objective analysis of the objective situation. It is making a wrong analysis of the current national and international situation. It has embraced an adventurist line and has become a victim of impatience in the background of the

The Growth of the Maoist Movement

failure of its past political lines, predominance of its petty bourgeois character and its inability to compete with other parties peacefully owing to its defeated mentality. Its politics is extremist and its activities are terrorists in character.' CPN (UML). 'An Analysis of National Political Situation' (From the 6th Congress document), http://www.cpnuml.org/documents/6thcongress.html.

12   Kantipur, 27 February, 1996. Cited in Nepal Rastriya Buddhijibi Sangathan, 2054 BS, p. 135.

13   Gurung et al. 2001 p. 42.

14   Gurung et al. 2001 p. 44.

15   INSEC, *Human Rights Yearbook, 1997*, 1998, p. 21.

16   Press statement by Baburam Bhattarai, 10 August 1997.

17   CPN (UML), *Nekapa (Maobadi)ko Chirphar*, 2058 BS (b) (2001), p. 72.

18   *The Worker* no. 5, 1999.

19   Gurung et al. 2001, p. 44.

20   *The Worker* 1999.

21   Deputy Inspector General of Police Sahabir Thapa, quoted in *The Kathmandu Post*, 8 July 1998.

22   *The Worker* 1999.

23   Himal Association. *Political Opinion Survey Nepal 2001*. 2001.

24   Inspector General of Police Pradeep SJB Rana, quoted in *The Kathmandu Post*, 20 May, 2001.

25   Gurung et al. 2001, p. 45.

26   Shaha, Rishikesh. 'Idea and reality, Nepal and Rolpa', *Himal South Asia*, July 1996.

27   Sharma, Sudhindra and Pawan Kumar Sen. *General Election Opinion Poll: How Voters Assess Politics, Parties and Politicians*, 1999.

28   Himal Association 2001.

29   Subedi, Navin. 'Vox populi', *Nepali Times*, 11-17 October, 2002.

30   Private communication from Prachanda to Durga Subedi dated 13 Fagun, 2056 (25 February 2000). Nepali Congress member Subedi was acting as a go-between for the Bhattarai government and the Maoist leadership at the request of the former.

31   Amnesty International 2002 (a).

32   *The Rising Nepal* 23 March 2000.

33   *Deshantar* 26 March 2000.

34   *Kantipur* 4 December 2000.

35   *The Worker* 1997.

36   Schram 1974, p. 292.

37   Gurung et al. 2001, p. 39.

38   *Jana Awaj*, 3 Oct 2002.

39   *The Worker* 1997.

40   Mao Tse-tung, *Selected Military Writings of Mao Tse-Tung*, 1966, pp. 210-211.

41   Mao Tse-tung 1966, pp. 210-211.

42   Prachanda in *Janaawaj*, no. 39-40, 12-19, December 2002.

43   *The Worker* 1996.

44   *The Worker* 1997.

The Growth of the Maoist Movement

45   *The Worker* no. 4, 1998.

46   *The Worker* 1999.

47   *The Worker* 1999.

48   *The Worker* 1999.

49   *The Worker*, no. 6, 2000. Alok is learnt to have been expelled from the party and sent to 'labour camp'.

50   A notable case at that time was of former minister and long-time Rastriya Panchayat member from Rolpa, Reg Bahadur Subedi, and his son who were kidnapped and sent to 'labour camp' as 'punishment for their anti-people's war activities'. *The Worker* 2000.

51   *The Worker* 2000.

52   *The Worker* 2002.

53   *The Worker* 1998.

54   CPN (UML), 2058 BS (a).

55   *Himalaya Times*, 5 September 1997. Cited in Nepal Rastriya Buddhijibi Sangathan, 2054 BS, p. 151.

56   *A World to Win* no. 27, p. 46.

57   *Selected Works of Mao*, Vol IX, 'On Guerilla Warfare'. www.maoism.org.

58   *The Worker* 2002.

59   *The Worker* 1998.

60   *The Worker* 1998.

61   The Unity Society was banned by the Indian government not long after the emergency was imposed in Nepal.

62   *Himal Khabarpatrika*, 1-15 Saun, 2057 BS (2000).

63   Sharma, Sudheer, 2001.

64   Dhungel, Binod, 'Maobadi sena gathan prakriya Chinko bhanda pharak', *Samacharpatra*, 30 Aug 2000.

65   *The Worker* 1999.

66   Onesto, Li, *Revolutionary* Worker, no. 1023, 1999.

67   Sharma 2001.

68   *Drishti*, 12 December 2000.

69   *The Worker* 2000.

70   Seddon, David. 'The Maoist Insurgency in Nepal: Revolutionary Theory and Practice', 2002.

71   Sharma 2001.

72   Seddon 2002.

73   Seddon 2002, cites Arjun Karki. 'The Politics of Poverty and Movements from below in Nepal'. Unpublished PhD thesis, University of East Anglia, Norwich, UK, 2001.

Chapter 5: Two Momentous Years, 2001 and 2002

1   CPN Maoist 2001. In its editorial, *The Worker* (No 6, October 2000) had stated that the 'ideological synthesis of the experiences of the creative application of the science of Marxism-Leninism-Maoism (MLM) in the concrete condition of Nepal, particularly in the light of the preparation, initiation and development of the

Two Momentous Years, 2001 and 2002

People's War so far' had been 'tentatively synthesised as the "Guiding Thought of the Party"' by the CPN (Maoist)'s central committee.

2   CPN Maoist 2001.

3   *The Worker*, 1996.

4   Amnesty International 2002 (a).

5   CPN Maoist 2001.

6   *A World to Win*, 2001. The interview took place on 28 May 2001, just three days before the 1 June royal palace massacre.

7   *Drishti*, 13 March 2001.

8   They had called for a three-day bandh on 3, 4 and 5 June, but the events of the royal palace massacre overtook everything else around then.

9   *Kantipur*, 21 April 2001.

10   The provision of a National Defence Council was one of the compromises reached during the drafting of the 1990 constitution, thus allowing for less-than-total control by the civilian executive over the army. In November 2001, as a prelude to activating the army, Koirala had appointed a defence minister in a departure from the tradition of the prime minister looking after defence affairs.

11   A reference to the 1846 massacre of a large number of the country's noblemen by Jang Bahadur Rana, and the establishment of Rana rule.

12   Bhattarai, Baburam, 'Naya "Kotparba" lai manyata dinu hunna', *Kantipur*, 6 June 2001. English translation available at http://www.humanrights.de/doc_en/archiv/n/nepal/politics/080601_royal_massacre.htm.

13   The present king of Bhutan.

14   Kaji Lhendup Dorji, prime minister of Sikkim at the time of its annexation by India in 1975.

15   *Kantipur*, 6 June 2001.

16   Press release signed by Prachanda, 11 June 2001.

17   *Kantipur*, 6 June 2001.

18   Bhattarai, Baburam. 'Akasmik dhangale ganatantra ko janma bhaeko chha' (The bird of a republic), *Rajdhani*, 29 June 2001. English translation available at www.insof.org.

19   *The Kathmandu Post*, 24 June 2001.

20   Himal Association 2001.

21   *Saptahik Bimarsha*, 9 November 2001.

22   Only the United People's Front was for a constituent assembly and the general secretary of the party, Lila Mani Pokhrel, even addressed a Maoist-sponsored public meeting in Kathmandu in August 2001.

23   *The Kathmandu Post*, 22 November 2001.

24   The Maoists are known to have acquired a few automatic weapons from India as is evident from photographs printed in newspapers and magazines (such as the cover of *Himal South Asian*, May 2001). But there has been no evidence of these having been used in combat up to the second ceasefire.

25   *The Worker* 2002.

26   *The Kathmandu Post*, 25 November 2001.

27   CPN (Maoist) (no date). Maoist Information Bulletin-2. www.insof.org

28   *The Kathmandu Post*, 22 November 2001.

29   *The Kathmandu Post*, 20 November 2001.

Two Momentous Years, 2001 and 2002

30   Maoist Information Bulletin-1. www.insof.org

31   *Far Eastern Economic Review*, 13 December 2001.

32   *The Kathmandu Post*, 28 November 2001.

33   *The Kathmandu Post*, 30 November 2001.

34   *Nepali Times*, 1-7 February 2002.

35   See *Drishti*, 5 March, 2002, and *Nepal Samacharpatra*, 17 March, 2002, for the full texts of the CPN (UML) and Nepali Congress proposals.

36   Deuba said: 'It isn't necessary that we need [an] emergency to combat terrorism.' But he added, 'Still I will be holding talks with others [on the issue].' *The Kathmandu Post*, 16 May 2002.

37   Deuba said: 'It was on the request of the security forces who are bravely fighting against the Maoist terrorists that we had decided to seek extension of the emergency.' CNN.com/World, 22 May, 2002.

38   Statement by Baburam Bhattarai explaining reasons for the 5-day bandh from 2 to 6 April, 2002.

39   *The Times of India*, 2 December 2001.

40   At a press conference on 1 October, 2002, the army spokesman said that the Maoists were still using weapons looted from the Dang barracks in November 2001. *The Kathmandu Post*, 2 October, 2002.

41   CNN.com/Transcripts, Q&A with Jain Verjee, 'Terrorism in Nepal', aired 25 March, 2002. Maj-Gen Ashok Mehta, formerly of the Indian army, has observed that 'it is doubtful if it can muster a bayonet strength of more than 10,000 combatants for operations'. Rediff.com, 5 April, 2002.

Chapter 6: **Cost of the Conflict**

1   Huston, James V. 'Insurgency in Peru: The Shining Path', 1988, and 'Shining Path: Core of the RIM Project', 1995.

2   This figure represents a government estimate that is broadly accepted by human rights groups and other observers.

3   Despite the rapidly growing body of writing on the current state of the conflict in Nepal, there has been little serious analysis on the actual cost of the conflict not only because of the complexities required in assessing the indirect effects but also because of the difficulty in getting any reliable data. As a result, assessments on the cost of the conflict has had to rely on the rehearsal of second-hand data culled from media reports and extrapolations from available information.

4   *The Kathmandu Post*, 2 January 2003.

5   Yogi, Bhagirath. 'The cost of insurgency', *New Business Age*, May 2002.

6   *The Kathmandu Post*, 3 August 2002.

7   Seddon 2002.

8   *The Kathmandu Post*, 27 September 2002.

9   Asian Development Bank, *Annual Report, Nepal, 2001*, 2002, and Economic Intelligence Unit, 'Country Report: Nepal, Mongolia', 2003.

10   *The Kathmandu Post*, 6 May 2002.

11   For the year ending mid-July 2001, Nepal's GDP was estimated at Rs 392 billion while the figure for the previous year had been Rs 365 billion. That means on an average (for 365 days), the country's daily GDP is Rs 1 billion. However, because the bandhs affect urban economy more than rural and since the share of agriculture is nearly 37 per cent and that of the non-agriculture sector is around 63 per

Cost of the Conflict

cent of the GDP, the cost of the bandh can be calculated to be approximately Rs 630 million per day. Refer to Yogi 2002, for more details.

12 *The Kathmandu Post*, 26 December 2002.

13 *The Kathmandu Post*, 3 August 2002.

14 *The Kathmandu Post*, 16 January 2002.

15 USAID, 'Mitigating the Impact of the Maoist Conflict on Children and Youth in Nepal'. *Annual Programme Statement*, 2002.

16 Ministry of Finance. *Economic Survey 2001/02*, 2002.

17 Ministry of Finance. *Economic Survey 2001/02*, 2002.

18 *The Kathmandu Post*, 28 July 2002.

19 *The Kathmandu Post*, 28 July 2002.

20 *The Kathmandu Post*, 28 July 2002.

21 Mohan Mainali, 'Famine by February', *Nepali Times*, 22-28 November 2002.

22 Seddon 2002.

23 Kumar, Dhruba, 'Sankat ko Nikas: Sainya Katauti', *Himal Khabarpatrika*, 13-28 April, 2003.

24 Yogi 2002.

25 *The Kathmandu Post*, 9 July 2002.

26 UNDP. *Nepal Human Development Report, 2001*, 2002.

27 UNDP, 2002.

28 *The Kathmandu Post*, 9 July 2002.

29 Bhattarai, Binod. '$70,000,000: That's how much the army is spending over the next five years on weapons upgrades. Who is going to pay for it?' *Nepali Times*, 23-29 November 2001.

30 Seddon 2002.

31 Seddon 2002.

32 Seddon 2002.

33 *The Kathmandu Post*, 19 January 2002. Deuba also made high-profile visits to Washington DC and London in May 2002, during which he received assurances of continued support in his fight against the Maoists.

34 *The Kathmandu Post*, 28 November 2001.

35 Dixit, Kanak Mani. 'Insurgents and innocents: The Nepali army's battle with the Maobaadi', *Himal South Asian*, June 2002.

36 Dixit 2002. According to one calculation, in the half-year of the emergency, the government has announced the detention of only 60 wounded Maobaadi during the action by security forces as opposed to the death of nearly 3,000 'Maoists'.

37 Mainali, Mohan, 'Unfriendly Fire', *Nepali Times*, 2-8 March 2001.

38 Dixit 2002.

39 Shrestha 2003.

40 *The Kathmandu Post*, 4 February 2003.

41 *Himal Khabarpatrika*, 15-29 January 2003.

42 International Crisis Group. 'Nepal Backgrounder: Ceasefire — Soft Landing or Strategic Pause?' ICG Asia Report # 50, Kathmandu/Brussels, 10 April 2003.

43 *The Kathmandu Post*, 26 July 2002.

44 Shrestha 2003.

45 Tiwari 2001.

Cost of the Conflict

46   Dixit 2002.

47   Gautam, Shobha. *Women and Children in the Periphery of People's War*, 2001. p. 39.

48   Gautam et al. 2001. p. 240.

49   UNDP, *Nepal Human Development Report 1998*, 1999.

50   Azad, Nandini. Engendered Mobilisation – the Key to Livelihood Security: IFAD's Experience in South Asia, 1999.

51   UNDP, 1999, note. 3. 'Beyond Beijing mid-decade meet in South Asia: Nepal monitoring platform, pledge and performance', report presented by Beyond Beijing Committee, Lalitpur, August 1999.

52   The measure for equality is 1.0. As a comparison, Canada ranks the highest in the world in terms of GDI (0.928) and other countries in South Asia such as Sri Lanka, India, Bangladesh have GDI index marked at 0.712, 0.525, and 0.428 respectively. See UNDP, 2002 for more details.

53   UNDP 2002.

54   Gautam, Shobha et al. 2001. p. 215.

55   Onesto, Li, *Revolutionary Worker*, no. 1032, 1999.

56   Gautam 2001. p. 66

57   Seddon 2002.

58   Gautam, et al. 2001. p. 226. A study by the Asian Institute of Technology in three villages in Kabhrepalanchowk district found that male migration meant a doubling in women's physical work burden. Azad, Nandini. *Engendered Mobilisation – the Key to Livelihood Security: IFAD's Experience in South Asia*, 1999.

59   Gautam 2001. pp. 49-54.

60   Child Workers in Nepal Concerned Centre (CWIN), *The State of the Rights of the Child in Nepal 2003*, CWIN, 2003.

61   The national average of teacher-student ratio stands at 1:40. See Timsina, Nitya Nanda, 'Maoist violence leaves over 700 schools closed', *The Kathmandu Post*, 13 November, 2002.

62   Economic Intelligence Unit 2003.

63   Gautam 2001, pp. 72-79.

64   CWIN 2003.

65   Gautam 2001. p. 75.

Chapter 7: Ceasefire Again

1   *Janaawaj*, no. 38, 5 December 2002.

2   The JVP re-emerged in the 1980s as a Sinhala chauvinist group, only to be decimated once again. It has since reappeared in Sri Lankan politics as a parliamentary party.

3   Banerjee, Sumanta. *In the Wake of Naxalbari: A History of the Naxalite Movement in India*, 1980. p. 350.

4   It is probable that they had believed such a time had come with the general state of chaos following the 1 June 2001, massacre of King Birendra and his family. Baburam Bhattarai's famous 'The new "Kot massacre" should not be accepted' article (Bhattarai 2001, *Kantipur*, 6 June 2001) exhorted the 'Royal Army officers and soldiers' not to shift their allegiance to the new king, Gyanendra.

5   Nickson, 1992, writes of a similar situation in Peru where 'the political impotence experienced by the parliamentary left under Peru's anachronistic presi-

dential system of government has already undermined its electoral support and has fuelled desertions to the senderista camp.' p. 384.

6   Mao Tse-tung 1966, p. 183.

7   Gautam, Pushkar, 'Maobadiko khel: Aru kati Almaline?', *Himal Khabarpatrika*, 2 October-1 November 2002.

8   Mao Tse-tung 1966, p. 212

9   *The Worker* 2000.

10   Gautam 2002.

11   *Janaawaj*, no 48, 18 February 2003.

12   Joint appeal signed by Prachanda and Baburam Bhattarai. 6 October 2002.

13   Press statement by Prachanda, 24 October 2002.

14   Pahari, Anup. 'Negotiating an end to internal war in Nepal'. In Deepak Thapa (ed) *Understanding the Maoist Movement of Nepal*, 2003, p. 340.

15   Major Mohan Khatri, ex-Royal Nepal Army officer in an email to a friend a few months before he was hacked to death by Maoists in his resort in eastern Nepal in October 2002. *Nepali Times*, 25-31 October 2001.

16   National Security Adviser in the Johnson administration, Walt Whitman Rostow, 'Containing guerrilla act'. In Franklin Mark Osanha (ed), *Modern Guerrilla Warfare*. Cited in Banerjee, 1980. p. 369.

Chapter 8: **Update**

1   Thapa, Deepak. 'Tentative Progress on Negotiations', South Asia Intelligence Review, Vol 1, No. 37, 31 March 2003.

2   *The Kathmandu Post*, 28 April 2003.

3   *The Kathmandu Post* and *The Himalayan Times*, 10 May 2003.

4   *The Kathmandu Post*, 12 May 2003. Interestingly, Baburam Bhattarai claimed at a public rally at a latter date that the restrictions on the army had had the approval of the king. *The Kathmandu Post*, 9 June 2003.

5   The five parties claimed to represent the last parliament. Missing from the grouping were Rastriya Prajatantra Party, the party of Prime Minister Lokendra Bahadur Chand, and Deuba's Nepali Congress (Democratic), which was anathema to the Nepali Congress. The Nepal Sadbhavana Party (Anandi Devi) had split from the one led by Deputy Prime Minister Badri Prasad Mandal.

6   The team consisted of the finance minister, Prakash Chandra Lohani, and the information and communication minister, Kamal Thapa.

7   Bhattarai, Baburam. 'To the Negotiation Team, The Old State Establishment (His Majesty's Government)', 26 July 2003.

8   See, for instance, International Crisis Group, 'Back to the Gun', 22 October, 2003; and Upreti, Bishnu Raj, 'Breaking the barriers and building a bridge: A road map for structuring negotiation and peace process in Nepal', paper presented at the 'Seminar on Management of Conflicts in Nepal: A Preparation for Negotiation' organised by the Centre for the Study of Democracy and Governance, Kathmandu, 2 December 2003.

9   Informal Sector Service Centre, www.insec.org.np.

10   An investigation by the National Human Rights Commission ten days after the incident concluded that the killings were 'contrary to the International Humanitarian Law and, and, especially, the Common Article 3 of the Geneva Conventions' and that 'even in the national context the above-mentioned act ran contrary

Update

to the Constitution of the Kingdom of Nepal, the Army Act, the Police Act and the Armed Police Act'. National Human Rights Commission, 'Doramba Incident, Ramechhap, On-the-spot Inspection and Report of the Investigation Committee', 2003. See www.nhrc-org.np for its report on Doramba.

11 Press statement from Prachanda, 27 August 2003.

12 Interview with Prachanda in 'Maoist Information Bulletin - 4', 15 September 2003, www.cpnm.org. Prachanda's rhetoric can be understood in the context of the comment by the International Crisis Group that 'A number of foreign diplomats publicly praised the position paper the government presented at the third round in August 2003 as a response to the paper forwarded by the Maoists in April. This was quickly viewed by the Maoists as further evidence that the international community was in bed with the monarchy.' International Crisis Group, 'Back to the Gun', 22 October 2003.

13 Two days before the truce had been called off, former prime minister, Sher Bahadur Deuba, had had a fortuitous escape when his motorcade came under a Maoist barrage of bullets in western Nepal.

14 www.nepalnews.com, 18 April 2004

15 Ibid.

16 Hencke, David. 'Blair "sneaked aid to Nepal military"', *The Guardian*, 5 August, 2002. The helicopters were delivered in March 2003.

17 Khadka, Navin Singh. 'Alms Race', *Nepali Times*, 28 May-3 June, 2004.

18 Kumar, Dhruba. 'Consequences of the militarisation conflict and the cost of violence in Nepal', *Contributions to Nepalese Studies*, Vol 30, No 2, p. 182.

19 *The Worker* 2003.

20 Another guard was killed in November 2002.

21 According to *Time* magazine, 'Up to 50 US special-forces trainers are now pushing 20 battalions of 700-800 men each—a quarter of the entire army—through a 12-week counterinsurgency program...' Perry, Alex. Living on the brink', *Time* (Asia edition), 15 September 2003.

22 Executive Order 13224 blocks 'the CPN (M)'s assets in the US or held by U.S. persons wherever located and bars most transactions or dealings with the organisation'. US Embassy press release, 1 November 2003.

23 The list means that 'members and those providing material support to such entities' are barred from the United States. US Embassy press release, 30 April 2004.

24 Remarks to the Heritage Foundation, Washington DC, 3 March, 2003. http://www.state.gov/p/sa/rls/rm/18474.htm. It is also significant that the US ambassador to Nepal, Michael Malinowski, said to a Kathmandu audience: 'The Maoists have shown themselves to be a ruthless enemy by their tactics in the field and through terrorist attacks against both government and innocent civilian targets...[W]orking in tandem, and with the full approval and coordination of the government of Nepal—in a spirit of cooperation not interference—our governments can help Nepal defeat the Maoist threat.' Remarks at a programme of the Foundation of Nepalese in America, Nepal Branch, 12 September, 2003. http://www.state.gov/p/sa/rls/rm/24249.htm. In response, in the form of an 'open letter' to the ambassador dated 24 September, Baburam Bhattarai accused him of displaying 'super-power arrogance and imperialist designs' and asked 'all foreign powers, particularly the USA and our immediate neighbours India and China, not to interfere in our internal affairs and let the Nepalese people choose their destiny themselves'.

25 Sharma, Sushil. 'Nepal row over US support', http://news.bbc.co.uk/1/hi/world/south_asia/1564467.stm.

Update

26   That the Maoist leadership spends part of its time in India was underscored once again when the general secretary of the CPN (UML), Madhav Kumar Nepal, met Prachanda and Baburam Bhattarai in the north Indian city of Lucknow in November 2003. This was the second meeting between Nepal and Prachanda on Indian soil, the first having taken place in West Bengal's Siliguri in August 2001.

27   Muni, S.D. *Maoist Insurgency in Nepal: The Challenge and the Response*, 2003, p. 58.

28   *The Rising Nepal*, 10 July 2004. Shyam Saran's statement is considered all the more significant since he has now become the foreign secretary of India.

29   Apart from Yadav and Magar, the rest are still in Indian custody. This is probably because since those sent to Nepal earlier had been set free during the second ceasefire, the Indians do not want to take the chance of sending them to Nepal and having them released again.

30   Bhattarai, Baburam. 'Raised Questions [sic] on the Arrest of Com Kiran', *The Newsletter*, fortnightly newsletter published by the 'Voice of the Struggle For Democracy', 16-30 April 2004, 1st issue.

31   *The Kathmandu Post*, 17 April, 2004.

32   See footnote 10.

33   The group of ten consisted of Canada, Denmark, the European Commission, Finland, France, Germany, the Netherlands, Norway, Switzerland and the United Kingdom.

34   Joint Donor Statement for Nepal Development Forum 2004, 4 May 2004.

35   Amnesty International, 'Nepal: A spiralling human rights crisis', 4 April 2002.

36   United Nations, 'Report of the Special Rapporteur on extrajudicial, summary or arbitrary executions, Ms Asma Jahangir, submitted pursuant to Commission on Human Rights resolution 2000/31, Addendum, Mission to Nepal', 9 August 2000.

37   United Nations, 'Civil and Political Rights, Including the Questions of: Disappearances and Summary Executions, Question of enforced or involuntary disappearances', Report of the Working Group on Enforced or Involuntary Disappearances, 21 January, 2004.

38   International Bar Association, 'Nepal in Crisis: Justice Caught in the Cross-fire', September 2002.

39   International Commission of Jurists, 'Human Rights and Administration of Justice: Obligations Unfulfilled', June 2003.

40   For instance, of the two main accused in the widely publicised execution of three civilians in Chisapani of Khotang District that was found to be motivated by personal vendetta, one was discharged from service while the other was discharged and sentenced to just two years in jail. The army, however, has refused to charge anyone for the Doramba incident.

41   See International Crisis Group, 'Nepal: Dangerous Plans for Village Militias', 17 February 2004, for a critique highlighting the pitfalls of the government's plan.

42   Baburam Bhattarai's communication to International Crisis Group (ICG), 26 September 2003. Maoist Information Bulletin - 5, 28 September 2003.

43   Prachanda, 'A Brief Introduction to the Policies of the CPN (Maoist)', Maoist Information Bulletin – 8, 20 January, 2004.

44   Baburam Bhattarai's communication to International Crisis Group (ICG), 26 September 2003. Maoist Information Bulletin - 5, 28 September 2003.

45   International Crisis Group, 'Nepal: Back to the Gun', 22 October, 2003.

46   Baburam Bhattarai's communication to International Crisis Group (ICG), 26 September 2003. Maoist Information Bulletin - 5, 28 September 2003.

Update

47 International Crisis Group, 'Nepal: Back to the Gun', 22 October, 2003.

48 See, for example, Baruah, Amit, 'Foreign mediation not needed in Nepal: India', *The Hindu*, 2 February, 2003. Explaining India's position on external involvement, Stephen Cohen writes: 'New Delhi's support for ... international intervention elsewhere is strongly conditioned by its concern with setting the wrong example [on Kashmir]'. Cohen, Stephen. *India: Emerging Power*, Brookings Institute, 2001, p. 58.

49 In his comments to a group of Nepali journalists, the Indian ambassador, Shyam Saran, said, 'I do not think that it is necessary for any third party to come in to enable one Nepali to talk to another Nepali.' Face–to-Face Programme at the Reporters' Club, Kathmandu, 13 August, 2003.

50 Maoist Information Bulletin - 8, 20 January, 2004.

51 Karki, Arjun and Binod Bhattarai (eds), *Whose War: Economic and Socio-Cultural Impacts of Nepal's Maoist-Government Conflict*, 2004, p. 78.

52 Khadka, Navin Singh. 'Alms Race', *Nepali Times*, 28 May-3 June 2004.

53 'King Gyanendra: Extended Interview', http://www.time.com/time/asia/2004/nepal_king/nepal_intvu_extended.html, posted 26 January 2004.

The ubiquitous memorial arch found in Maoist strongholds all over Nepal. The slogans read (clockwise): 'Long live the great people's war', 'Arch and platform built in memory of all the martyrs', and 'Red salute to all the great and brave martyrs'. Rolpa, 2002.

References

In Nepali

Acharya, Narahari (2000). 'Maobadi gatibidhi ko pristhabhumi' (Background to Maoist activities). Paper outlining the Nepali Congress position and strategies for resolution at a seminar organised by the High-Level Committee to Provide Suggestions to Solve the Maoist Problem.

Bhattarai, Baburam (2001a). 'Naya "Kotparba" lai manyata dinu hunna', *Kantipur*, 6 June 2001.

Bhattarai, Baburam (2001b). 'Akasmik dhangale ganatantra ko janma bhaeko chha', *Rajdhani*, 29 June 2001.

CPN (Masal) (2059 BS) (2002/03). *Rato Tarwar* (Red Sword). Kathmandu: Central Committee of CPN (Masal).

CPN (UML) (2058 BS [a]) (2001). 'Maobadi tatha rajyadwara hinsa ra atanka sambandha adhyayan karyadal prativedan, 2058' (Report of the working group to study violence and terror by the Maoists and the state, 2001).

CPN (UML) (2058 BS [b]) (2001). *Nekapa (Maobadi)ko Chirphar* (A 'surgery' of the CPN–Maoist). Kathmandu: CPN (UML) Central Secretariat.

Dhungel, Binod (2000). 'Maobadi sena gathan prakriya Chinko bhanda pharak' (Maoists' military formation different than China's), *Samacharpatra*, 30 Aug 2000.

'Ekikrit antarik surakshya tatha bikas yojana' (Integrated Internal Security and Development Programme), 2057 BS (2000-01).

Gautam, Pushkar (2002). 'Maobadiko khel: Aru kati almaline?' (Maoist game: How long will it go on?), *Himal Khabarpatrika*, 2 October-1 November 2002.

Gautam, Shobha and Amrita Banskota (2055 BS) (1998/99). 'Maobadi janyuddhale mahila tatha bal-balikama pareko prabhavbareko adyayan prativedan' ('Study report on the effect of the Maoist people's war on women and children'), Sancharika Samuha.

Gautam, Shobha (2058 BS) (2001/02). *Janyuddhako Serophero bhitra Mahila ra Balbalika* (Women and Children in the Periphery of People's War). Kathmandu: IHRICON.

Gyawali, Sambhu Prasad (2038 BS) (1981/82). *Jivan ra Kanoon* (Life and Law). Lalitpur: Nalini Gyawali.

KC, Surendra (1999). *Nepalma Communist Andolan ko Itihas* (The History of the Communist Movement in Nepal). Kathmandu: Bidyarthi Pustak Bhandar.

Kumar, Dhruba (2003). 'Sankat ko Nikas: Sainya Katauti' (A way out of the impasse: Demilitarisation), *Himal Khabarpatrika*, 13-28 April, 2003.

Nepal Rastriya Buddhijibi Sangathan (2054 BS) (1997). *Nepal ma Yanayuddha – Bhag Ek* (The People's War in Nepal – Part One). Kathmandu: Nepal Rastriya Buddhijibi Sangathan (Nepal National Intellectuals' Organisation).

Rawal, Bhim (2047 BS) (1990/91). *Nepal ma Samyabadi Andolan: Udbhav ra Bikas* (The Communist Movement in Nepal: Origins and Evolution). Kathmandu: Pairavi Prakashan.

In English

A World to Win, No 27, 2001.

Ahmad, Eqbal (1970). 'Revolutionary warfare and counterin-surgency'. In Gerard Chaliand (ed), *Guerrilla Strategies: An Historical Anthology from the Long March to Afghanistan*. Berkeley, Los Angeles and London: University of California Press, 1982. Extracted from N. Miller and E. Aya (eds), *National Liberation and Revolution*. New York: The Free Press.

Amnesty International (2002 [a]). 'Nepal: A spiralling human rights crisis'. London: Amnesty International.

Amnesty International (2002 [b]). 'Nepal: A deepening human rights crisis'. London: Amnesty International.

Asian Development Bank (2002). 'Annual Report, Nepal, 2001'.

Azad, Nandini (1999). *Engendered Mobilisation – The Key to Livelihood Security: IFAD's Experience in South Asia*. Rome: IFAD.

Baldauf, Scott (2002). 'In Nepal's Maoist hunt, villagers are hit hardest', *The Christian Science Monitor*, 8 May, 2002.

Banerjee, Sumanta (1980). *In the Wake of Naxalbari: A History of the Naxalite Movement in India*. Calcutta: Subarnarekha.

Baral, Lok Raj (1977). *Oppositional Politics in Nepal*. New Delhi: Abhinav Publications.

Bhattarai, Baburam (1998). *Politico-Economic Rationale of People's War in Nepal*. Kathmandu: Utprerak Publications.

Bhattarai, Binod (2001). '$70,000,000: That's how much the army is spending over the next five years on weapons upgrades', *Nepali Times*, 23-29 November, 2001.

Blaikie, Piers, John Cameron, and David Seddon (2001). *Nepal in Crisis: Growth and Stagnation at the Periphery*. Delhi: Adroit Publishers.

Brown, T Louise (1996). *The Challenge to Democracy in Nepal: A Political History*. London, Routledge.

Child Workers in Nepal Concerned Centre (2003). *The State of the Rights of the Child in Nepal 2002*. Kathmandu: Child Workers in Nepal Concerned Centre.

CPN (Maoist) (2001). *The Himalayan Thunder*, Vol 1 no 1.

CPN (Maoist) (no date). Maoist Information Bulletin-2. www.insof.org (accessed May 2003).

CPN (UML). 'An Analysis of National Political Situation' (From 6th Congress document), www.cpnuml.org/documents/6thcongress.html (accessed 2003).

Dixit, Kanak Mani (2001). 'Bahuns and the Nepali State', *Nepali Times*, 19-25 October 2001.

Dixit, Kanak Mani (2002). 'Insurgents and innocents: The Nepali army's battle with the Maobaadi', *Himal South Asian*, June 2002.

Economic Intelligence Unit (2003). 'Country Report: Nepal, Mongolia'. London: Economist Group Business.

Enabling State Programme (2001). *Pro-Poor Governance Assessment Nepal*. Kathmandu: Enabling State Programme.

Gaige, Frederick (1975). *Regionalism and National Unity in Nepal*. Berkeley: University of California Press.

Gautam, Shobha, Amrit Baskota, and Rita Manchanda (2001). 'Where There Are No Men: Women in the Maoist Insurgency in Nepal'. In Rita Manchanda (ed). *Women War and Peace in South Asia: Beyond Victimhood to Agency'*. Delhi: Sage.

Gautam, Shobha (2001). *Women and Children in the Periphery of People's War*. Kathmandu: Institute of Human Rights Communications.

Gupta, Anirudha (1993). *Politics in Nepal, 1950-60*. New Delhi: Kalinga Publications.

Gurung, Harka, Ananda Aditya, Surendra KC, Chuda Bahadur Shrestha and Sudheer Sharma (2001). 'An overview of recent armed conflict in Nepal'. Kathmandu: New Era.

Hachhethu, Krishna (2002). *Party Building in Nepal: Organisation, Leadership and People*. Kathmandu: Mandala Book Point.

Hencke, David (2002). 'Blair "sneaked aid to Nepal military"', *The Guardian*, 5 August, 2002.

Himal Association (2001). *Political Opinion Survey Nepal 2001*. Kathmandu: Himal Association.

Hoftun, Martin, William Raeper, and John Whelpton (1999). *People, Politics and Ideology: Democracy and Social Change in Nepal*. Kathmandu: Mandala Book Point.

Huntington, Samuel P (1996 [1968]). *Political Order in Changing Societies*. New Haven and London: Yale University Press.

Huston, James V (1988). 'Insurgency in Peru: The Shining Path'. Paper presented at 'War in the Modern Era', Virginia, May 1988.

Huston, James V (1995). 'Shining Path: Core of the RIM Project'. In Executive Intelligence Review, 17 November, 1995.

Hutt, Michael (2001). 'Drafting the 1990 constitution'. In Michael Hutt (ed). *Nepal in the Nineties*. New Delhi: Oxford University Press

The Independent (1995). 'The phobia of guerilla war is hounding the reactionaries'. Interview with Baburam Bhattarai, *The Independent*, 13-19 December, 1995.

INSEC (1993, 1994, 1996, 1998, 2002, and 2003). *Human Rights Yearbook, 1992, 1993, 1995, 1997, 2001, and 2002*.

International Bar Association (2002). 'Nepal in Crisis: Justice Caught in the Cross-fire'. London: International Bar Association.

International Commission of Jurists (2003). 'Human Rights and Administration of Justice: Obligations Unfulfilled'. Geneva: International Commission of Jurists.

International Crisis Group (2003). 'Nepal Backgrounder: Ceasefire — Soft Landing or Strategic Pause?'. Kathmandu/Brussels, 10 April.

International Crisis Group (2003 [a]). 'Back to the Gun'. Kathmandu/Brussels, 22 October.

Karki, Arjun and Binod Bhattarai (eds) (2004). *Whose War: Economic and Socio-Cultural Impacts of Nepal's Maoist-Government Conflict.* Kathmandu: NGO Federation of Nepal.

The Kathmandu Post (2002). 'Maoists kill 65 in Arghakhanchi: Toll could soar, as dozens reported missing'. The Kathmandu Post, 10 September 2002.

Khadka, Navin Singh (2004). 'Alms Race', *Nepali Times*, 28 May-3 June, 2004.

Kumar, Dhruba (2004). 'Consequences of the militarisation conflict and the cost of violence in Nepal', *Contributions to Nepalese Studies*, Vol 30, No 2, p. 182.

Lal, CK (2001). 'Nepal's Maobaadi', *Himal South Asian*, November 2001.

Lecomte-Tilouine, Marie (2001). 'Ethnic claims within Maoism — The Magar dilemma between two regroupings: nationality and class'. Paper presented at 'The Maoist Movement in Nepal: Context, Causes and Implications', a conference organised by the School of Oriental and African Studies in London, 2-3 November, 2001.

Maharjan, Pancha N (1993). 'Role of the Extra-Parliamentary Political Party in Multi-party Democracy: A Study of the CPN–Unity Centre', *Contributions to Nepalese Studies*, vol 20 no 2, 1993.

Maharjan, Pancha N (2000). 'The Maoist Insurgency and Crisis of Governability in Nepal'. In Dhruba Kumar (ed). *Domestic Conflict and Crisis of Governability in Nepal.* Kathmandu: Centre for Nepal and Asian Studies.

Mainali, Mohan (2001). 'Unfriendly fire', *Nepali Times*, 2-8 March 2001.

Mainali, Mohan (2002 [a]). 'Famine by February', *Nepali Times*, 22-28 November 2002.

Mainali, Mohan (2002 [b]). 'Our descendants are doomed', *Nepali Times*, 6-12 December 2002.

Mao Tse-tung (1966). *Selected Military Writings of Mao Tse-tung*. Peking: Foreign Languages Press.

Mao Tse-tung. *Selected Works of Mao*, Vol IX, 'On Guerilla Warfare'. www.maoism.org (accessed 2003).

Maoist Information Bulletin, No 5, 28 September 2003; No 8, 20 January 2004.

Mikesell, Stephen L (1993). 'The paradoxical support of Nepal's Left for Comrade Gonzalo'. *Himal*, Mar/Apr 1993.

Ministry of Finance (several years). *Economic Survey*. Kathmandu: HMG/ Ministry of Finance.

Muni, S.D. (2003), *Maoist Insurgency in Nepal: The Challenge and the Response*. New Delhi: Rupa.

National Planning Commission (1991). *Approach to the Eighth Five Year Plan, 1992-97*. Kathmandu: National Planning Commission.

Nickson, R Andrew (1992). 'Democratisation and the Growth of Communism in Nepal: A Peruvian Scenario in the Making?', *Journal of Commonwealth and Comparative Politics*, Vol 30 No 3, November 1992.

Ogura, Kiyoko (2001). *Kathmandu Spring: The People's Movement of 1990*. Kathmandu: Himal Books.

Onesto, Li (1999). 'Dispatches: Report from the People's War in Nepal', *Revolutionary Worker*, nos 1020, 1023 and 1032, 1999.

Pahari, Anup (2003). 'Negotiating an end to internal war in Nepal'. In Deepak Thapa (ed) *Understanding the Maoist Movement of Nepal*. Kathmandu: Martin Chautari.

Panday, Devendra Raj (2000). *Nepal's Failed Development: Reflections on the Mission and the Maladies*. Kathmandu: Nepal South Asia Centre.

Pandey, J and Rudra Khadka (2002). 'Maoist terror: loot, burn & kill', *The Kathmandu Post*, 11 July 2002.

Pant, Shastra Dutta (1995). *Comparative Constitutions of Nepal*. Kathmandu: Research Centre for South Asia.

Pant, Suvecha and Ujir Magar (2002). 'First-hand accounts of massacre; Mental trauma of injured soldiers'. *The Kathmandu Post*, 11 September 2002.

Pfaff-Czarnecka, Joanna (1999). 'Debating the state of the nation: Ethnicisation of politics in Nepal — A position paper'. In Joanna Pfaff-Czarnecka, Darini Rajasingham-Senanayake, Ashis Nandy, and Edmund Terence Gomez (eds). *Ethnic Futures: The State and Identity Politics in Asia*. New Delhi: Sage Publications.

Regmi, Mahesh Chandra (1995). *Kings and Political Leaders of the Gorkhali Empire, 1768-1814*. Hyderabad: Orient Longman.

Revolutionary Internationalist Movement. 'Declaration of the Revolutionary Internationalist Movement'. www.awtw/org/rim/ declaration_eng.htm (accessed May 2003).

Revolutionary Worker (2000). 'Inside the Revolution in Nepal: Interview with Comrade Prachanda' by Li Onesto, *Revolutionary Worker*, no. 1043, 2000.

de Sales, Anne (2000). 'The Kham Magar country, Nepal: Between ethnic claims and Maoism', *European Bulletin of Himalayan Research*, no 19, Autumn 2000.

Schram, Stuart R. (1974). *The Political Thought of Mao Tse-tung.* New York, Washington and London: Praeger Publishers.

Seddon, David, Jagannath Adhikari, and Ganesh Gurung (2001). *The New Lahures*, Kathmandu: Nepal Institute of Development Studies.

Seddon, David (2001). 'Democracy and development in Nepal'. In Michael Hutt (ed). *Nepal in the Nineties.* New Delhi: Oxford University Press.

Seddon, David (2002). 'The Maoist Insurgency in Nepal: Revolutionary Theory and Practice' Paper presented to the 'Symposium on South Asia — Conflict in South Asia', organised by the Research group on South Asia in the School of Development Studies, University of East Anglia, on 18 June 2002.

Shaha, Rishikesh (1996), 'Idea and reality, Nepal and Rolpa', *Himal South Asia*, July 1996.

Shakya, Sujeev (2002). 'The squandering of a promising economy'. In Kanak Mani Dixit and Shastri Ramachandaran (eds), *State of Nepal.* Kathmandu: Himal Books.

Sharma, Sudheer (2001). 'The Maoist movement: an evolutionary perspective'. Paper presented at 'The Maoist Movement in Nepal: Context, Causes and Implications', by the School of Oriental and African Studies, London, November, 2001.

Sharma, Sudhindra and Pawan Kumar Sen (1999). *General Election Opinion Poll: How Voters Assess Politics, Parties and Politicians.* Kathmandu: Himal Association.

Sharma, Sushil (2001). 'Nepal row over US support', http://news.bbc.co.uk/1/hi/world/south_asia/1564467.stm.

Shrestha, Manesh (2003). 'Internal displacement in Nepal: A problem unprepared for' (forthcoming).

Subedi, Navin (2002). 'Vox populi', *Nepali Times*, 11-17 October, 2002.

Thapa, Deepak (2001). 'Day of the Maoist', *Himal South Asia*, May, 2001.

Thapa, Deepak (2001). 'Radicalism in the Left and the Emergence of the Maoists'. Paper presented at 'The Maoist Movement in Nepal: Context, Causes and Implications', a conference organised by the School of Oriental and African Studies, London, November, 2001.

Thapa, Deepak (2002). 'Erosion of the Nepali World', *Himal South Asia*, April 2002.

Thapa, Deepak (ed) (2003). *Understanding the Maoist Movement of Nepal.* Kathmandu: Martin Chautari.

Thapa, Deepak (2003 [a]). 'Tentative Progress on Negotiations', South Asia Intelligence Review, Vol 1, No. 37, 31 March.

Thapa, Manjushree (2003). 'The war in the west', *Himal South Asian*, January 2003.

Timsina, Nitya Nanda (2002), 'Maoist violence leaves over 700 schools closed', *The Kathmandu Post*, 13 November, 2002.

Tiwari, Chitra K (2001). 'Maoist insurgency in Nepal: Internal dimensions', Paper No. 187, South Asia Analysis Group, January 2001.

UNDP (1999). *Nepal Human Development Report 1998*, Kathmandu.

UNDP (2002). *Nepal Human Development Report 2001*, Kathmandu.

United Nations (2000). 'Report of the Special Rapporteur on extrajudicial, summary or arbitrary executions, Ms Asma Jahangir, submitted pursuant to Commission on Human Rights resolution 2000/31, Addendum, Mission to Nepal'. Geneva: United Nations.

United Nations (2004). 'Civil and Political Rights, Including the Questions of: Disappearances and Summary Executions, Question of enforced or involuntary disappearances', Report of the Working Group on Enforced or Involuntary Disappearances. Geneva: United Nations.

United People's Front Nepal (1991). Election Manifesto.

Upadhya, Sanjay (2002). 'A dozen years of democracy: Games that parties play'. In Kanak Mani Dixit and Shastri Ramachandaran (eds), *State of Nepal*. Kathmandu: Himal Books.

USAID (2002). 'Mitigating the impact of the Maoist conflict on children and youth in Nepal'. Annual Programme Statement. Kathmandu: USAID.

Whelpton, John (1997). 'Political identity in Nepal: State, nation, and community'. In David N. Gellner, Joanna Pfaff-Czarnecka and John Whelpton (eds), *Nationalism and Ethnicity in a Hindu Kingdom: The Politics of Culture in Contemporary Nepal*. Amsterdam: Harwood Academic Publishers.

Whelpton, John (2001). 'The general elections of May 1991'. In Michael Hutt (ed), *Nepal in the Nineties*. New Delhi: Oxford University Press.

The Worker, No. 2, June 1996; No. 3, February 1997; No. 4, May 1998; No. 5, October 1999; No. 6, October 2000; No 7, January 2002; No 8, January 2003.

World Bank (1999). *Nepal: Poverty at the Turn of the Twenty-First Century, Main Report and the Background Studies*. Washington DC: World Bank.

Yogi, Bhagirath (2002). 'The cost of insurgency', *New Business Age*, May 2002.